AF594884

POSTCARD HISTORY SERIES

# *Amsterdam*

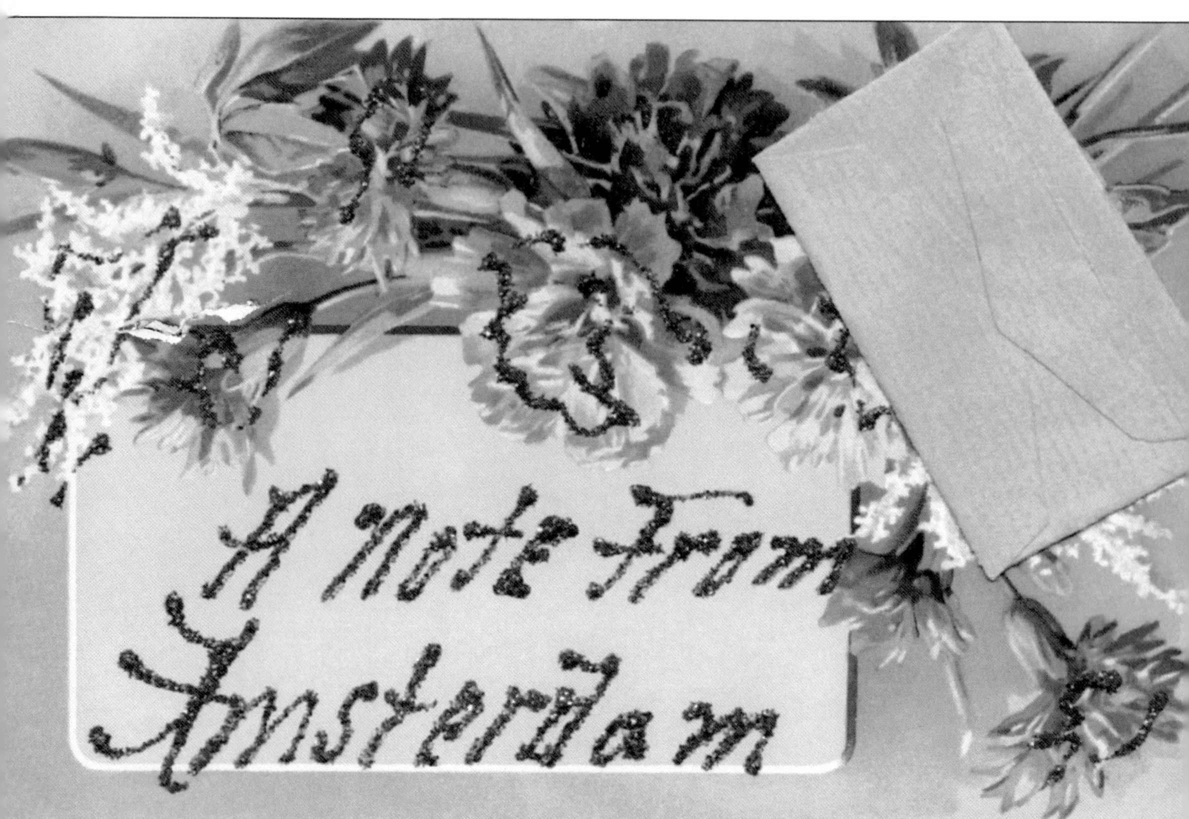


This is a typical novelty card from the height of the postcard's popularity. The tiny envelope is folded paper glued to the card, and the message is glued sparkles. Although the city or town name could be easily substituted on this kind of card, it is a reminder that Amsterdamians, then as now, like to see the name of their own city in print. (Courtesy of Rob von Hasseln.)

**ON THE FRONT COVER:** Here is Market Street, as seen north from Main Street sometime around the dawn of the 20th century. Although an industrial powerhouse, the city retains its human, urban scale. The downtown is easily walked, and streetcars run to all outlying parts. (Courtesy of Gerald R. Snyder.)

**ON THE BACK COVER:** Here are the McCleary, Wallin, and Crouse Mills, as viewed from Lyon Street. Originally an independent concern, when combined with one of the other two firms that made Amsterdam the "Carpet City," they became the upper mills of Mohawk Mills—a brand name known throughout the United States and abroad. (Courtesy of Gerald R. Snyder.)

POSTCARD HISTORY SERIES

# *Amsterdam*

*Gerald R. Snyder and Robert von Hasseln*

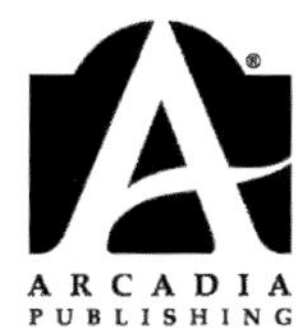

Copyright © 2010 by Gerald R. Snyder and Robert von Hasseln
ISBN 978-0-7385-7253-6

Published by Arcadia Publishing
Charleston, South Carolina

Printed in the United States of America

Library of Congress Control Number: 2009936091

For all general information contact Arcadia Publishing at:
Telephone 843-853-2070
Fax 843-853-0044
E-mail sales@arcadiapublishing.com
For customer service and orders:
Toll-Free 1-888-313-2665

Visit us on the Internet at www.arcadiapublishing.com

*To Kathy and Mike (GRS) and Maria and Erich (RvH)*

# Contents

# ACKNOWLEDGMENTS

First and foremost, the authors wish to acknowledge their debt to John Arthur Maney (1870–1935). Neither an Amsterdam native nor a professional photographer, he was the single most prolific and significant recorder of Amsterdam's appearance in its industrial heyday. His works graced numerous local commercial and historical volumes and were the basis for many of the postcards in this collection. Our appreciation also extends to Montgomery County historian Kelly Yacobucci Farquhar and to Rebekah Collinsworth, our editor at Arcadia. Unless otherwise noted, all images are courtesy of Gerald R. Snyder.

# Introduction

The history of postcards and the history of Amsterdam converge in a fascinating way. In the latter half of the 19th century, changes in postal practices, photography, and printing combined to create a simple, cheap, and visually interesting way to send mail without letters or envelopes. What happened next was not expected; this good idea became a collecting craze that lasted into the first decades of the 20th century. At the same time, Amsterdam was at the height of a transformation fueled by its rapid economic and population growth: the old fabric of the earlier village was being replaced by the shape the city would keep until it was torn apart by urban renewal in the 1960s and 1970s.

The postcards from that period are a visual record of these important changes. Many of them have not been seen other than by collectors since they were first published. Either of these two points would be reason enough to publish them, but there is a third reason that is important, if not more important, than the other two. The postcards are a collection, and seen together, they offer information beyond what is printed on all the individual cards.

As a collection, we derive an idea of what Amsterdamians and visitors thought interesting, attractive, or significant about the city. We do so by seeing which sites have more views published and which were not published at all. For example, there are at least two shots each of the Chalmers Mill for both construction and the finished buildings; four shots of the landscaping and ramps at the rail depot; and none of Green Hill Cemetery. Hotels and churches run about even with each other. What does this tell us? That the new mill on the south side was considered a major civic accomplishment; that Amsterdamians were proud of the appearance of the main entry way to their city; that a large number of persons stayed at hotels; and that attitudes towards the cemetery had shifted greatly in the decades since it was seen as a novel addition to the city and a matter of civic pride.

When organizing this book, we have tried to limit the number of similar images without imprinting our own "frequency analysis" on the collection or preventing the reader from making his or her own discoveries. We have also arranged the images geographically by the traditional sections of the city rather than the more common method of topic. We did this because, in a heavily developed city such as ours, it becomes difficult to tell one mill or schoolhouse from another, let alone relate them to each other and fit them into a mental picture of the city overall. It is even harder to do this in a city where so many visual prompts that could have helped tie it all together have been swept off the landscape by urban renewal and arterial roadway construction.

By arranging the areas in the sequence in which they developed, the reader also gets a feel for what shaped the city as it grew. As an aid to this, and also because many of these have not been widely available, we start each section with a historical map centered on the area discussed.

Although a great deal of history is encapsulated in each image, this book is not intended to be a general history of Amsterdam; for that, we recommend the Images of America series book on Amsterdam. Rather, this book is intended to bring together images long unseen, to look at them in new ways, and to discover new information about the city. We hope it will allow the reader to better see and feel the Amsterdam that once was and understand how the memory of it informs and shapes today's city.

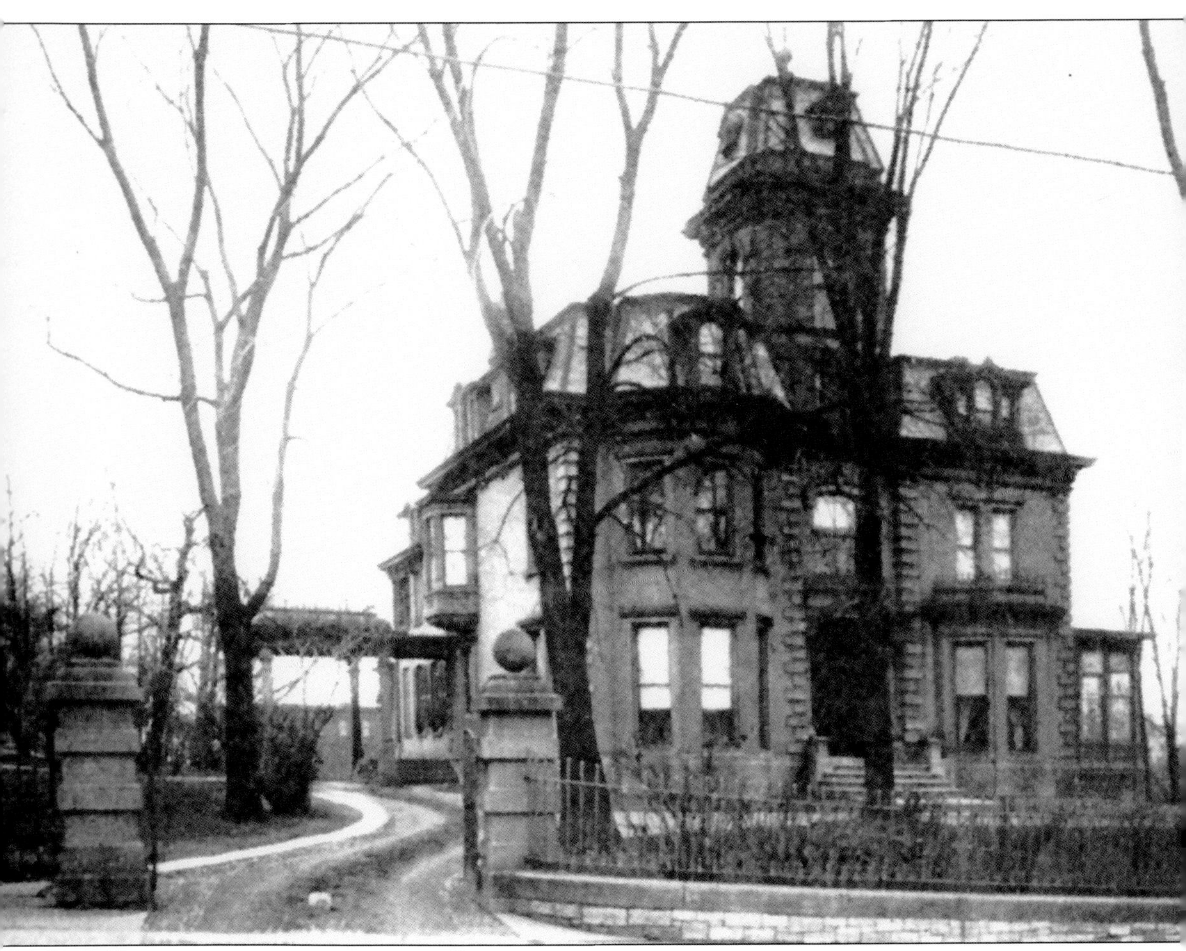

Perhaps no single image is more evocative of Amsterdam's past and its continuing resonance today, than this image of the Stephen Sanford mansion before its major 1913 renovation. The Sanford family started the first carpet mills in what would become the "carpet city" and were involved in many of the civic enhancements represented in the postcards contained in this volume. Their last benefice was to donate the mansion to the city as its first permanent city hall (see page 103).

# *One*

# Downtown

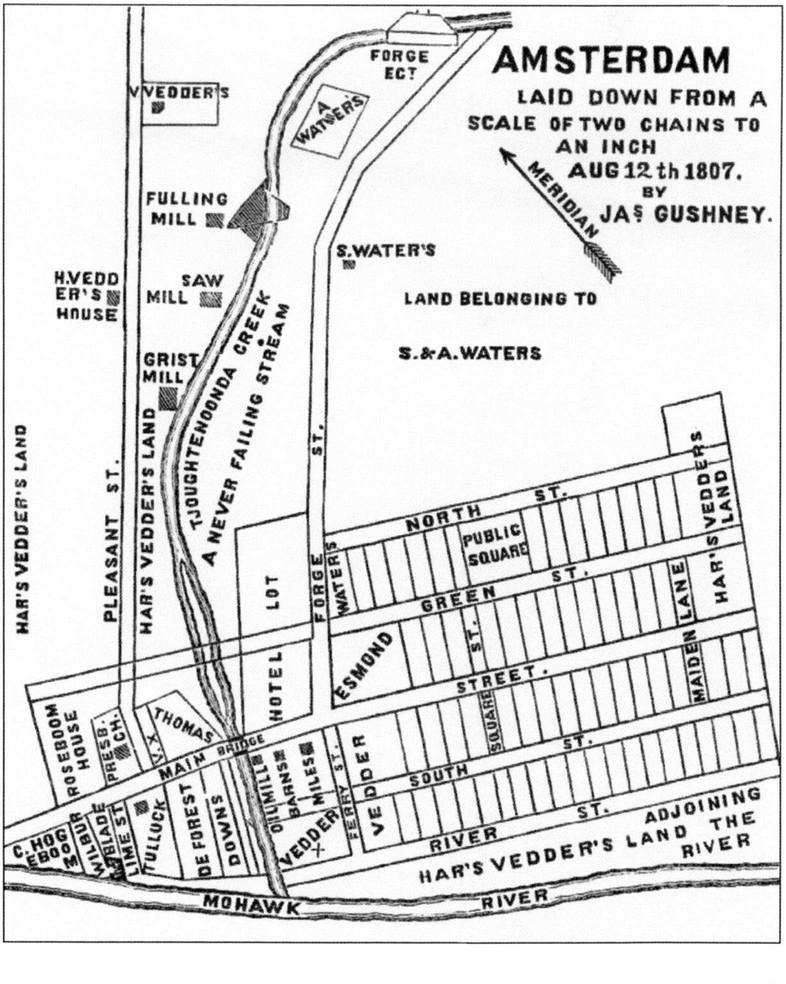

This is the earliest-known map of Amsterdam. It was created shortly after the name was changed from Veddersburg and shows the beginning of the village along the banks of the North Chuctanunda Creek where it joins the Mohawk River. (Courtesy of Montgomery County Department of History and Archives.)

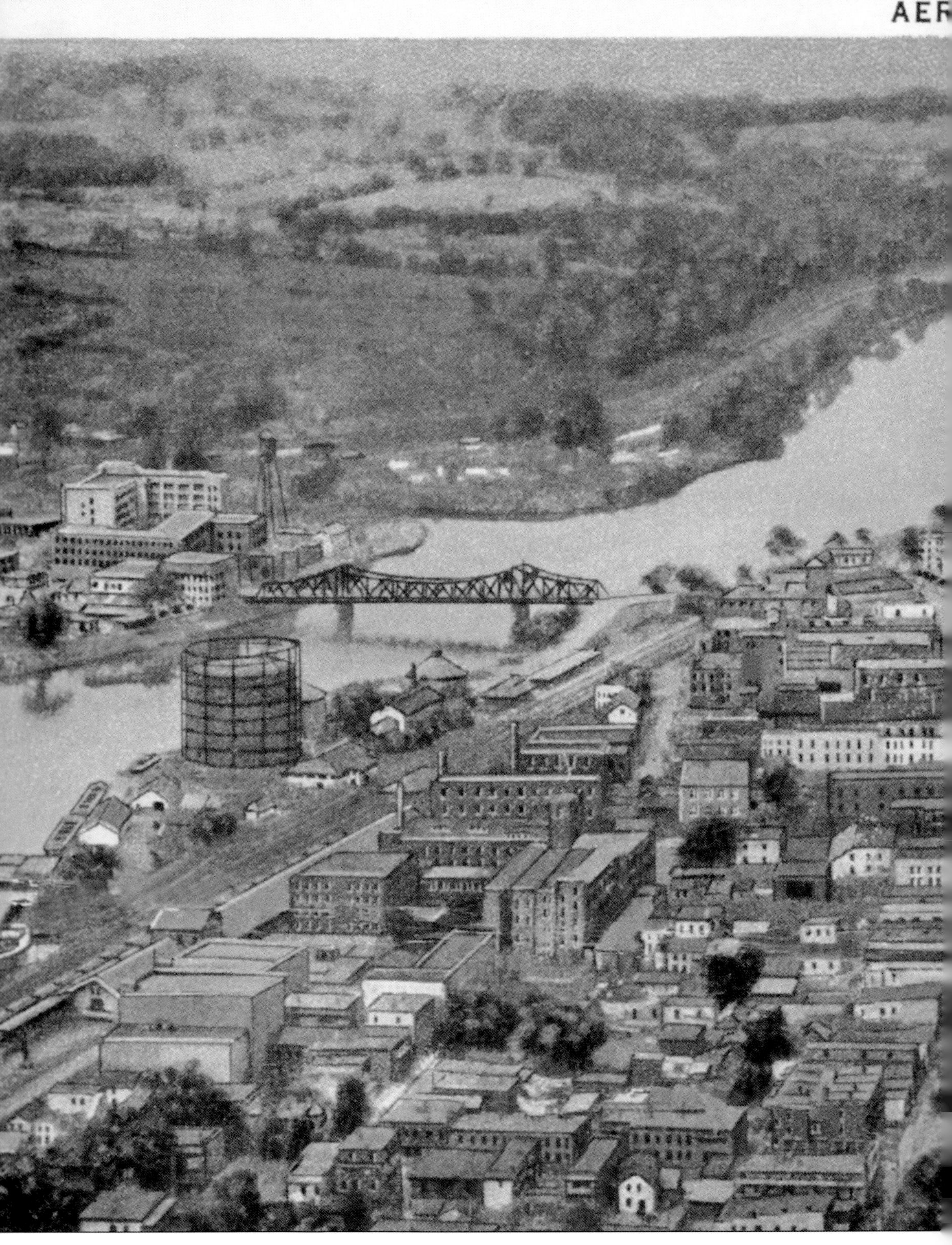

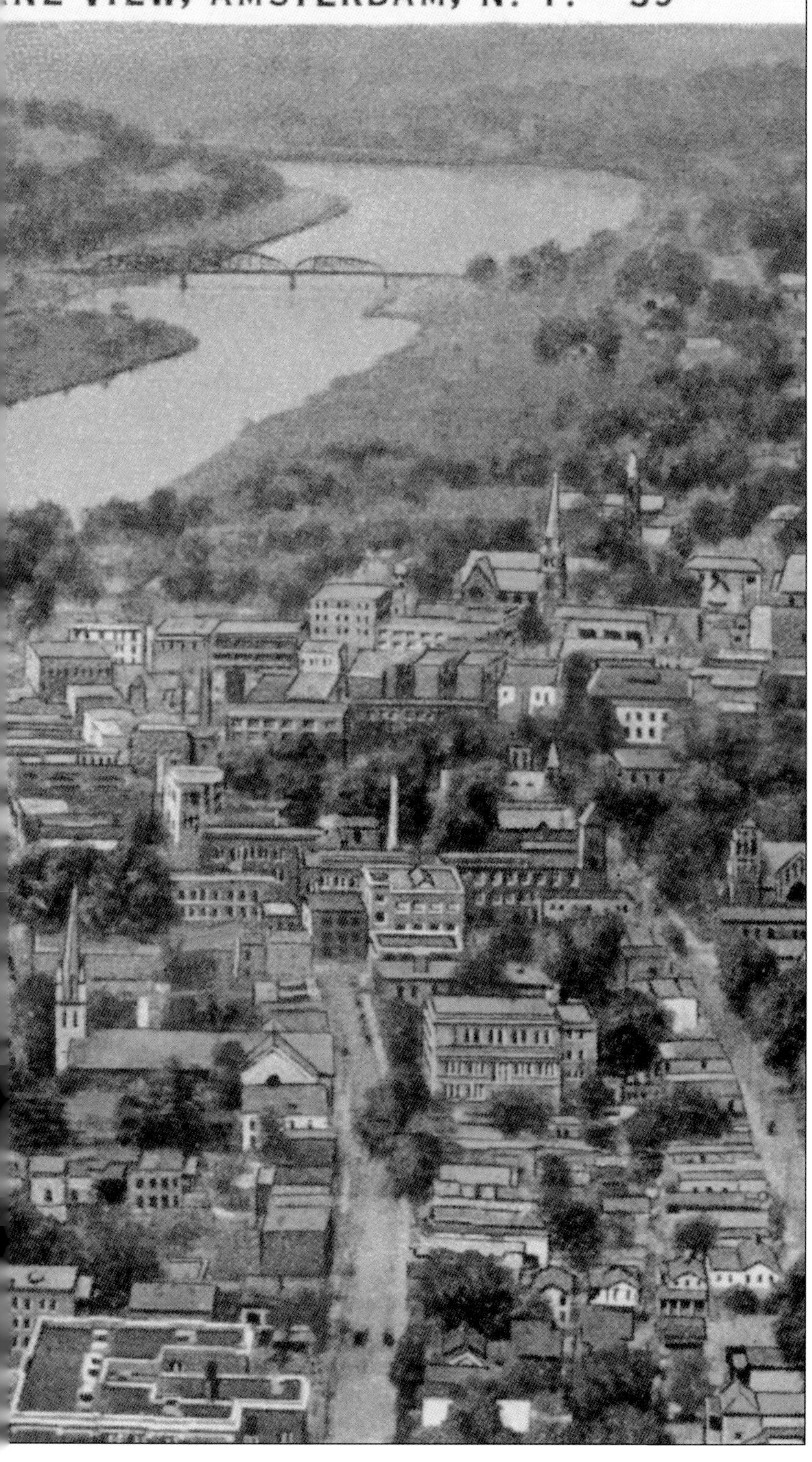


The focal point of this view is the 1916 bridge over the Mohawk River. To the south of the bridge is the Chalmers Mill (1913–1916), and to the east on the north bank is the gas works. The dense, urban fabric depicted in this photograph was ripped apart by urban renewal and arterial construction in the late 1960s and early 1970s. Over 400 buildings (approximately 100 from the 19th century) in the center of this picture were destroyed and replaced with modern structures and roadways, completely altering the nature of the city.

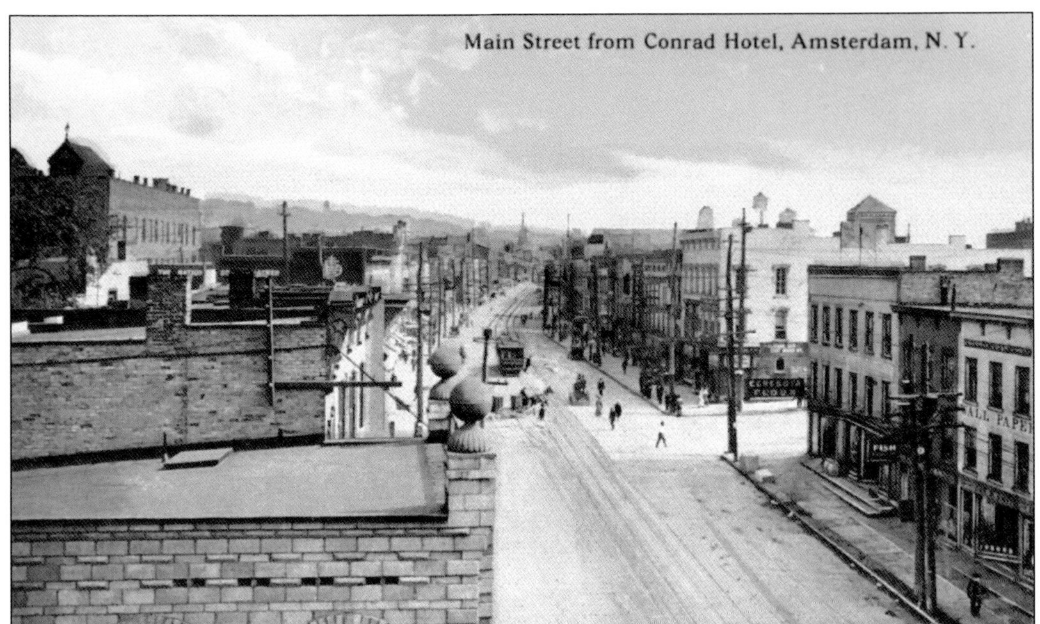


Above, the Hotel Conrad (as it was more commonly called) sat on the western edge of the traditional downtown area. Below, the hotel was built in 1910 on either side of the Old Voorhees Homestead, which had been the Roseboom Tavern, Amsterdam's first stagecoach stop in 1790. Later the building housed Wil-Ton Bowling. The buildings were torn down to make room for arterial construction.

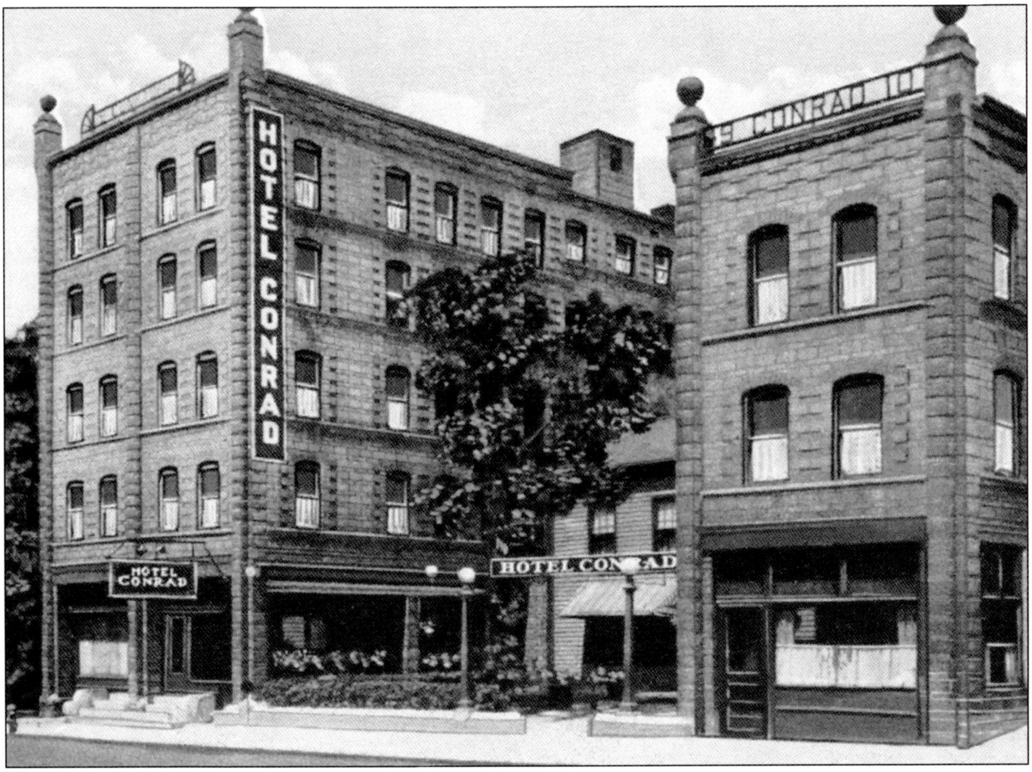

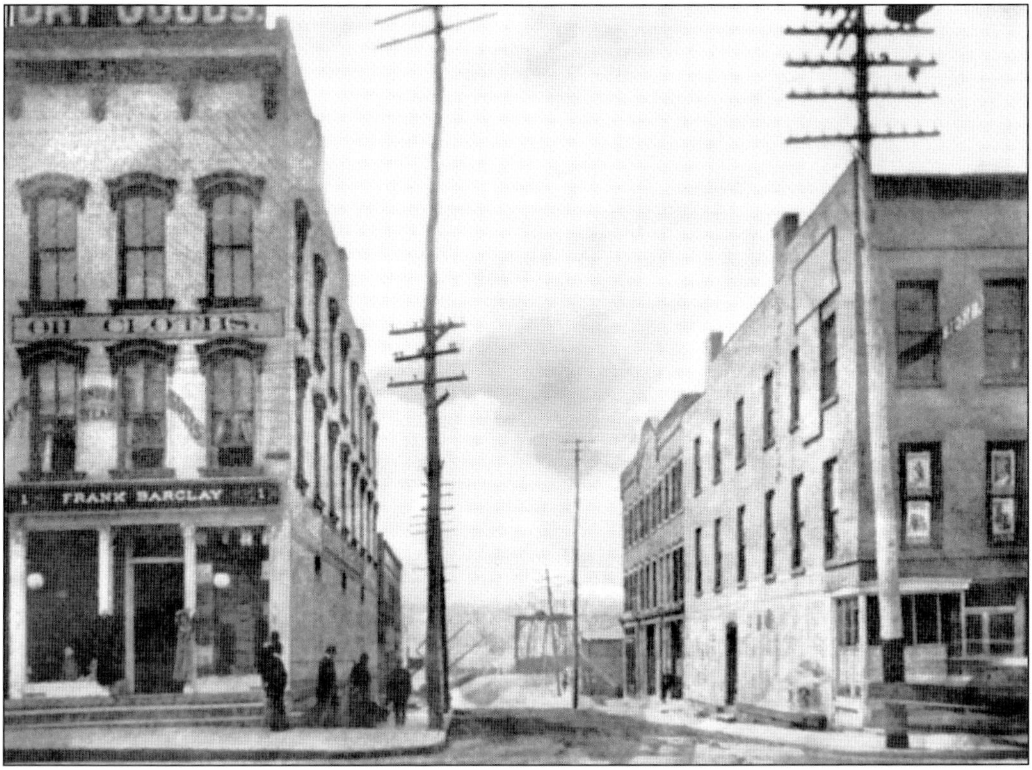

Here are north and south views from the heart of downtown at the intersection of Bridge, Main, and Market Streets. The above view looks to the south across the railroad tracks and onto the bridge over the Mohawk River. The view at right looks north up Market Street towards Market Hill and the high ground that runs parallel to the river.

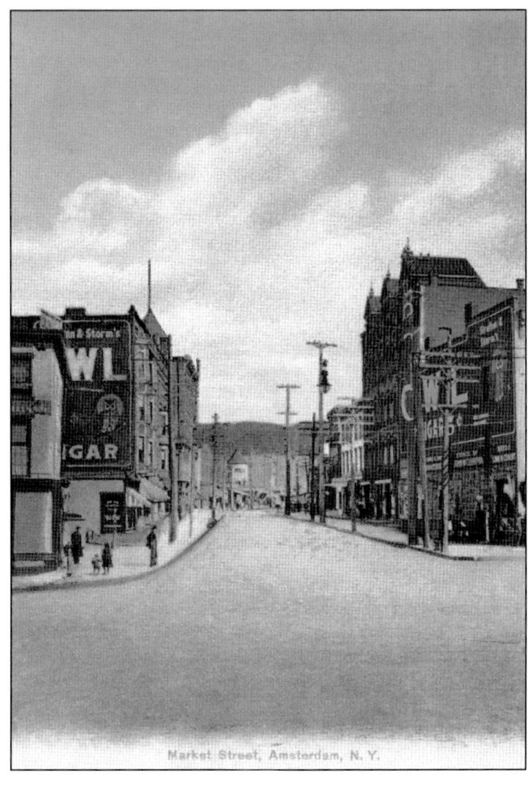

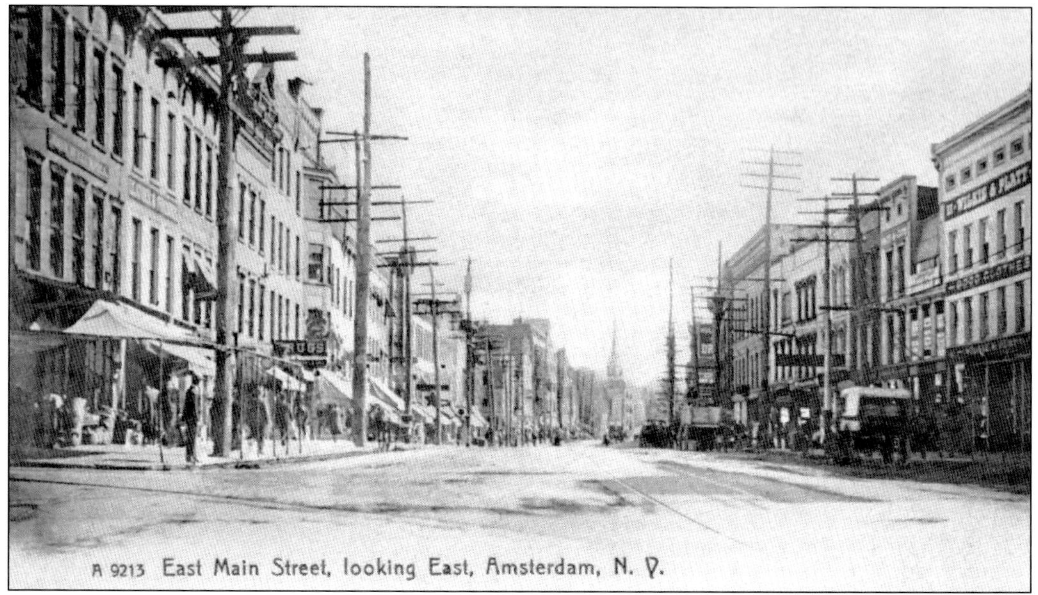


Looking east from Market Street, the spire of St. Mary's Roman Catholic Church is visible in the center background. At far right is a portion of the Willkie and Platt clothing store. Utility poles line both sides of the street. The electrification of downtown began in December 1887. Slightly over a year later, the great blizzard of 1888 demonstrated that overhead wiring was not a permanent solution in Upstate New York.

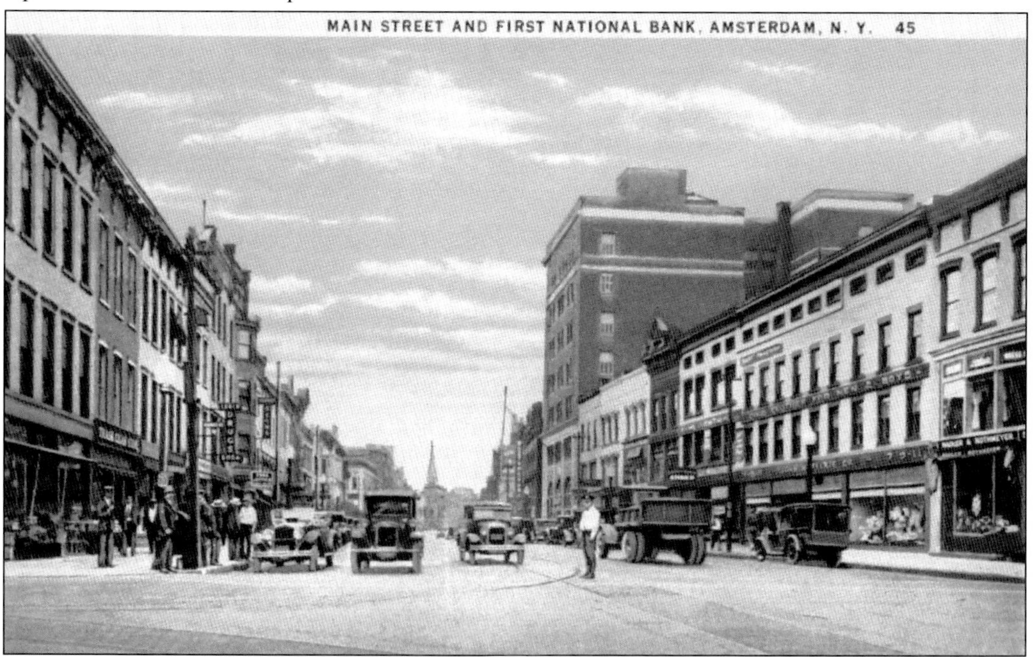


This photograph was taken from same location as above several decades later. The clothing goods store has expanded its facade and the utility poles are gone. At right center, the bank building, Amsterdam's modern high-rise office structure, now straddles the Chuctanunda Creek where the Morris Hall building was destroyed by a spectacular fire on January 16, 1927. Constructed in 1929, it still dominates the few blocks of this portion of Main Street that escaped urban renewal.

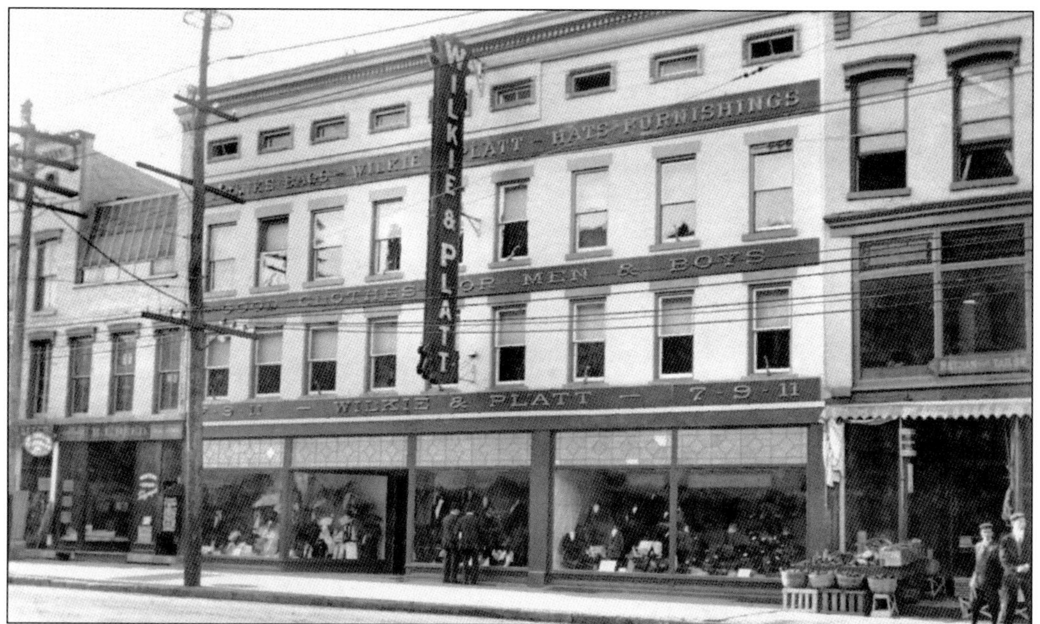


The Willkie and Platt department store at 7–11 East Main Street is shown before the expansion of its storefront. Illustrations of this block from 1897 show it as Quiri and Willkie, the original firm name. The three- or four-story block building became the downtown norm, arising first in the oldest part of town and replacing earlier one- or two-story commercial buildings and commercialized residences.

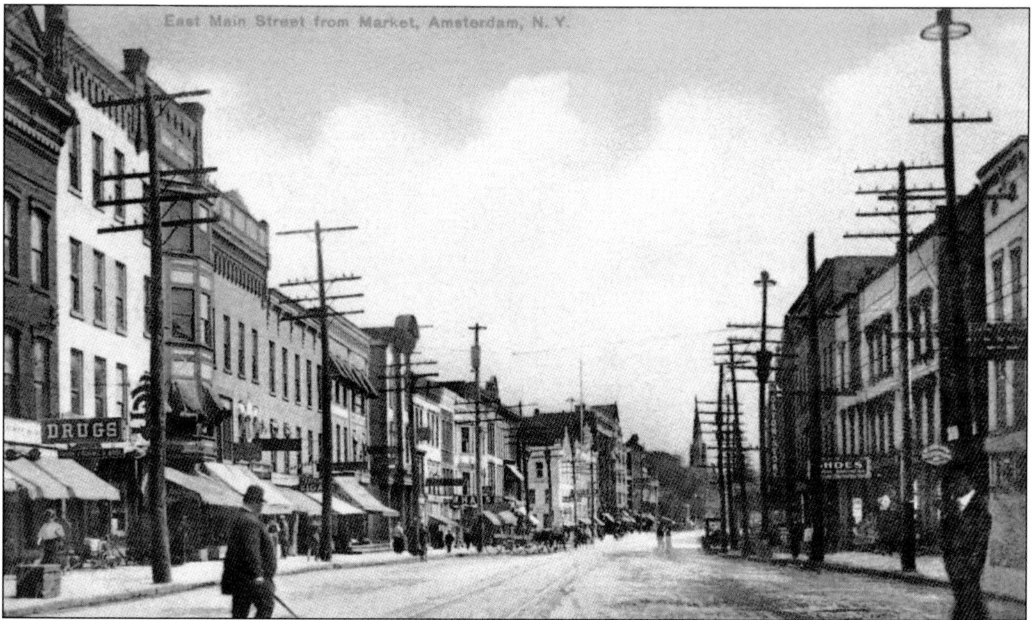


This view, taken farther to the east, shows a number of buildings that managed to escape urban renewal and are now a section of modern East Main Street. Halfway down the left-hand side of the street is the old First National Bank building, a reference for later images. The circular devices at the top of the utility poles spread wires to individual buildings; the wires may have been removed from the photograph when the card's original image was colorized (see page 16).

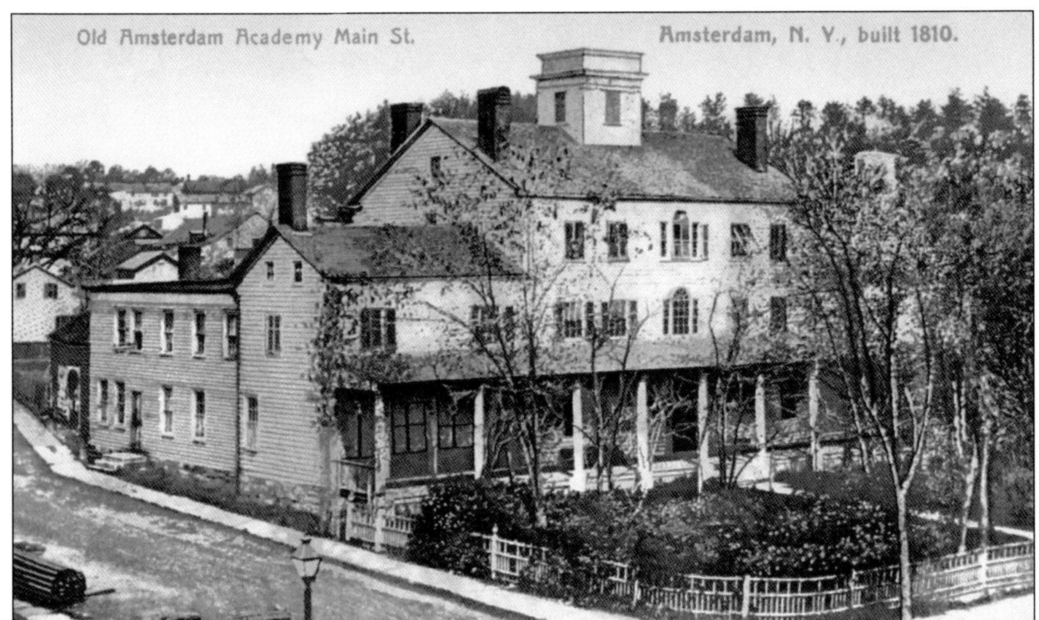


Originally the Globe Hotel, this building, located on the northeast corner of Main and Chuctanunda Streets, was a stage house on the old Mohawk Turnpike. In 1839, it became the Amsterdam Female Seminary, which provided dormitory rooming for female students and a coeducational program by day. After the school moved to new quarters and expanded its charter, the old building was torn down in the 1860s.

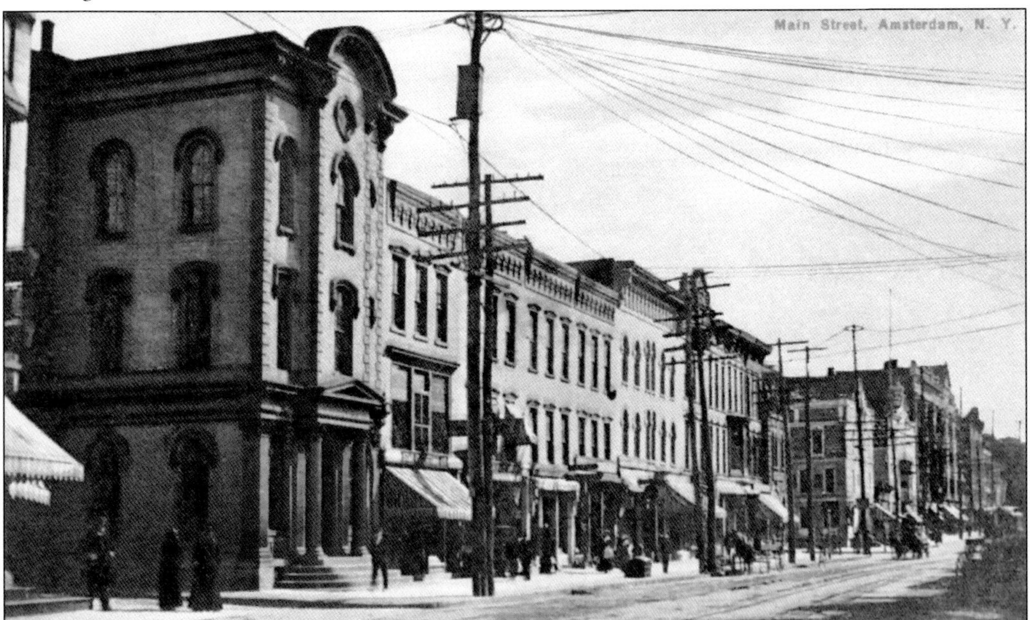


The First National Bank was organized in 1860, federally chartered in 1865, and occupied the former site of the Globe Hotel. The bank used the lower stories, and the upper stories served various purposes, including housing the YMCA at one time. All of the buildings on the second (lower right) block were destroyed to create the new Route 30 arterial and the Amsterdam Mall. Many of the buildings of the closest block (including the bank building) still exist.

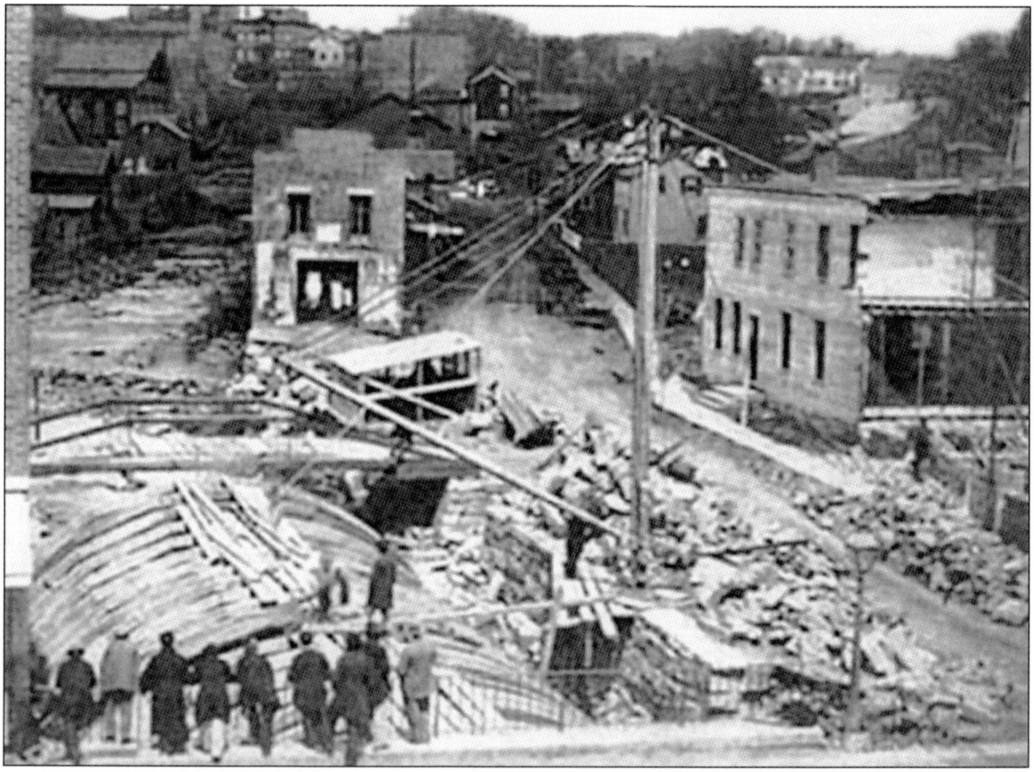

Above, the old firehouse, built in 1839 for a volunteer company, is seen at left center between the Chuctanunda Creek and Chuctanunda Street. To the right in this image, the former Globe Hotel is being demolished. The activity in the foreground appears to be the construction of the culvert, which would carry the creek under Main Street and the rail tracks to the Mohawk. At the top center on Market Street is a house with a cupola, which was the home of mill founder William Greene. In the image to the right is the old firehouse as it appeared after being modified and expanded in the 1890s. The tower was added to permit the hanging of fire hoses to dry out between uses to avoid mildew and rot. After the fire department moved to its new central station (see page 69), this became the police headquarters until the new public safety building opened in 1974.

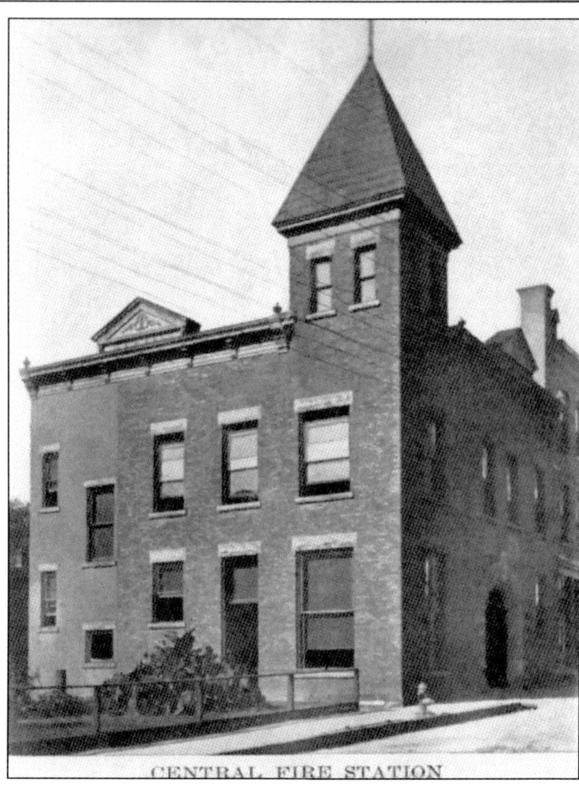

CENTRAL FIRE STATION

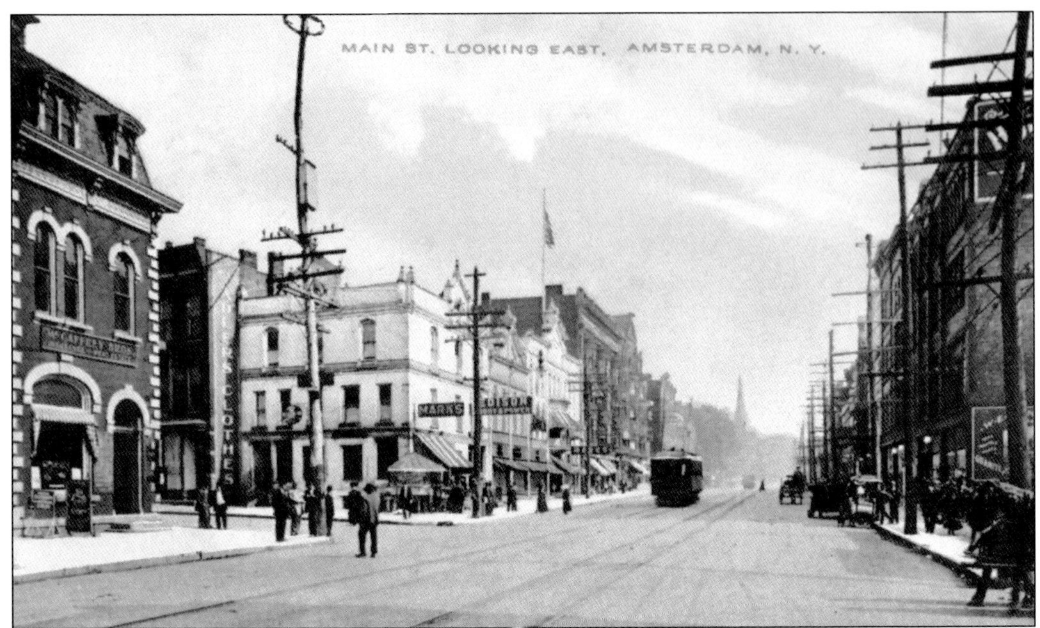


These views are from essentially the same point and roughly the same time. Above at right is the McCaffery Brothers building, which housed Amsterdam's first telephone and telegraph exchange. Farther left in the same picture and at the right in the one below is the Reynolds business school; the post office was located here in the 1890s, and later it was the waiting room for the Fonda, Johnstown and Gloversville interurban trolley service. At center in the photograph below, the building with the large painted advertisement is the Behr Block, which housed the local National Guard company before the armory was built. City trolley service originated in 1873 with the founding of the Amsterdam and Rockton Street Railway, which was later known as the Amsterdam Street Railroad Company, and absorbed into the Fonda, Johnstown and Gloversville in 1901.

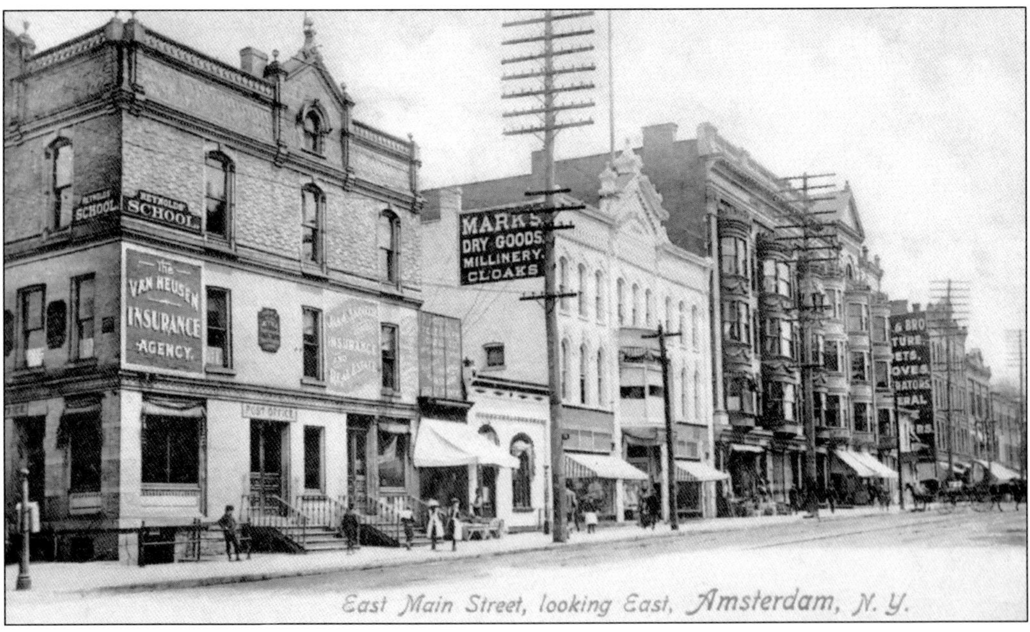

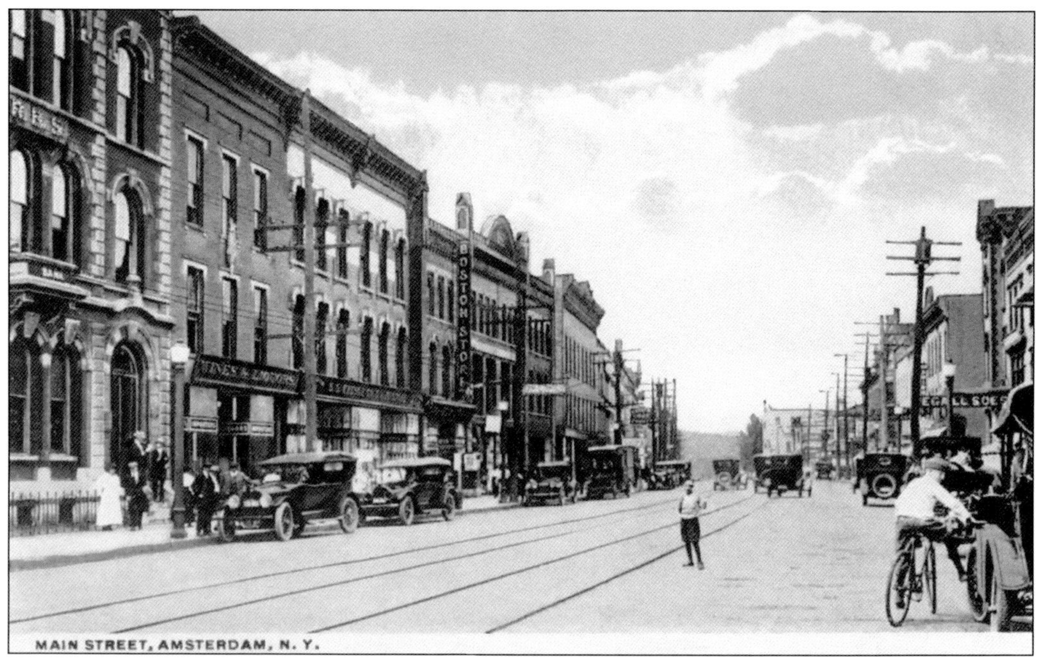
MAIN STREET, AMSTERDAM, N. Y.

In these two views, the perspective is to the west, with the Hotel Conrad in the distance. Railroad Street is to the left in both frames, and Chuctanunda Street is halfway down the right side. Amsterdam's first bank was the Farmers Bank, organized in 1839. After a series of locations, the bank constructed its own building in 1875; it is seen on the far left and still stands. The First National Bank (the reorganized Bank of Amsterdam) constructed its own building, which is the prominent overhang on the right on the corner of Chuctanunda Street.

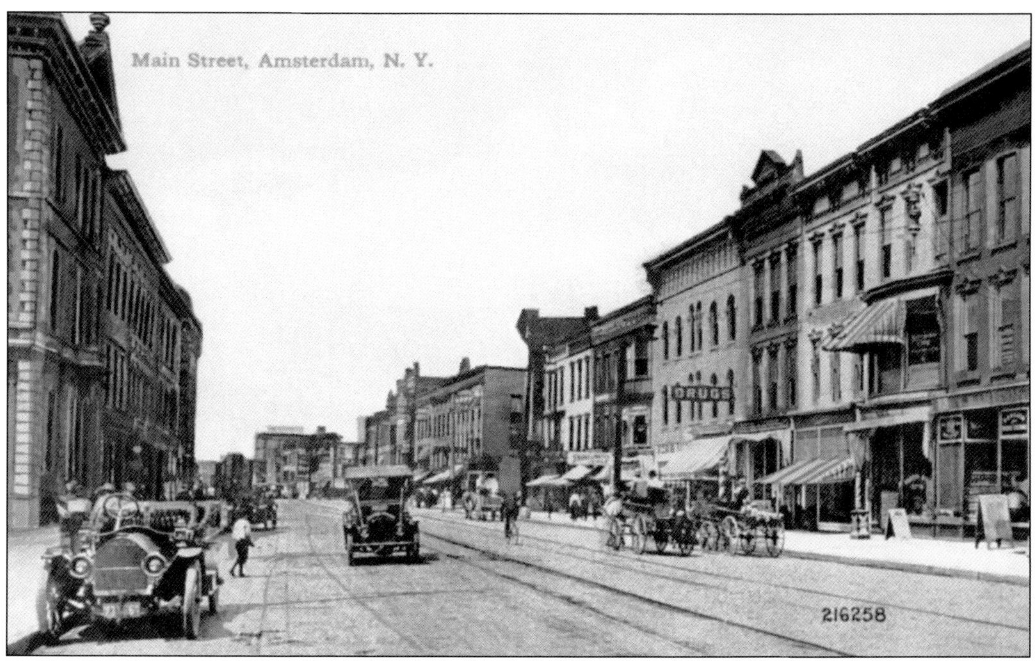

Main Street, Amsterdam, N. Y.

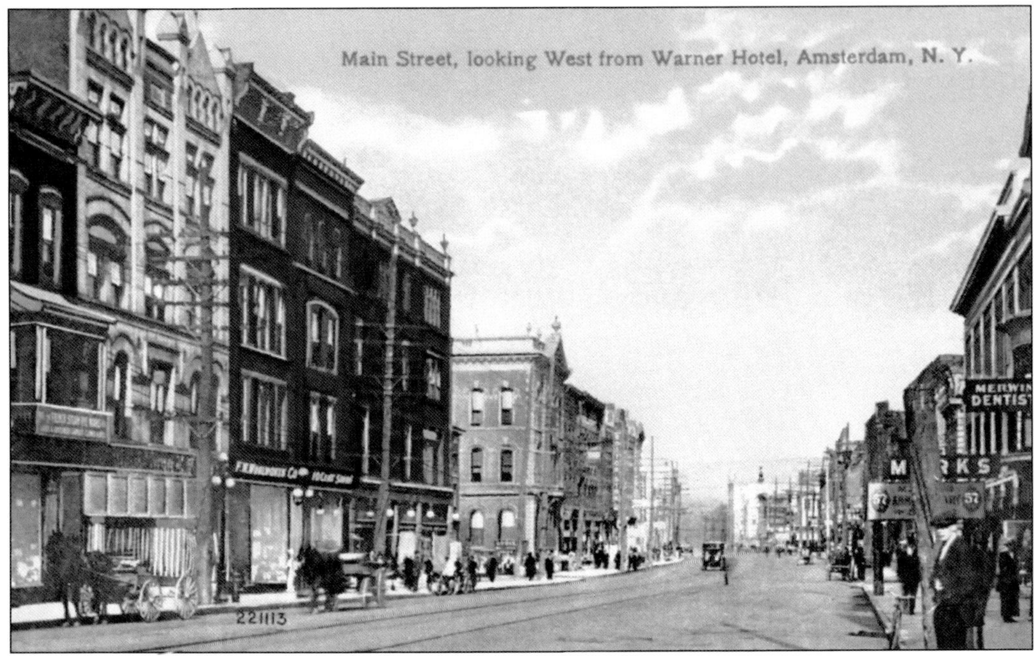


In the above picture, the perspective has moved back, with the bank building at the far left in the last picture now in the left middle at the intersection. The picture below show the area further east along Main Street to just short of where the Hotel Warner was later built. For reference, the Cassidy Blocks (*c.* 1890) appear on the right-hand side of the pictures below on both this page and the next. Standing in this position today, one would be inside the downtown mall. In some of these downtown views, the streets are paved, but in others they are not. For example, East Main Street was bricked in 1891 while West Main Street was not paved until 1911.

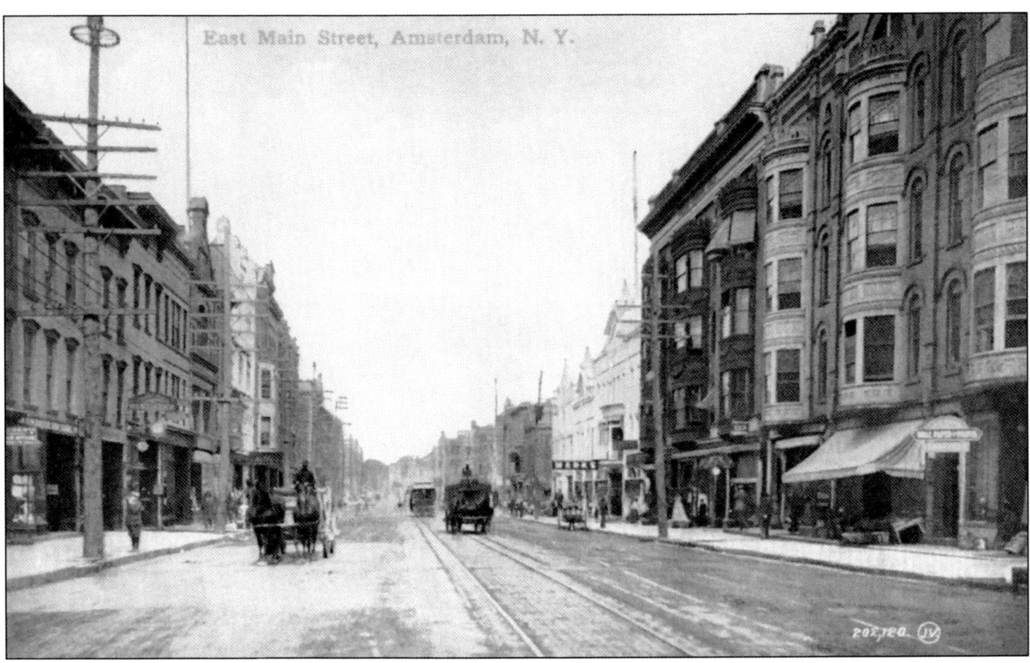

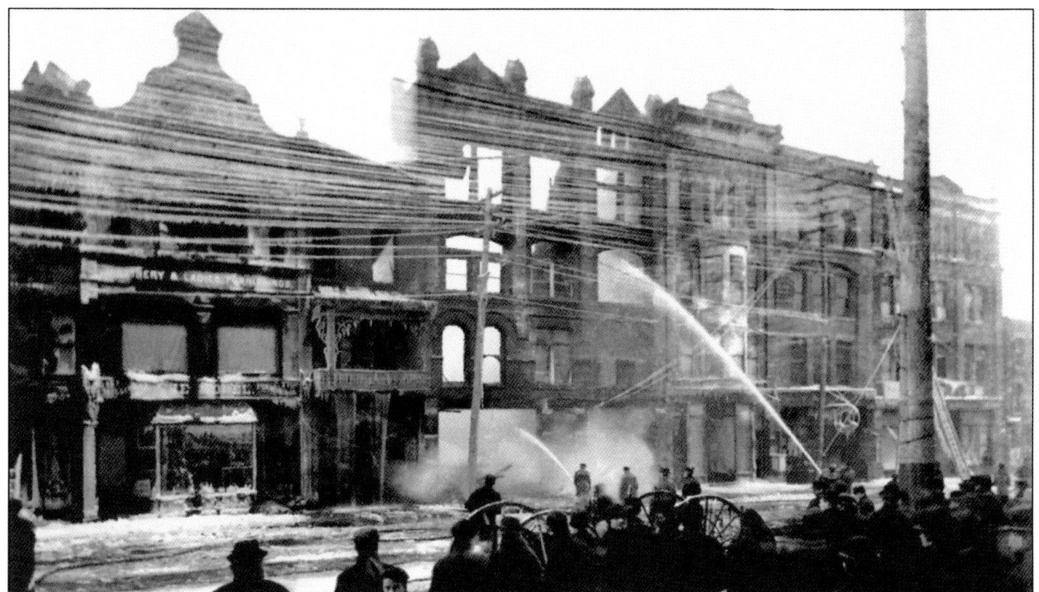

Amsterdam volunteer firemen fight a fire in the Arnold Block building on February 3, 1897. Over $75,000 in damage was suffered by the store, offices, and flats in this block, the Parr Block to the west, and the Yund Block to the east. The fire was covered in the *New York Times* the next day.

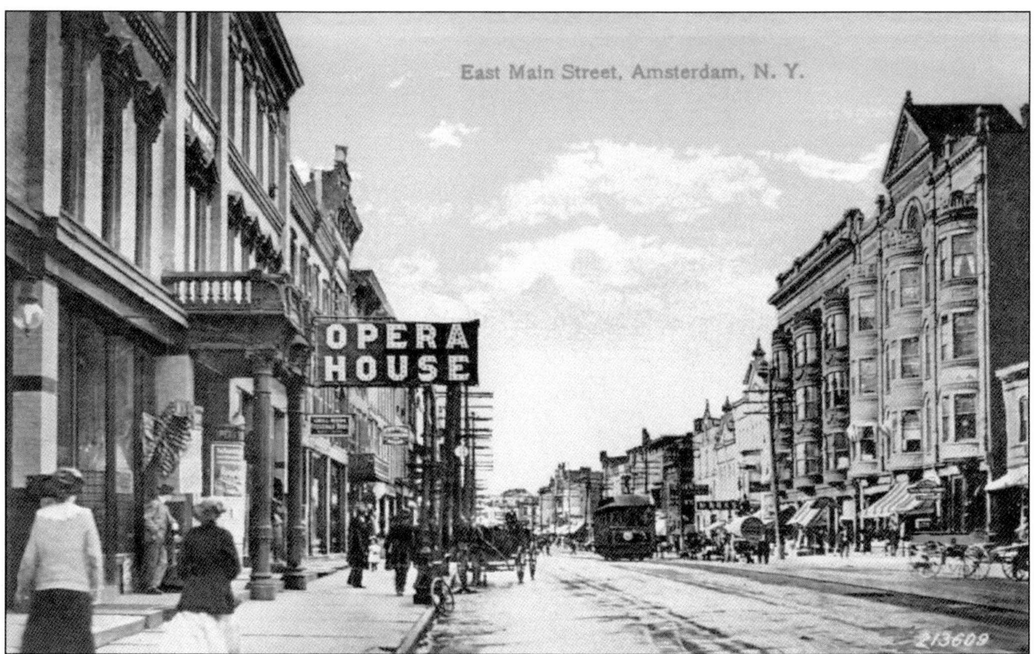


Amsterdam's East Main Street Opera House was actually a playhouse that featured the likes of concerts by John Phillip Sousa, exhibition boxing by John L. Sullivan, and oratory by William Jennings Bryan. Although the opera house was actually located at the rear of the Hotel Warner, the sign and entrance for it were located at the front of the hotel on East Main Street. Access was through a long arcade that ran through the hotel.

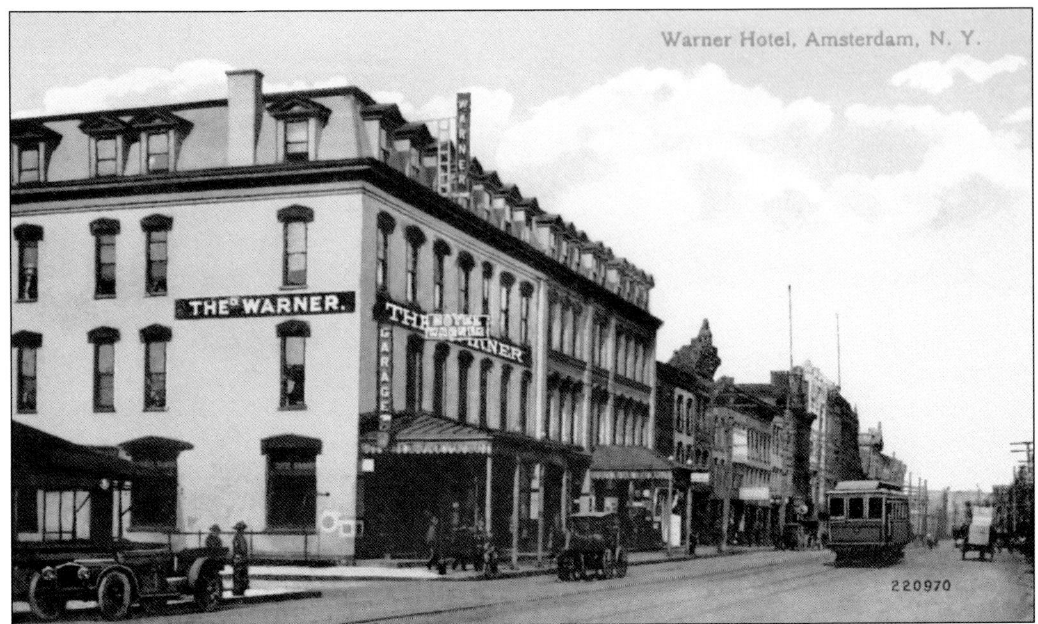


The Hotel Warner was the first large, modern hotel in Amsterdam, built in 1882 on the corner of Walnut and East Main Streets. An advertisement for the Warner from 1897 states its "cuisine equals any $2 hotel in the state." With 76 rooms, telephones, and electric lighting, the hotel was profitable enough that a fourth story was added in 1902. During the 1930s, the hotel was renamed the Hotel Amsterdam.

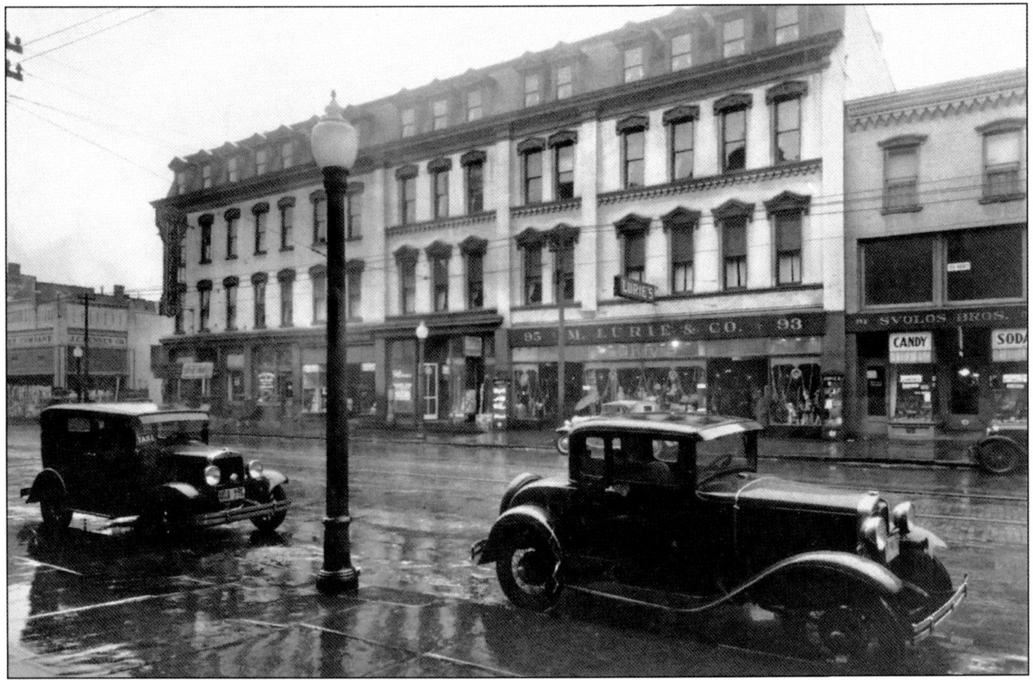


The license plate on the first car dates this photograph to 1934 or 1935. Part of the Hotel Warner is now Lurie's Department Store, famous to Amsterdam children of all ages for the pneumatic messenger system that whooshed payments from the cashiers to the central office.

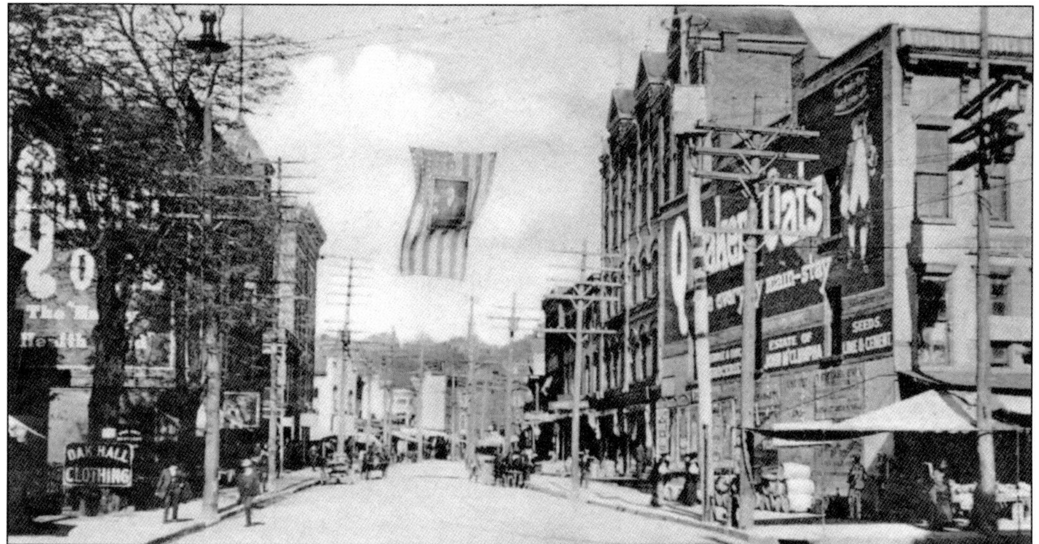

A banner promoting the election of Theodore Roosevelt flies above Market Street near Republican Party headquarters. Whether the view is from his gubernatorial campaign of 1898 or presidential campaign of 1904 cannot be readily established. The absence of trolley tracks on Market Street is interesting but not significant because they were present on either campaign date and may have been eliminated during the color lithography processing of the original photograph.

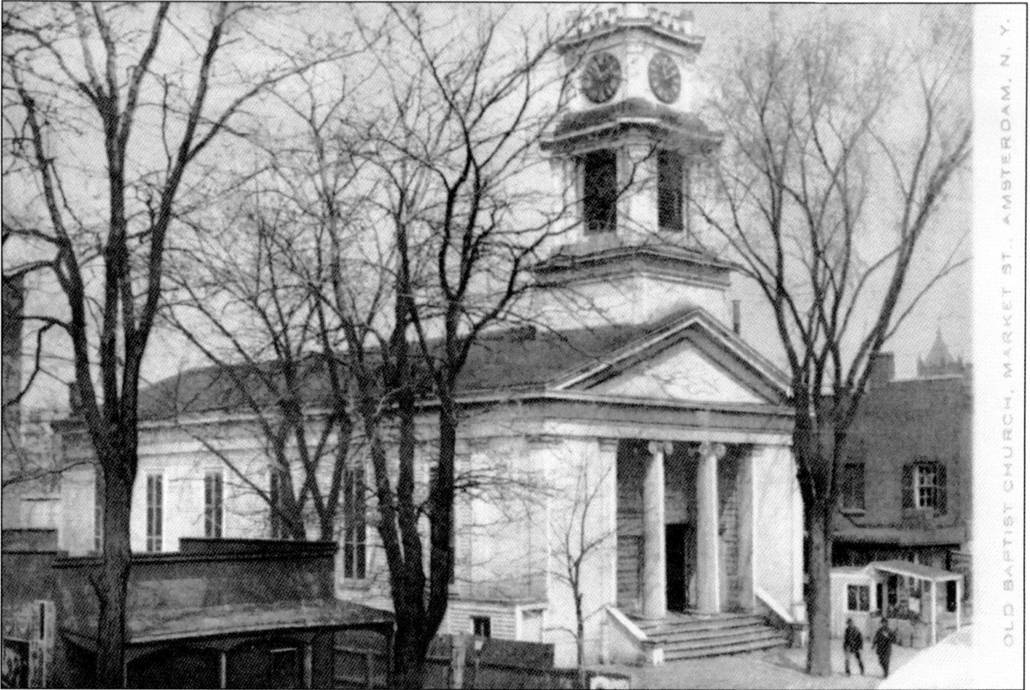

This Baptist congregation was first organized in 1825 and was initially established in a brick building on Main Street. The pictured wooden clapboard church was constructed in 1842 on lower Market Street, and its tower bell served as the local fire alarm. Still later, the congregation moved into a church on Division Street, which was torn down in 1969 to create room for fixed-income housing.

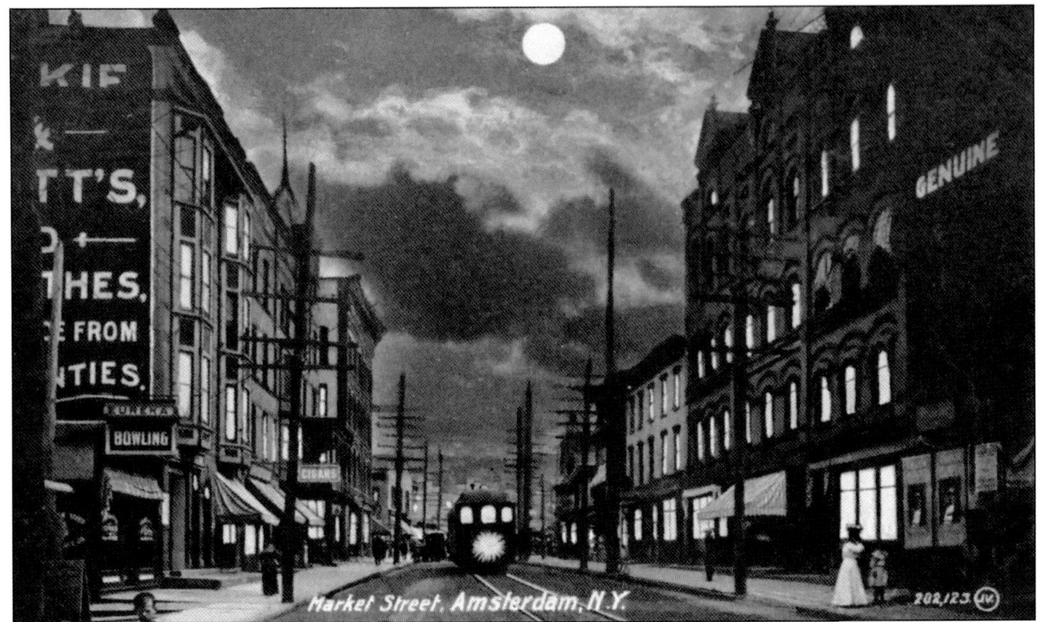


This is a night view of Market Street looking north. On the right is the Sanford Homestead building, erected in 1889. This prime location near Main Street was home to the first city hall and Board of Trade (later called the Chamber of Commerce). The Odd Figure Bazaar and Larrabee's stores occupied the first level. *Homestead* referred to this site's previous use as industrialist and developer Stephen Sanford's boyhood home.

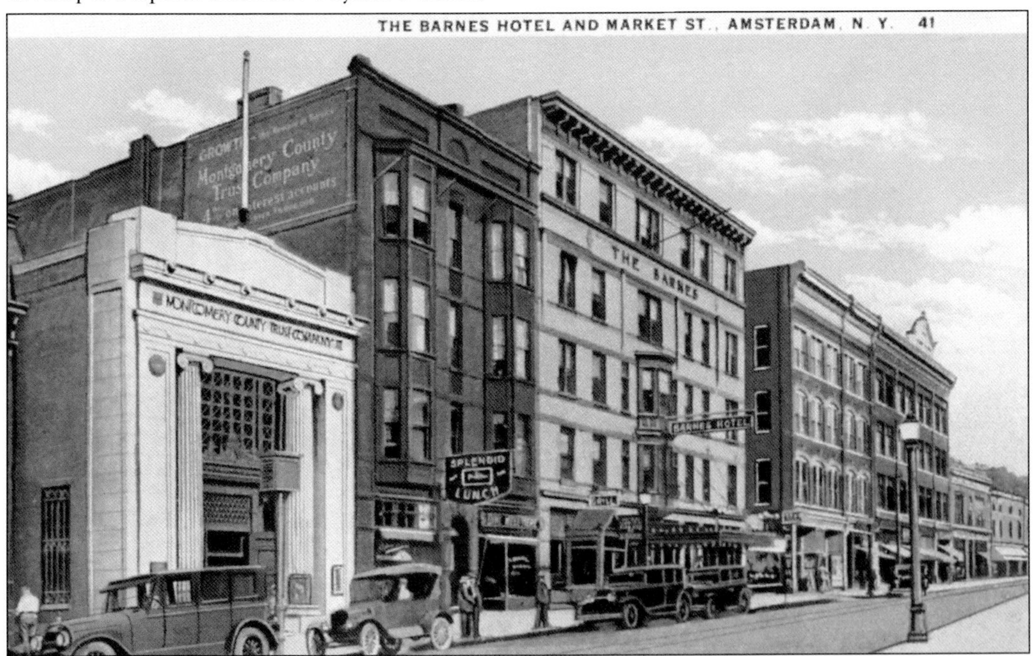


The Barnes Hotel is at center in this picture and the one above. To its left is the Rulison Block where the Splendid Lunch let its name do its advertising. This building also housed Amsterdam's first cinema, a nickelodeon. Farther left is the Montgomery County Trust Company, established in 1912.

Barnes Hotel, Amsterdam, N. Y.

The Barnes Hotel was the successor to the Central Hotel and was built in 1910 as a competitor to the Hotel Warner. Business was good enough that a fourth floor was added not long afterwards. The alleyway between the buildings led to a garage. As automobile use increased, paving and repair and service facilities also increased. Dust, mud, and horse droppings diminished but so did amenities, such as trees, awnings, and wide sidewalks, as the concern shifted to providing for safe traffic lanes and parking.

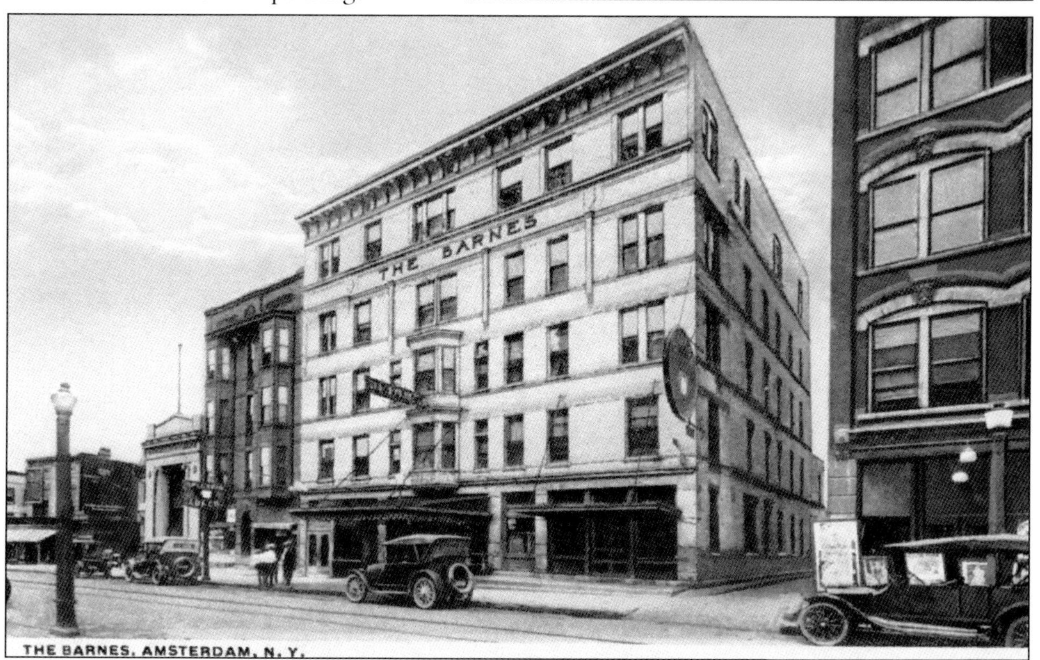

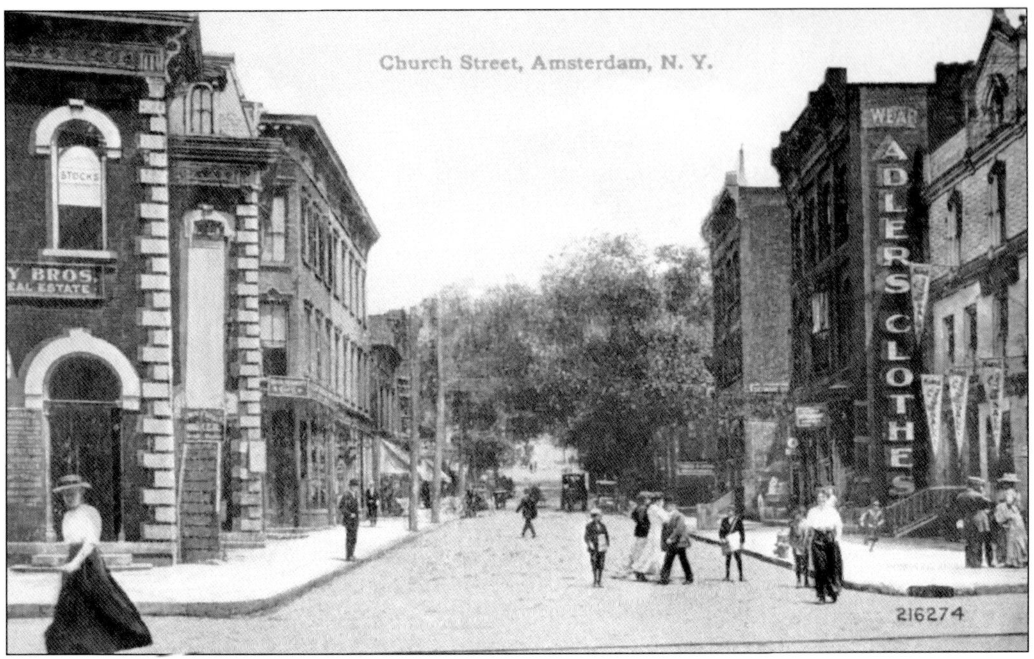


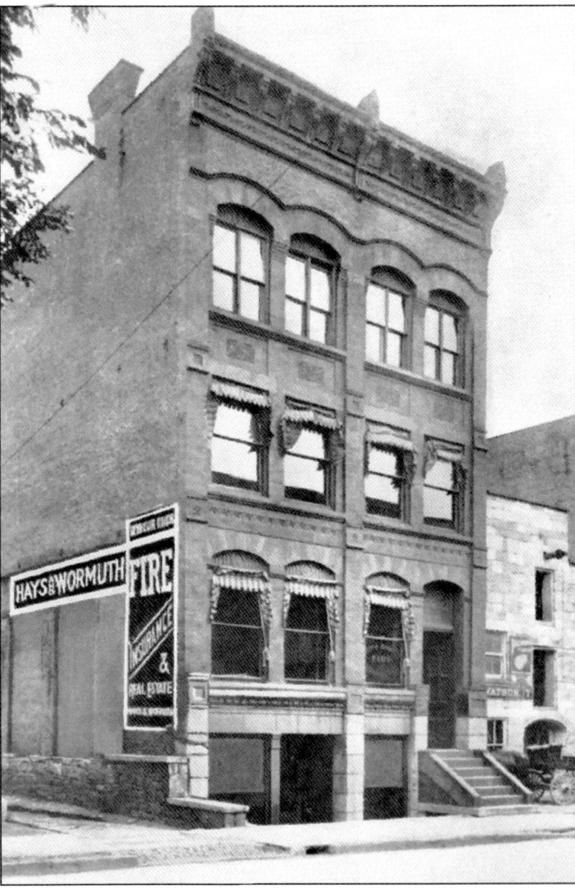


Above, looking north from Main Street on the near left is the McCaffrey Brothers building, which housed the central office for the first 50 telephone lines installed in the city in 1881. Farther up on the left is where Federal Street was later cut in to provide access to the post office when it is built in 1936. At left is the insurance building where Hays and Wormuth wrote policies for more than 80 years before moving to the north limits of the city. This building was where the first common council meeting was held after Amsterdam became a city in 1885 and was also frequently used for union meetings.

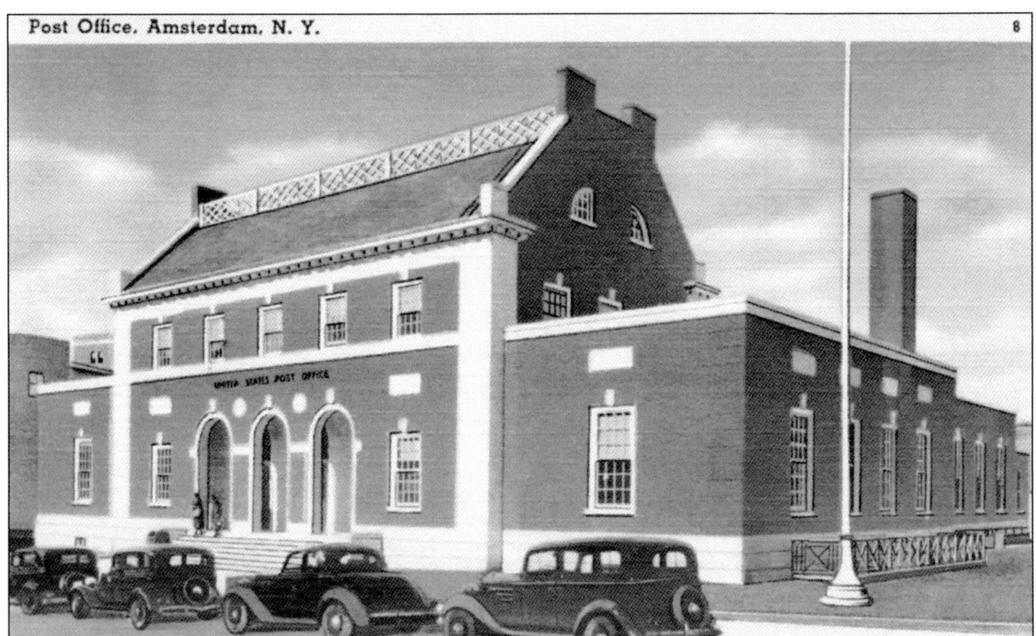


The current post office building, designed by Louis Simony in a Colonial Revival style, was constructed in 1936. It is located just south of the Amsterdam Public Library. Two Treasury Department arts program murals adorn the sides of its main lobby: one is of Sir William Johnson meeting with the Mohawk Indians, and the other is an Erie Canal scene. Both were painted by H. F. Schnakenberg in 1939 and retouched by local artist Lucy Suhr in 1974.

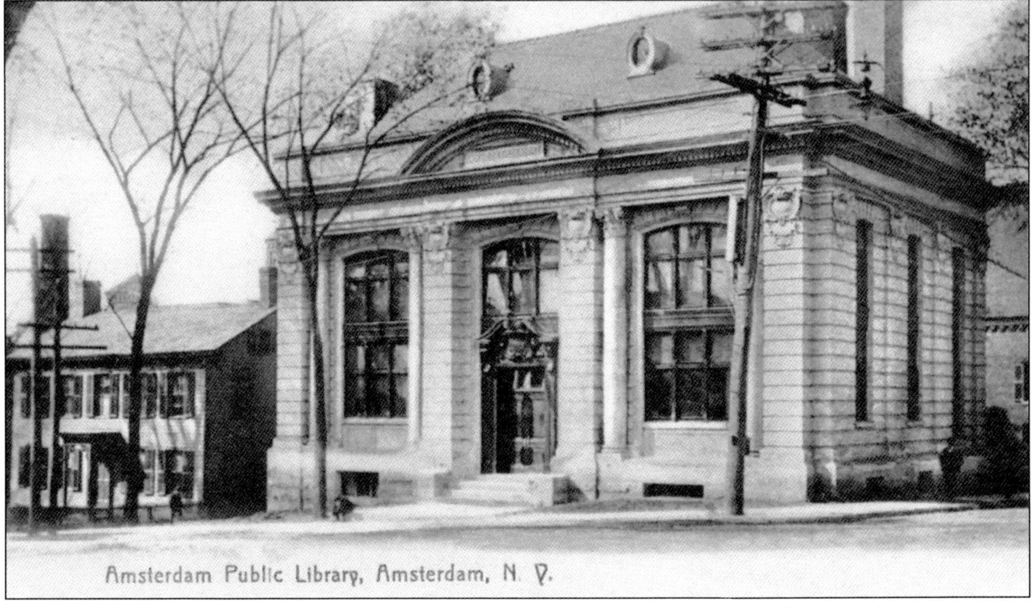


This, the first permanent library, was opened in 1903 with a $25,000 grant from Andrew Carnegie. Two conditions were set for this grant: the library should be "open to all" and the common council had to provide maintenance funds. The first was met when the words were inscribed over the main entrance. The second was arranged after serious drinking and arm-twisting at a local tavern. The rear of the building was extended in 1980.

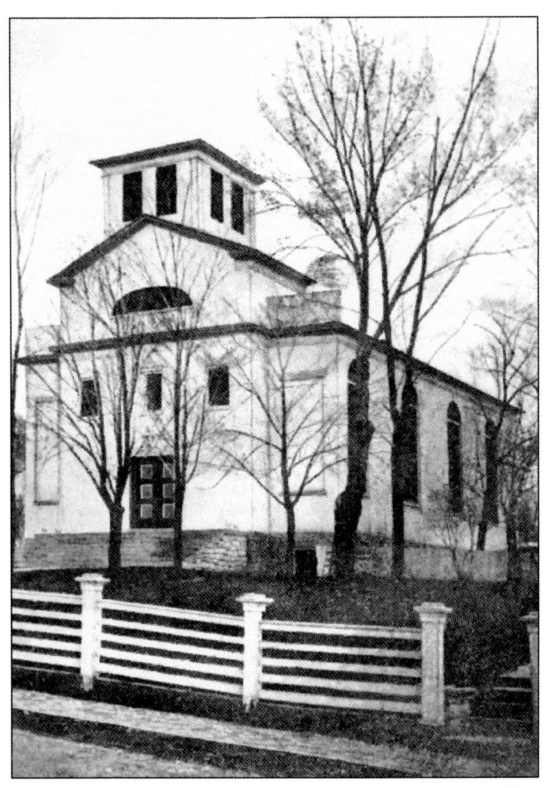

On the left, the Second Presbyterian Church, a wood-frame structure seen in this view from about 1865, was built on the corner of Church and Grove Streets in 1832. The *second* in the church's name referred to the congregation not the building; the first Presbyterian Church in the area was established outside the village in the Town of Amsterdam at Manny's Corners. Shown below, the 1832 structure was razed in 1869 to permit the erection of this imposing brick structure whose steeple once dominated the city skyline. The Sanford family, pioneers of the carpet business in the city, donated Tiffany windows, and the Shuttleworths, executives at Mohawk carpets, donated more modern windows, including one of Jesus blessing the mill workers. All were lost in a horrific fire in January 2000, which caught national media attention. A new, modern church building has since risen from its ashes at this location.

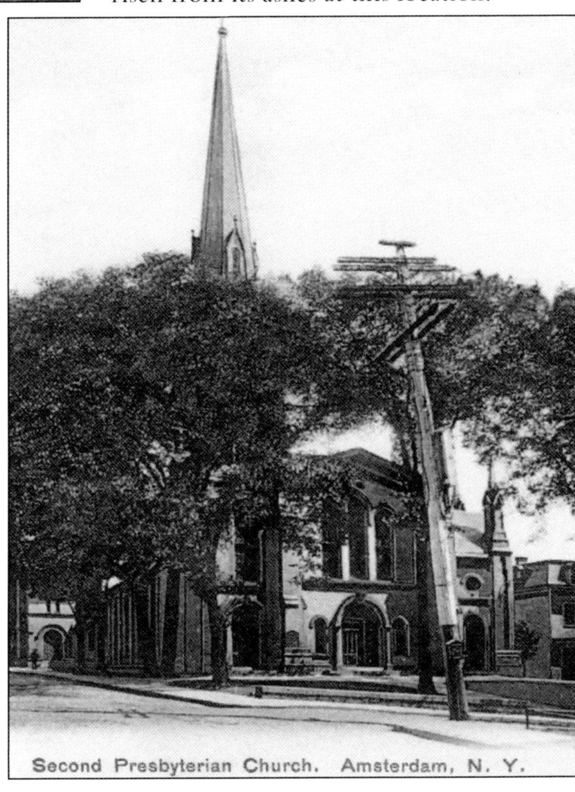

# *Two*

# The River and the Railroad

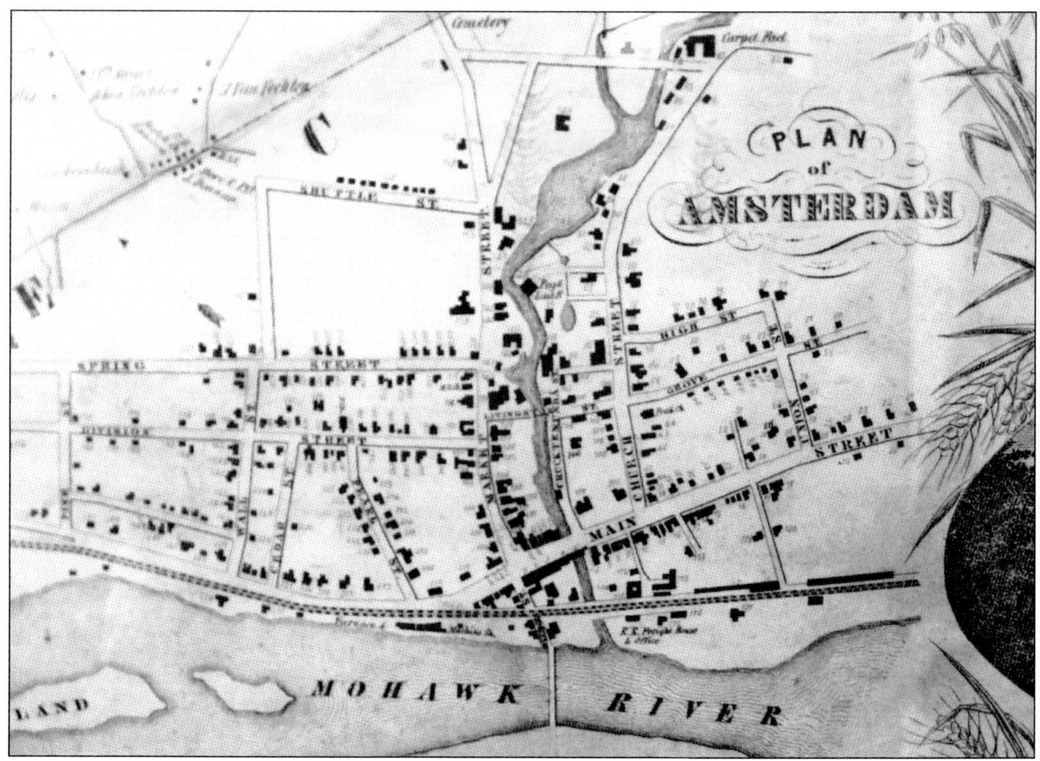


This plan of Amsterdam from an 1853 map shows how the village is beginning to take the shape of the future city. The railroad parallels the river, and a bridge connects the village to Port Jackson and the Erie Canal on the south bank. Mills shoulder the Chuctanunda Creek, which will make Amsterdam the "Carpet City," the largest manufacturer of carpets and rugs in the United States. (Courtesy of Montgomery County Department of History and Archives.)

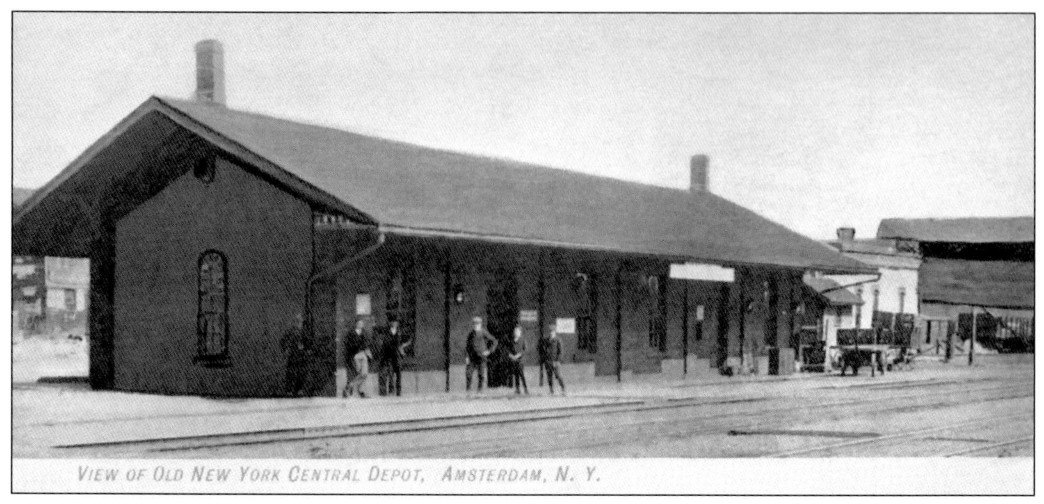
VIEW OF OLD NEW YORK CENTRAL DEPOT, AMSTERDAM, N. Y.

Amsterdam became one of the first American cities with regular rail service when the Utica and Schenectady Railroad reached it on August 1, 1836. The first train to arrive was the famous *DeWitt Clinton*, one of the first steam locomotives built in America, which was originally in the service of the Mohawk and Hudson Railroad. This was the first purpose built depot, erected north of the tracks in 1867 at the foot of Railroad Street.

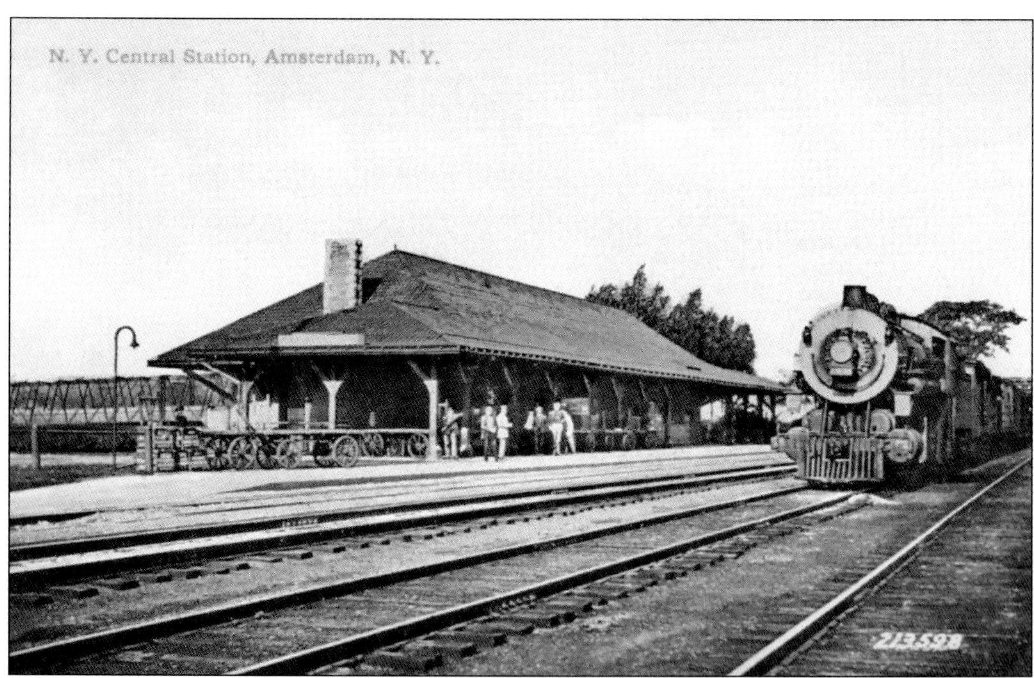
N. Y. Central Station, Amsterdam, N. Y.



This depot was built in 1899 on the south side of the tracks and was the first expressly for passengers. It remained in use until the new Route 30 bridge made its north shore landing here in the late 1960s. A smaller, modern building on the west side took its place in 1970. Portions of the original freight station are now used by a tire company immediately to the east of this site.

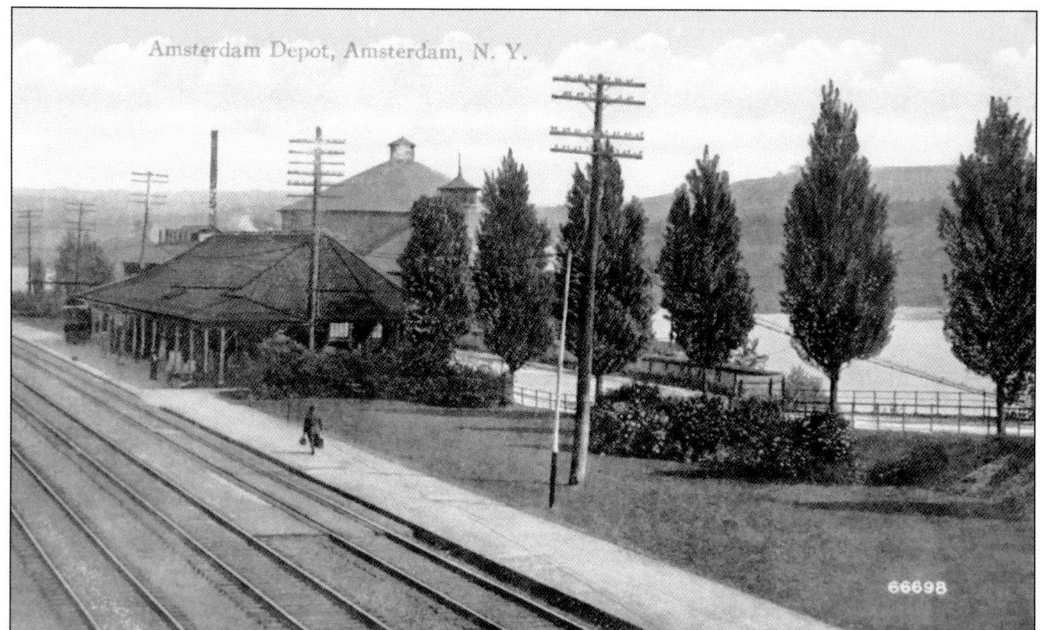


This view shows the 1899 depot in its relative position between the tracks and the Mohawk River and a platform that was extended as the city grew. The conical structure behind the station is part of the Chuctanunda Gas Light Company (see page 39).

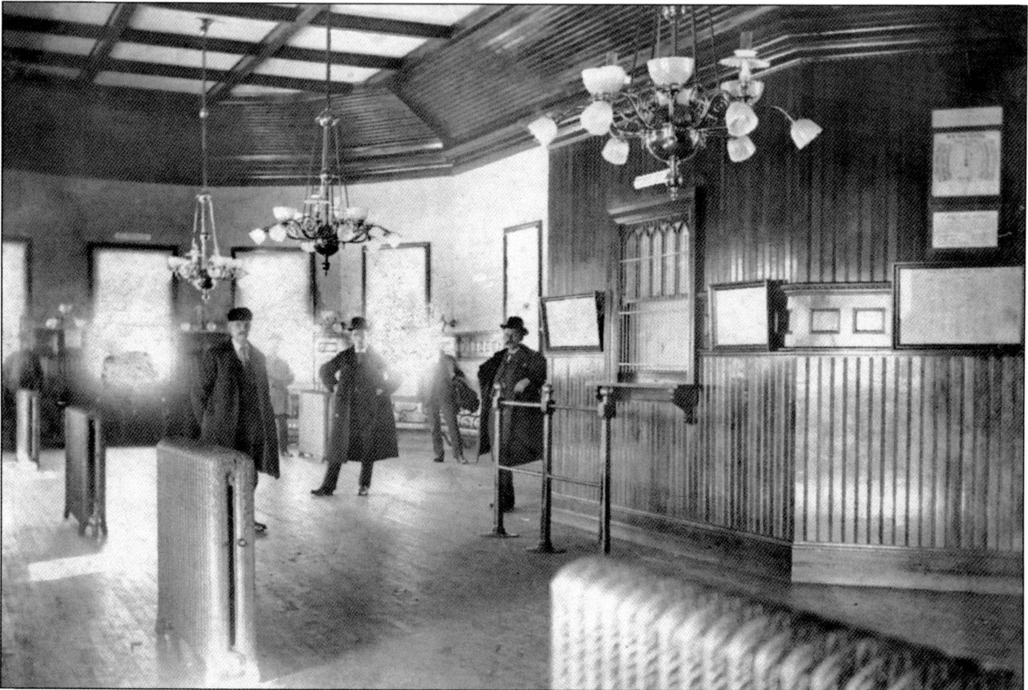

The 1899 depot was built to impress at a cost of $60,000. It was spacious and well appointed with steam heat, combination gas and electric chandeliers, polished woodwork, and coffered ceilings. The audience was the business traveler more than the local residents; Victorian business values—substantial but not frivolous—was the first thing they saw on arrival in Amsterdam.

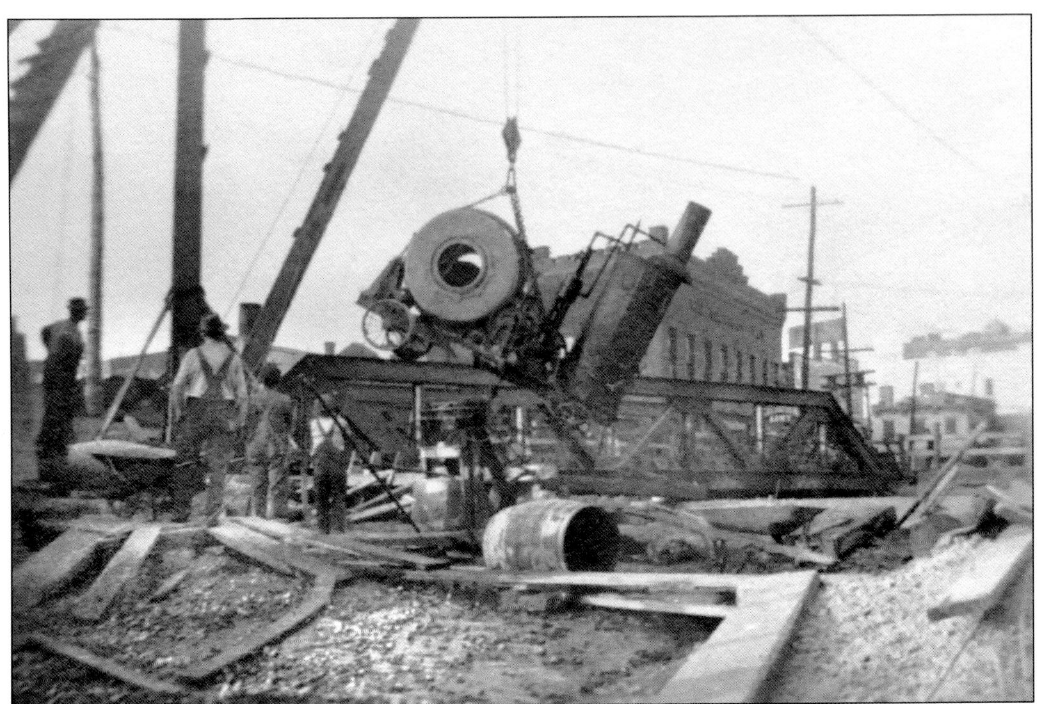

Steam equipment is shown being emplaced to assist with the construction of a new overpass over the New York Central Railroad tracks in 1915, replacing an earlier overpass built in 1895.

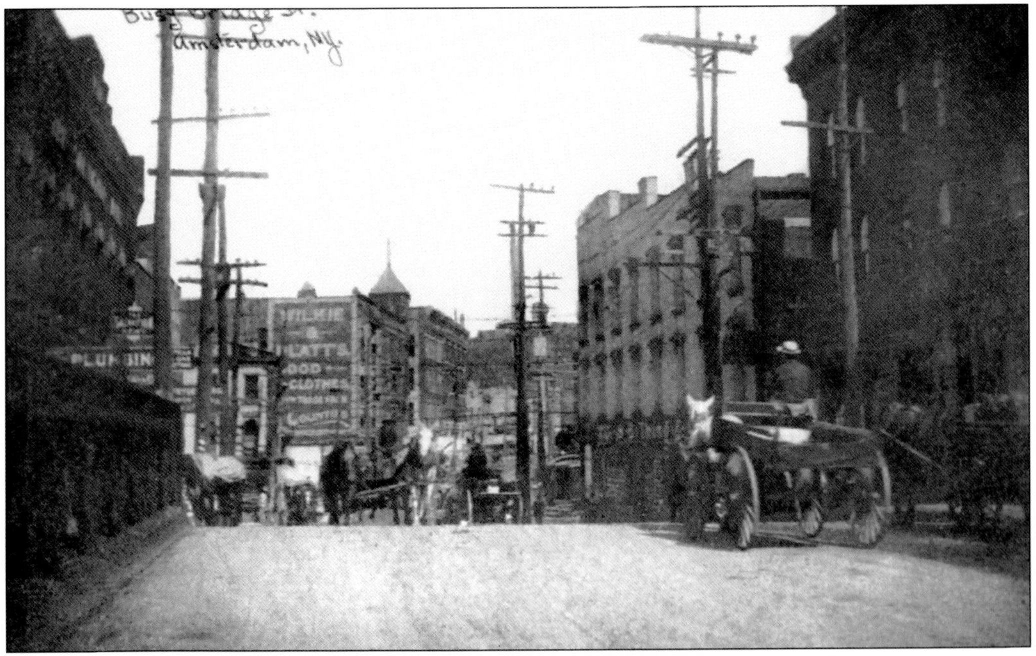


This view appears to have been taken on the 1895 overpass looking north. The number of accidents between high-speed trains and foot and vehicle traffic at grade-level crossings not only prompted the construction of overpasses but also was a factor in the creation of the city's first hospitals.

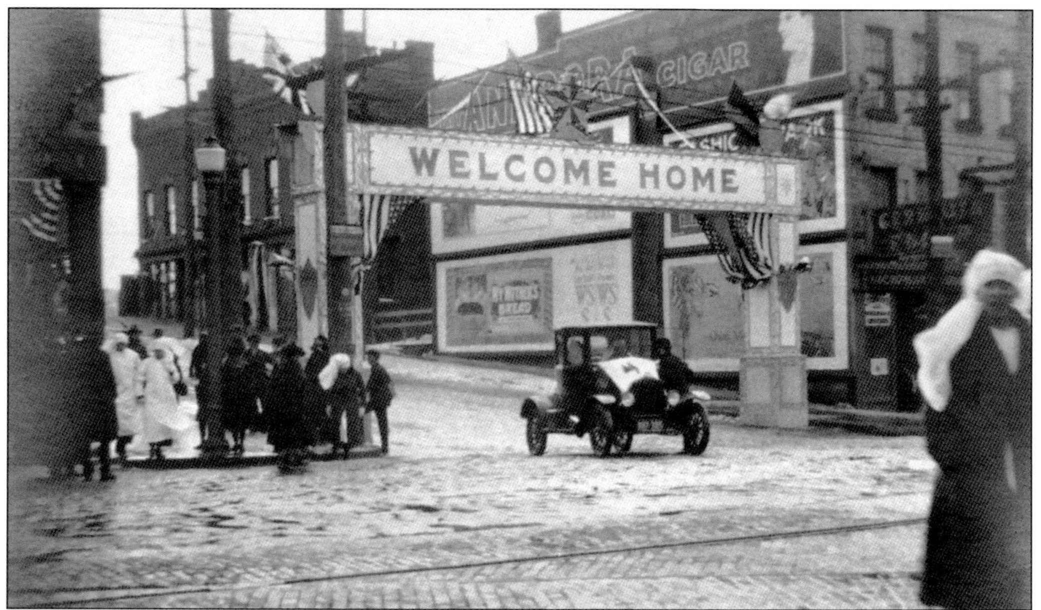


When the Bridge Street overpass was rebuilt in 1915, it was necessary to increase its height to meet that of the new Mohawk River bridge, which was then under construction. Therefore, certain buildings' ground floors became basements, and new entries were constructed into former second levels. It has been said that when one of these buildings was torn down for later roadway expansion, a complete bar room from 1916 was found intact. The banner greeted the local National Guard unit returning in 1919 from World War I.

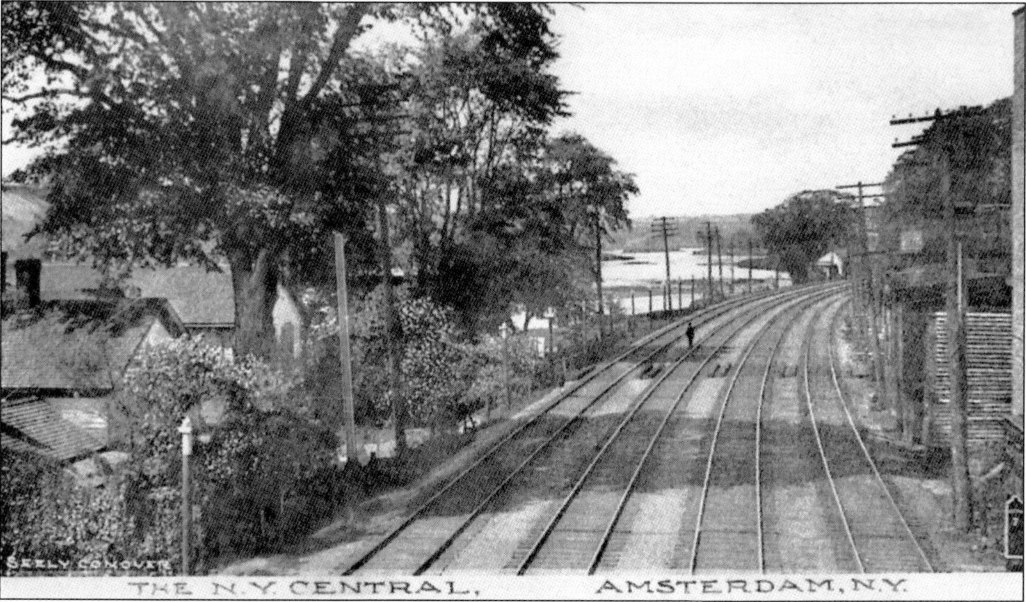


The New York Central Railroad is seen looking west from the Bridge Street overpass. The successor to Amsterdam's first railroad was consolidated into the New York Central Railroad system in 1853. The system stretched from New York City to Buffalo and beyond and permitted Amsterdam industries to ship and receive raw materials and finished product from all over the world faster and cheaper than by the canal.

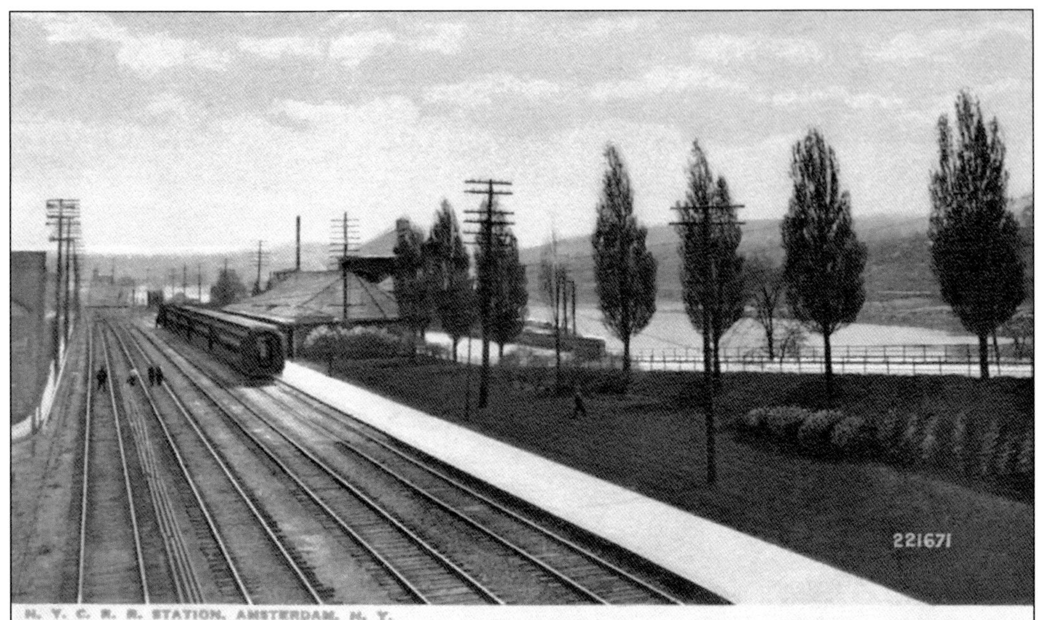


A passenger train departs eastbound from Amsterdam. The tracks through Amsterdam were part of one of the longest four-track runs in the world and helped keep freight and passenger traffic moving smoothly. Approximately one mile east of the city another important but local rail line branched off. Organized in 1879, the Amsterdam, Chuctanunda, and Northern Railroad extended northwest to shuttle freight to and from the upper mills, keeping that traffic off city streets.

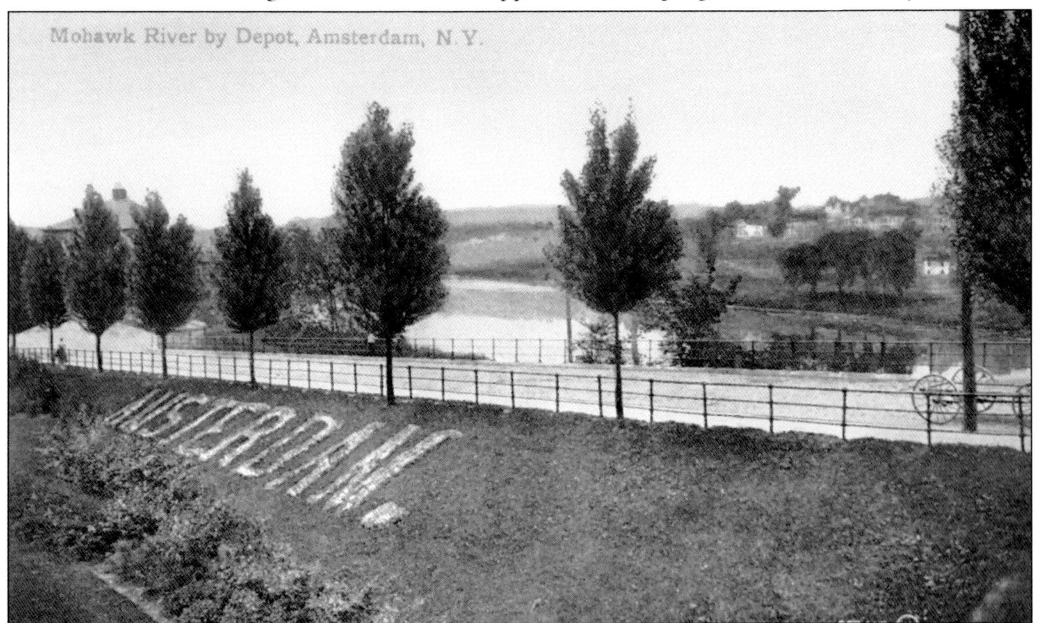


Here is the roadway that connected the rail station with the overpass. It was built in 1910. On a day such as the one pictured on this card, many passengers might prefer the longer walk to passing through the dank and dark pedestrian tunnel that passed from the station under the tracks to Railroad Street. The baggage cart at the far right might have been placed there for their assistance.

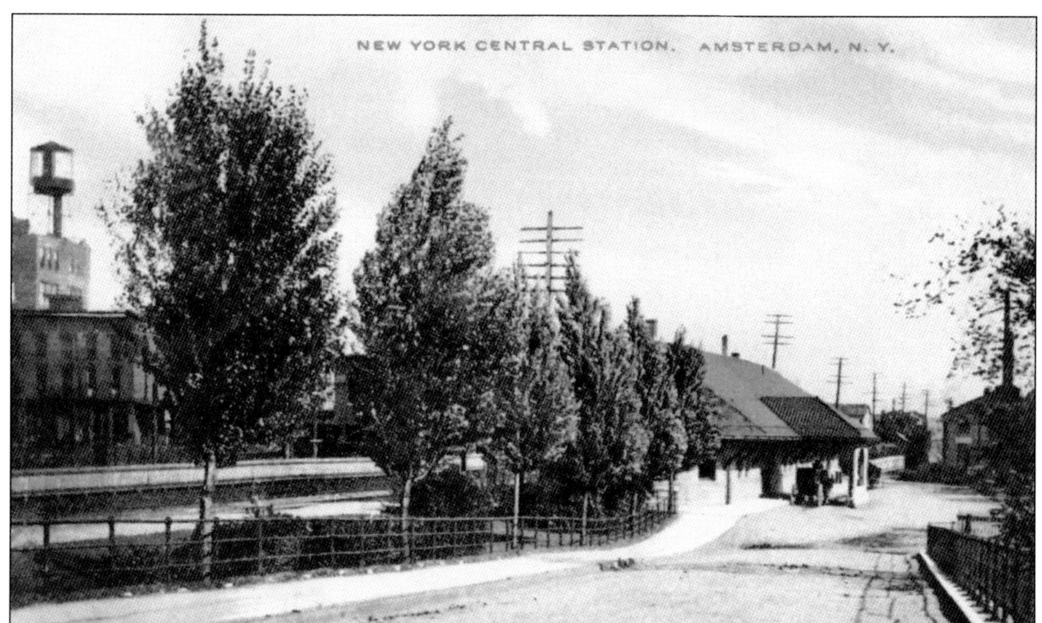


At the height of the rail era, 27 trains each day stopped at Amsterdam; today only a few do. Trucks and airplanes began to take business away from the New York Central Railroad as it had done from the canal. In 1957, the New York Central Railroad eliminated two tracks, and in 1968, it merged with the Pennsylvania Railroad in an attempt to prevent collapse. Soon after, passenger and freight operations were taken over by Amtrak and Conrail, respectively.

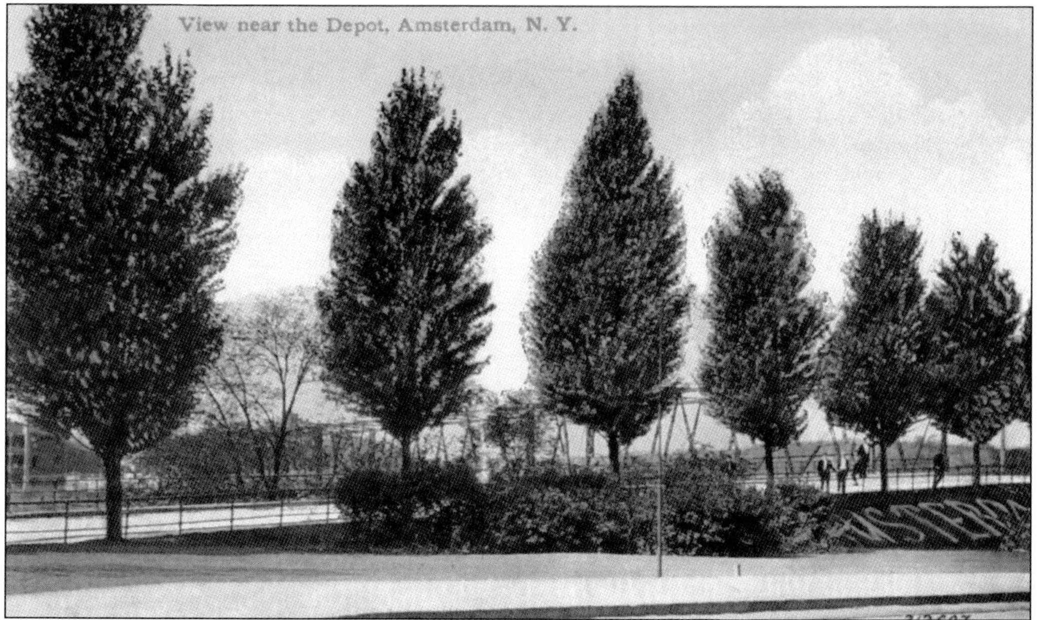


Civic planners today are considering ways to move the train station back to a downtown location. Perhaps then again Amsterdamians will be able to ride or see the great trains of their own day. In the past, these have included Abraham Lincoln's funeral train in 1865, Engine No. 999 (the fastest machine in the world at the time), the *Empire State Express*, the *20th Century Limited*, and the streamliners of the 1930s and 1940s.

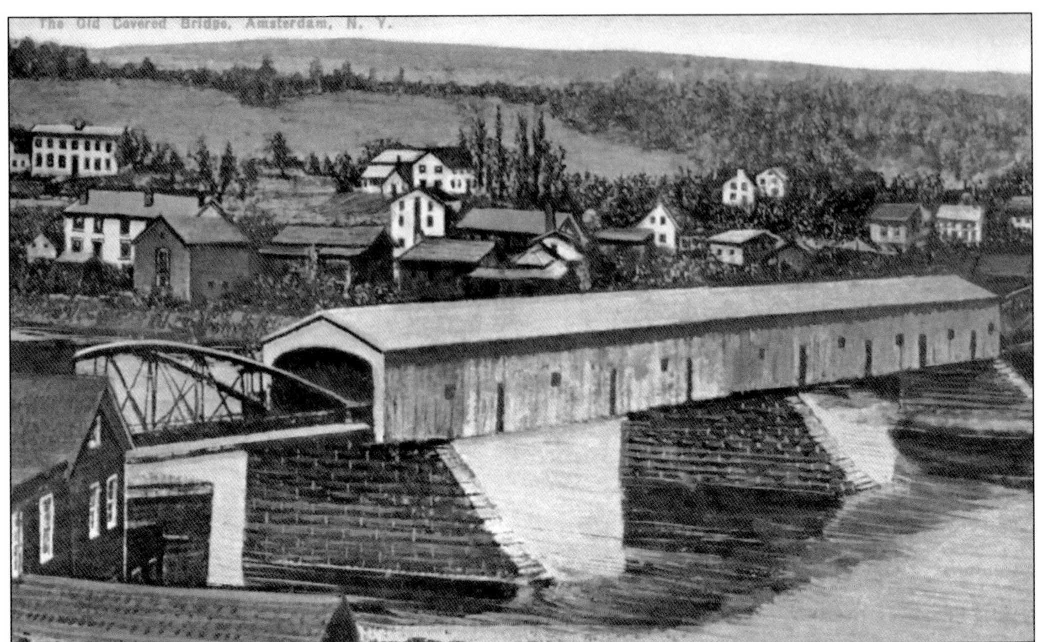


The first bridge over the Mohawk River was built in 1821, which was replaced by another in 1839. This span was built in 1842 and damaged by a boat at high water in 1865 (the metal span at the right may be a replacement for the damaged portion). The purpose of the bridge cover was not to keep the elements off travelers but rather off the bridge structural components.

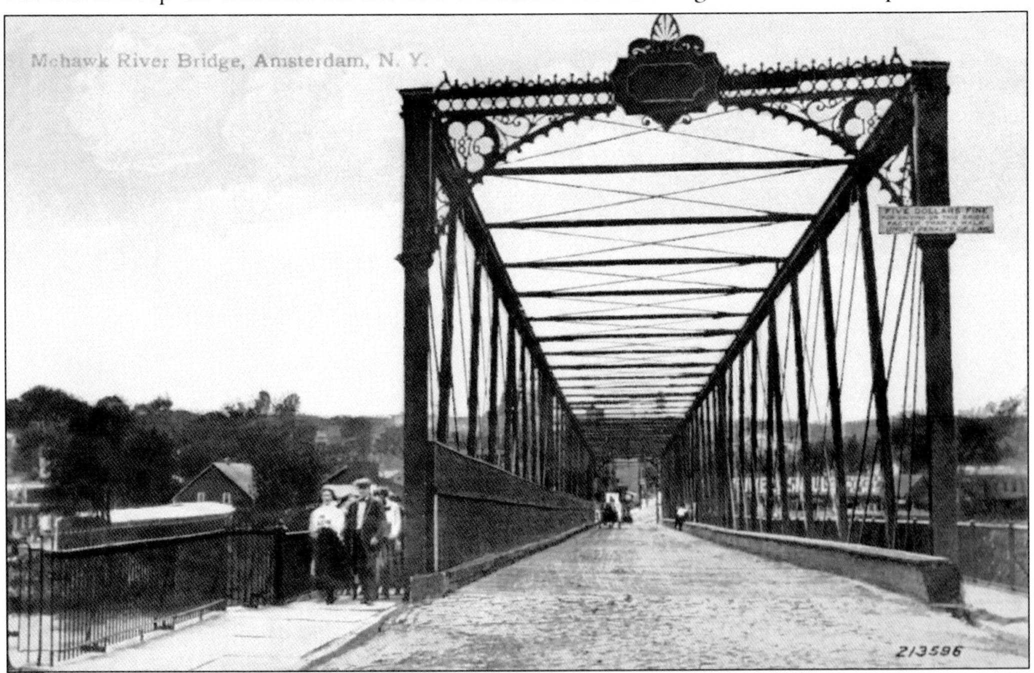


This bridge, built in 1876 (the date is fashioned into the filigree at the upper corners of the ironwork), replaced the above structure. Previous bridges had operated as private companies, but an 1864 law required free passage over the bridge. Nevertheless, the sign at right states, "Five dollar fine for driving on this bridge faster than a walk under penalty of law."

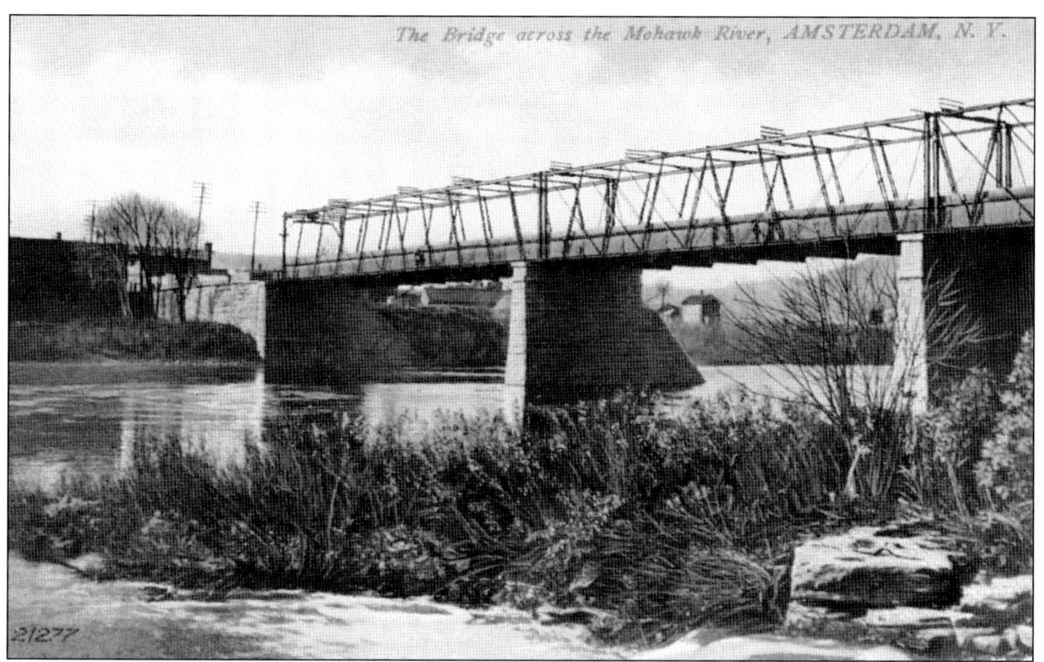


These two postcards represent the stresses on Mohawk River bridges. Both views show the same 1876 bridge from roughly the same position. Above, the river is calm and the water level is low. Below, an ice dam downriver has caused the water level to rise significantly. If either the Schoharie or Chuctanunda Creeks should crest at this time, the results could be catastrophic.

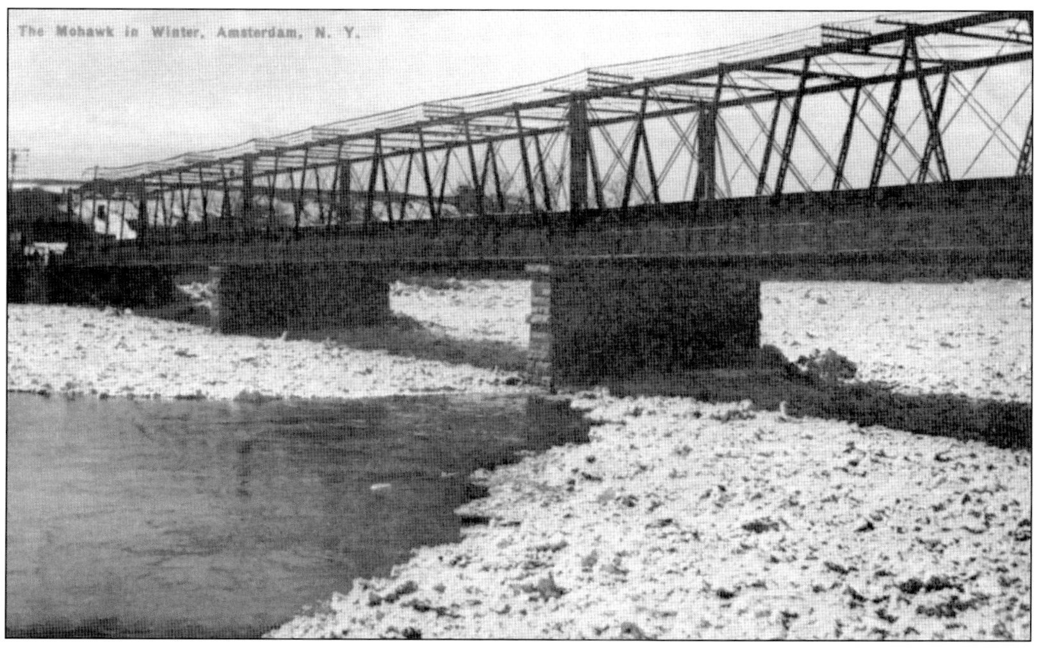

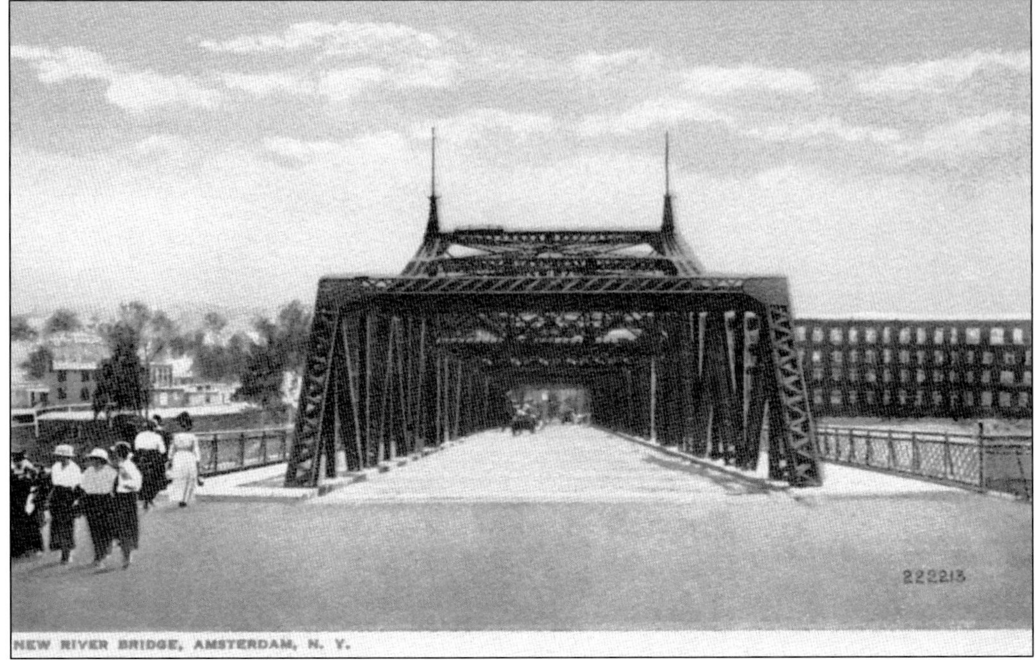


NEW RIVER BRIDGE, AMSTERDAM, N. Y.

These two views show the entrance and span of the 1916 bridge, which stood from January 1916 until December 1972. Although structurally more impressive than its predecessors, by the end of its service life, it was widely regarded as being held together by "pigeon glue." Trolley tracks were optimistically laid down its middle, but a streetcar connection to the south side never occurred.

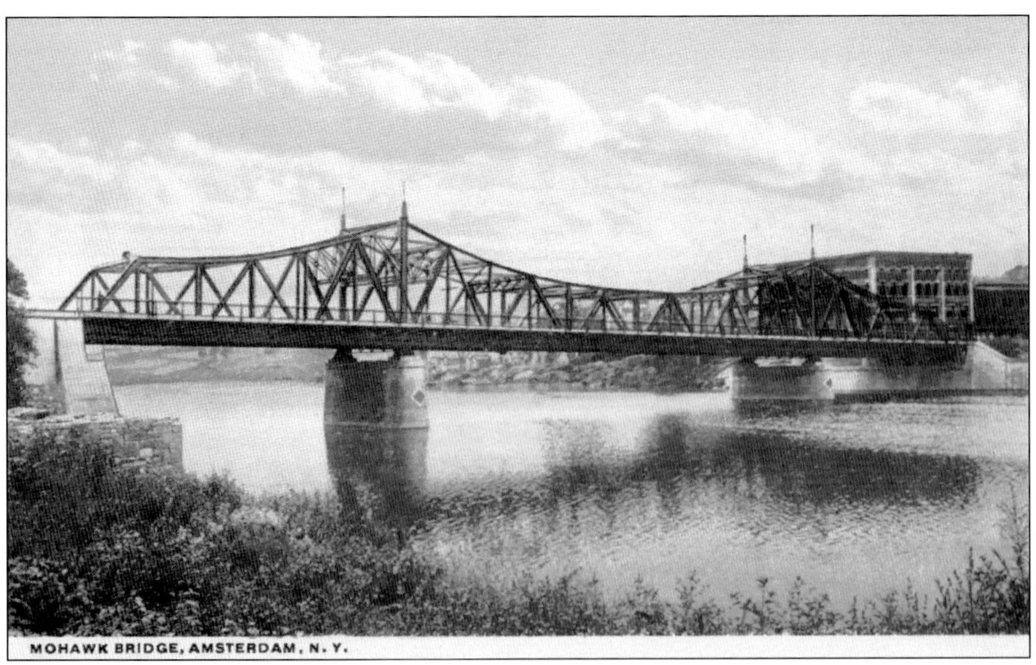

MOHAWK BRIDGE, AMSTERDAM, N. Y.

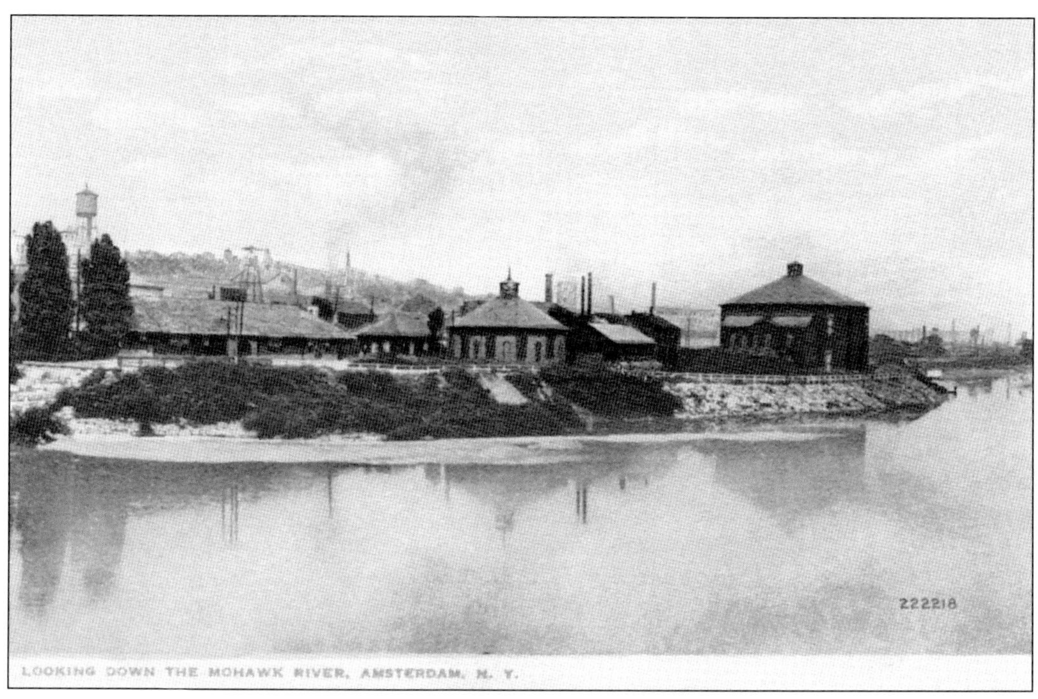


The round buildings on the north shore belong to the Chuctanunda Gas Light Company, organized in 1860. These buildings date to 1867 and processed coal into gas products that were piped throughout the city. The company was purchased in 1929 by New York Power and Light (later Niagara-Mohawk), which took the structures down in the late 1960s. The site today is a pending development as phase II of Riverlink Park.

**Protect Your Meter and Pipes From Frost.**

GAS STOVES ON SALE AT THIS OFFICE.

M J Howard Hanson

Street.

**To Chuctanunda Gas Light Company, Dr.**

For GAS consumed as follows:

STATE OF METER. AUG 1900 624 00

JUL 1900 551 00

Consumption, 6,900 Cu. Ft. at $1.25 per 1000 ft. $ 8.63

Received payment Aug 22 1900.

For the Company

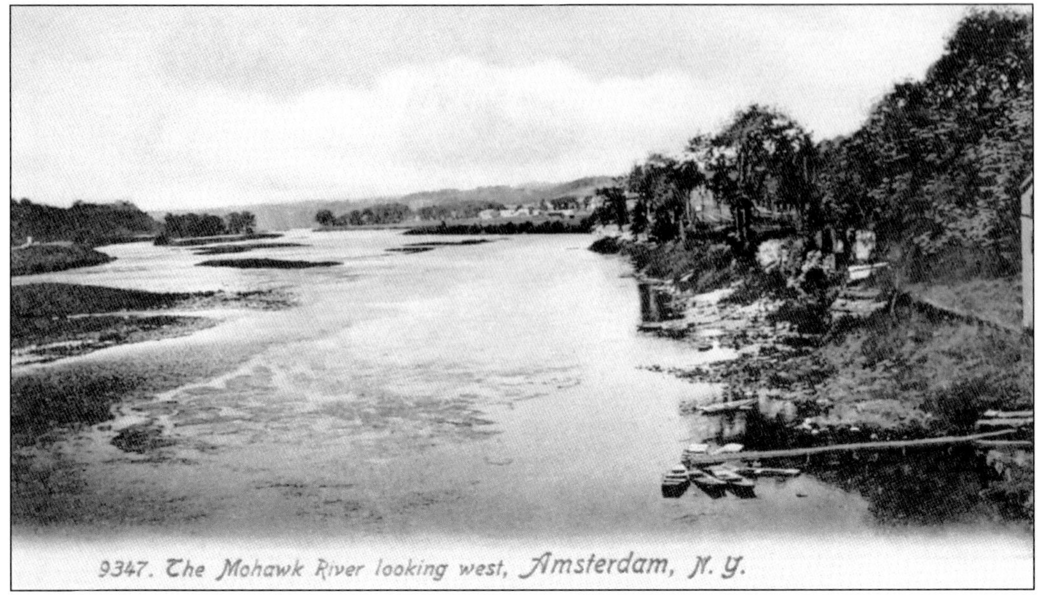

9347. The Mohawk River looking west, Amsterdam, N. Y.

The importance of the Mohawk River in history cannot be underestimated. The valley it carved was the only low-level passage through the Appalachian Mountains from Stone Mountain in Georgia to the St. Lawrence River Valley. This factor made it the natural site for turnpikes, canals, and railroads. It may have been the power of the Chuctanunda Creek that built the mill town, but it was the ability to move raw materials, product, and people along the river's path that turned the town into an industrial powerhouse.

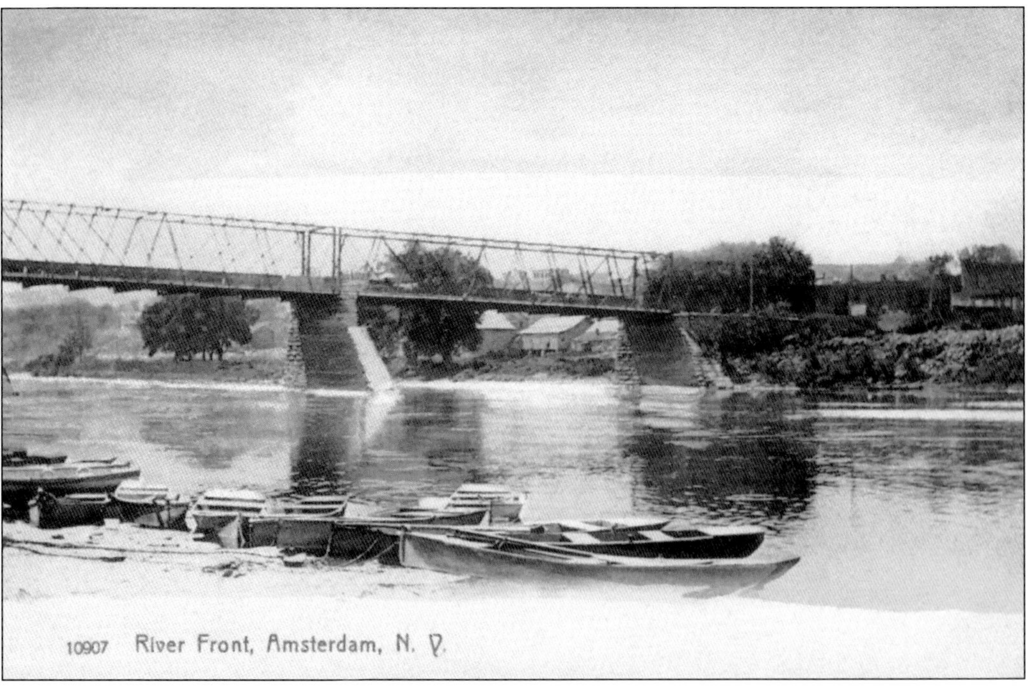

10907 River Front, Amsterdam, N. Y.

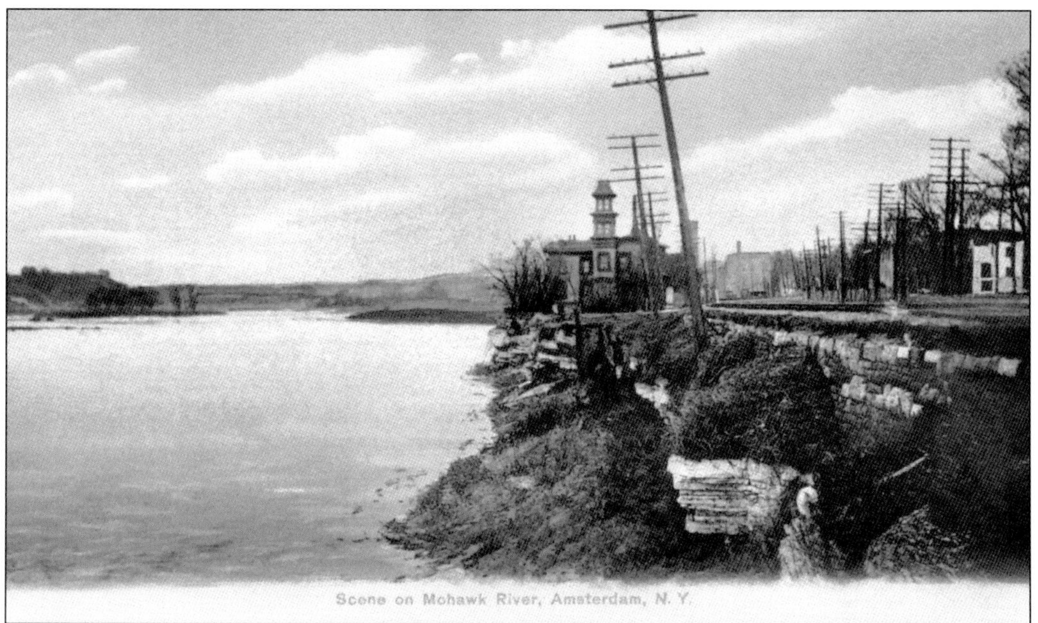


The Collins home at 96 West Main Street perches on the riverbank at the foot of Mohawk Place. Collins was an agent for the New York, West Shore and Buffalo Railway in Port Jackson. Also visible are the New York Central Railroad tracks leading out of town. East and west of the city, the tracks of the Fonda, Johnstown and Gloversville trolley system paralleled the train lines, making a six-track spread.

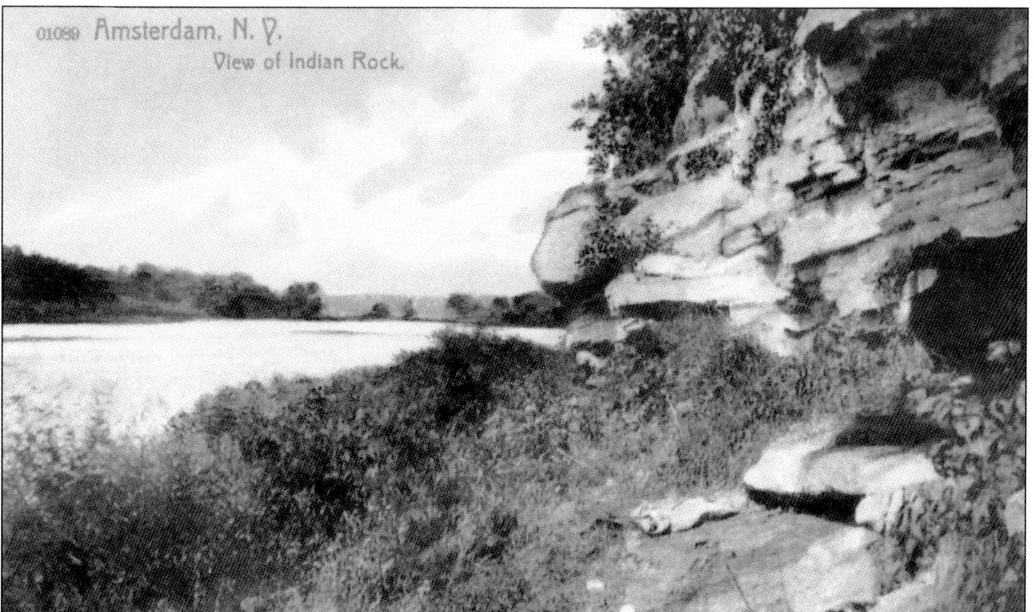


The "Indian Rock" caption may allude to the Painted Rocks, although the perspective is not consistent with the best modern analysis of where these rocks were located. First described by European Americans in the 1790s, the Native American pictographs of warriors and canoes were one of only several such in New York and visible until at least the 1880s. The exact location, fate, and meaning of them remain under investigation.

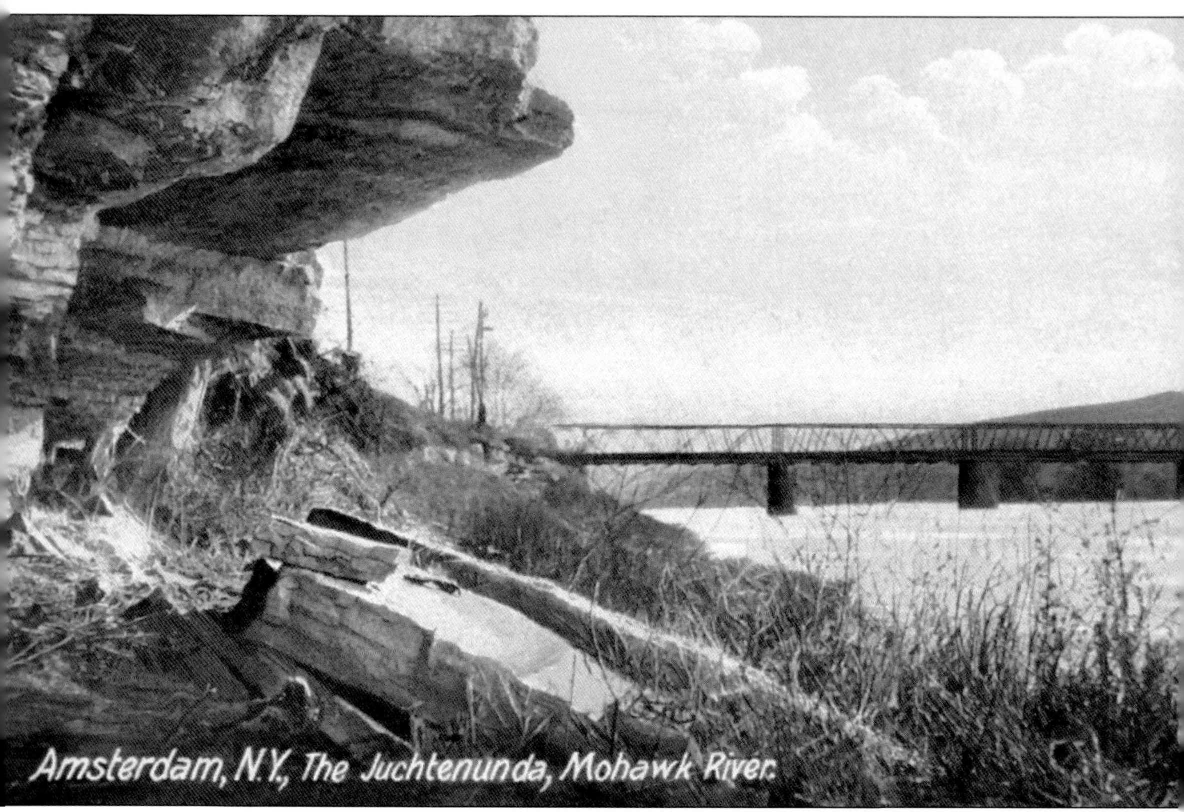


There are more variants in the spelling of "Chuctanunda" than there are nicknames and explanations of its meaning. The spelling on this card is unusual but would have been entirely recognizable to an 18th- or early-19th-century settler. While there is a north and south Chuctanunda, the north is often referred to simply as the Chuctanunda and sometimes as the "Chuck," the "Chuck 'em under," or some similar name. It is also reputed to be the model for the "Keepthemunda" in Bob Cudmore's satirical book on upstate living, *You Can't Go Wrong*. An early theory held that Chuctanunda means "the twin sisters" in reference to the nearly opposite exits of the north and south creeks, but the most informed opinion now is that it means "the stony place of shelter." As the area near the north creek mouth is one of the few places on the river with sheltering rock overhangs, it is entirely plausible that Mohawk Indians transiting the river would think it worth noting and name the area.

*Three*

# The East End

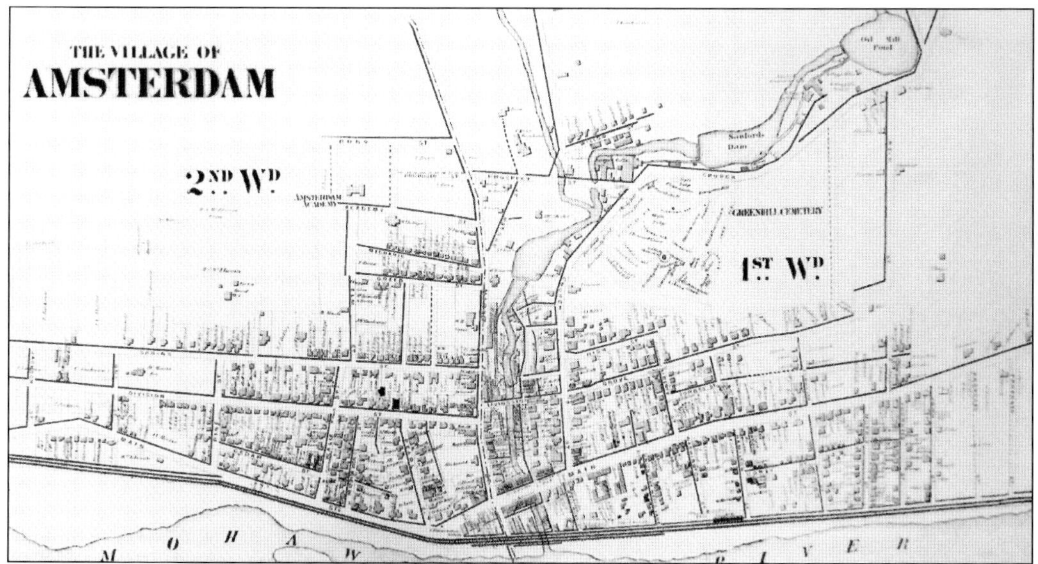


This 1868 rendering shows the quickening pace of development and infill and the increasing definition of neighborhoods. In an era before streetcars, the soon-to-be city organized itself on walking distances. Mill workers lived in duplexes on the east end, while supervisors and professionals built large homes on the west end. (Courtesy of Montgomery County Department of History and Archives.)

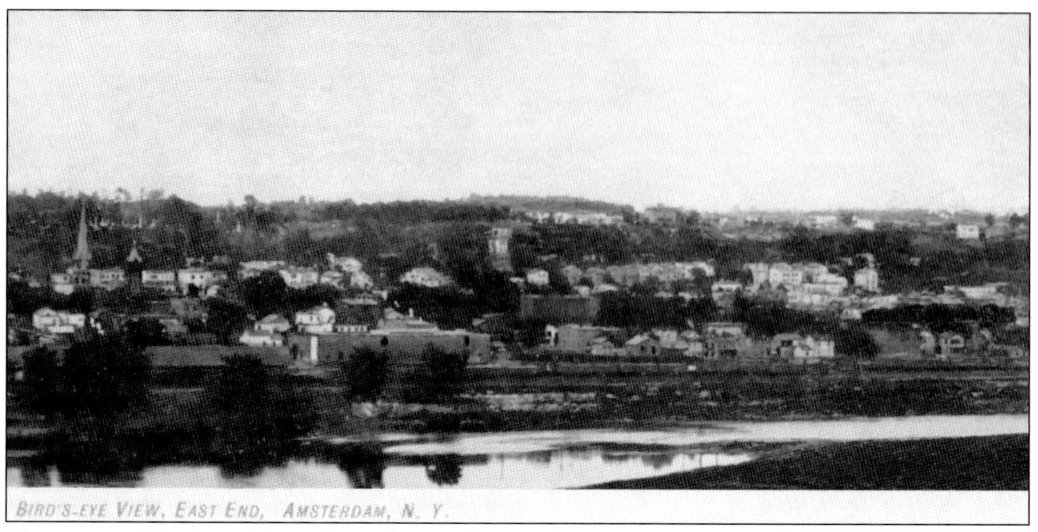


The east end is viewed here from the southwest; the distinctive steeple of St. Mary's Roman Catholic Church is visible on the left skyline. After the initial settlement in what became downtown, the next natural development of the village was along the flatlands to the east along the Mohawk Turnpike in the direction of the nearest city, Schenectady.

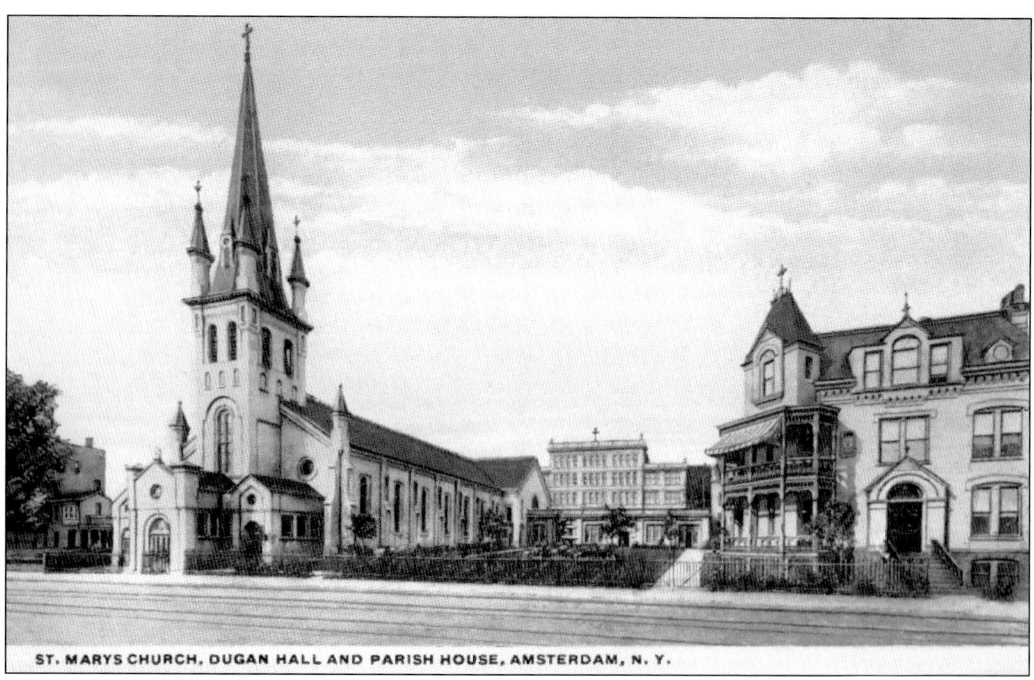


The parish of St. Mary's was originally established on the south side of the Mohawk in 1839, where many of the city's first Irish immigrants moved after building and working on the Erie Canal. As a new wave of Irish mill workers began to live on Reid (Cork) Hill in the east end, the decision was made to move the parish to the north side (1855) and erect a much more impressive church (1869).

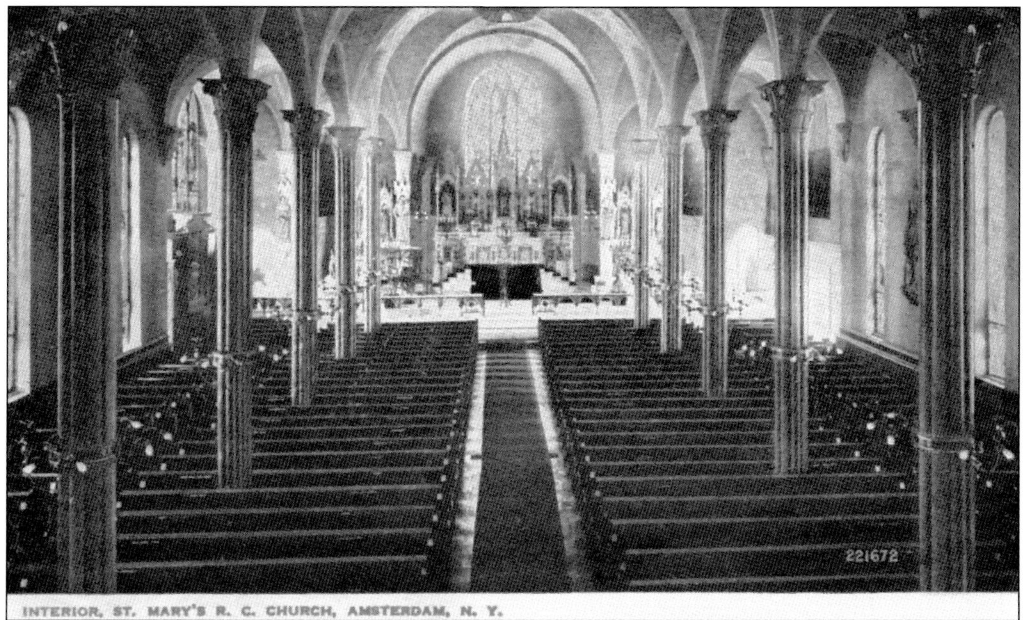


One hallmark of the Catholic churches in Amsterdam has always been the devotion of their parishioners to the suitable appointment of their interiors. Some were more solemn, and others were more ornate, but all were impressive in their ability to convey the faith of their worshippers. In 2009, when budget concerns promoted closing two churches, laymen and clergy honored that tradition by working to see that much of the sacred art and objects found suitable futures.

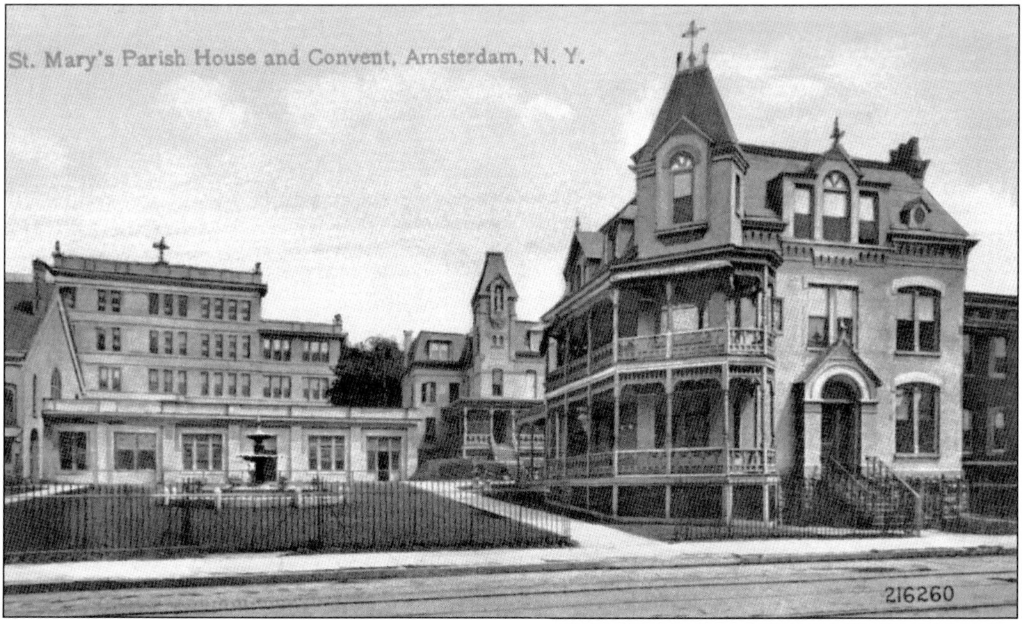


From left to right are St. Mary's Institute, the convent, and the rectory. Much of this property was lost to the arterial expansion of Route 5. Parish facilities are now housed in a modern structure immediately to the right (east) of the church. The original rectory was acquired in 1870 and damaged when the steeple blew down in 1873. The church itself has been expanded at least once and its exterior resurfaced.

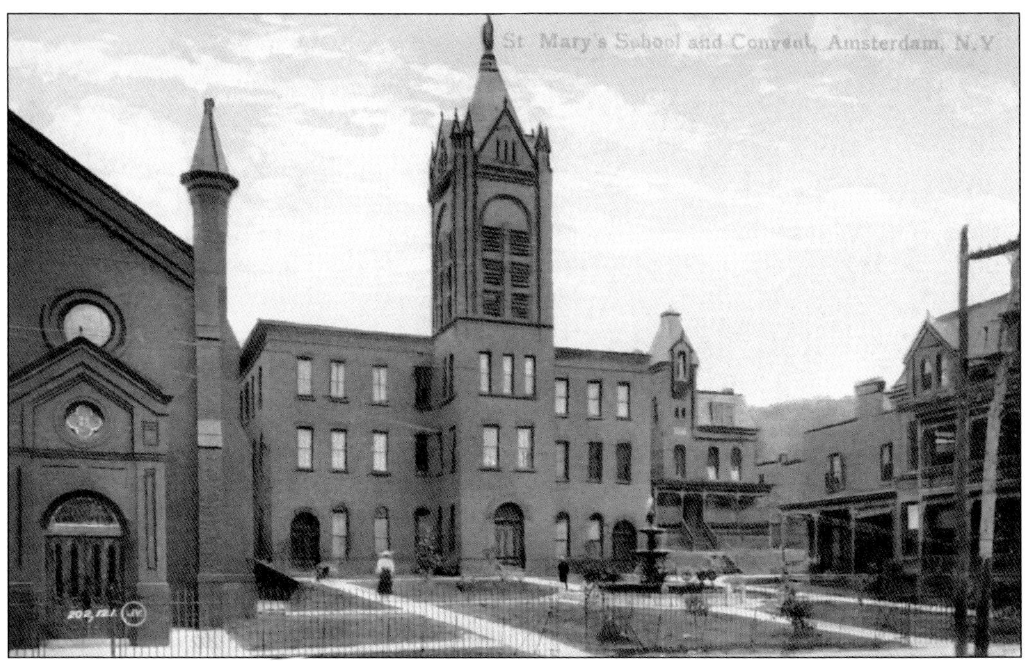


The original St. Mary's Institute building sat much closer to Main Street. St. Mary's was chartered in 1881 and was the first parochial school in Montgomery County. This building was replaced in 1909 by the structure seen in other images of the church grounds.

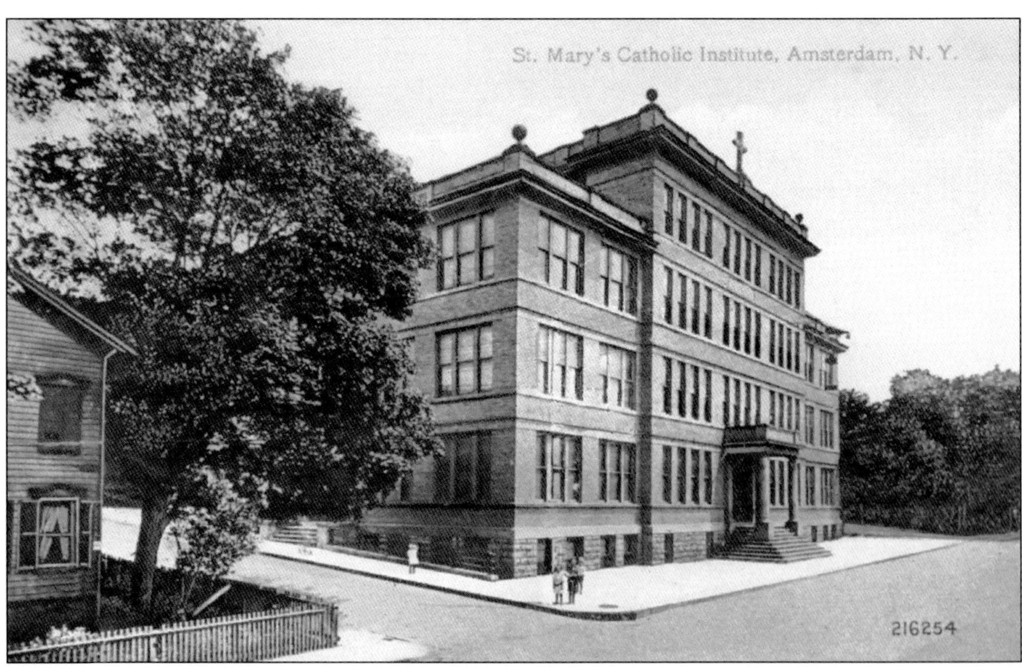


The front of the second St. Mary's Institute faced Forbes Street. At left is a typical narrow clapboard balloon-on-frame home of the mid-1800s. At one time, these homes were seen as a sign of prosperity and improvement in the original village; by the last decades of the 1800s, they are increasingly viewed as relics to be replaced.

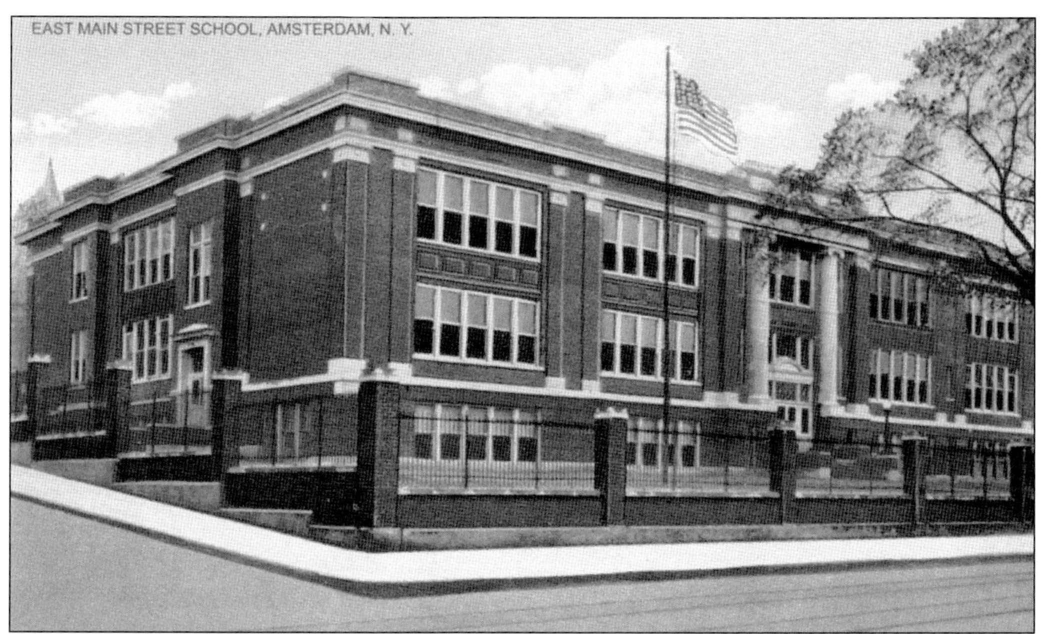


Here is East Main Street School, built in 1922. Later seen as excess by the school district, this became home to St. Mary's Institute when its 1909 building fell to the construction of the Route 5 arterial highway prior to its eventual relocation to the north. Today it is the Calvary of God Church.

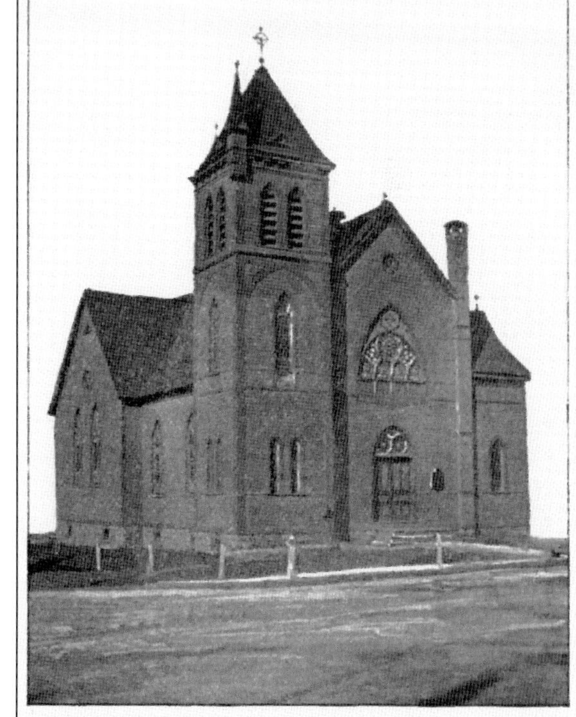

E. Main Street Methodist Episcopal Church, Amsterdam

This church, located at the foot of Vrooman Avenue on East Main Street, was established in 1888. Its first members were mainly immigrants from Great Britain who came to work in the Shuttleworth Mills. The first Methodist classes were organized in the village in 1827, with a church organized by 1831.

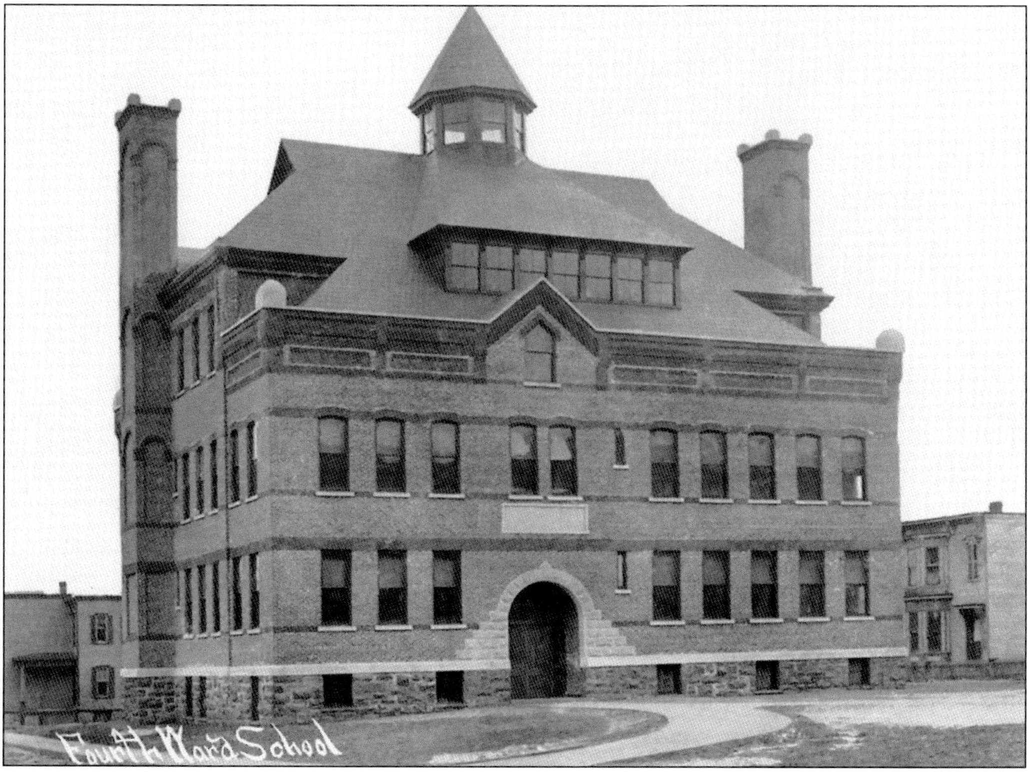

The Fourth Ward School was built on Vrooman Avenue south of Main Street in 1894. It was one of the last built in the city under the board of education constituted in 1855 prior to the consolidation of several school districts into the Amsterdam School District in 1895.

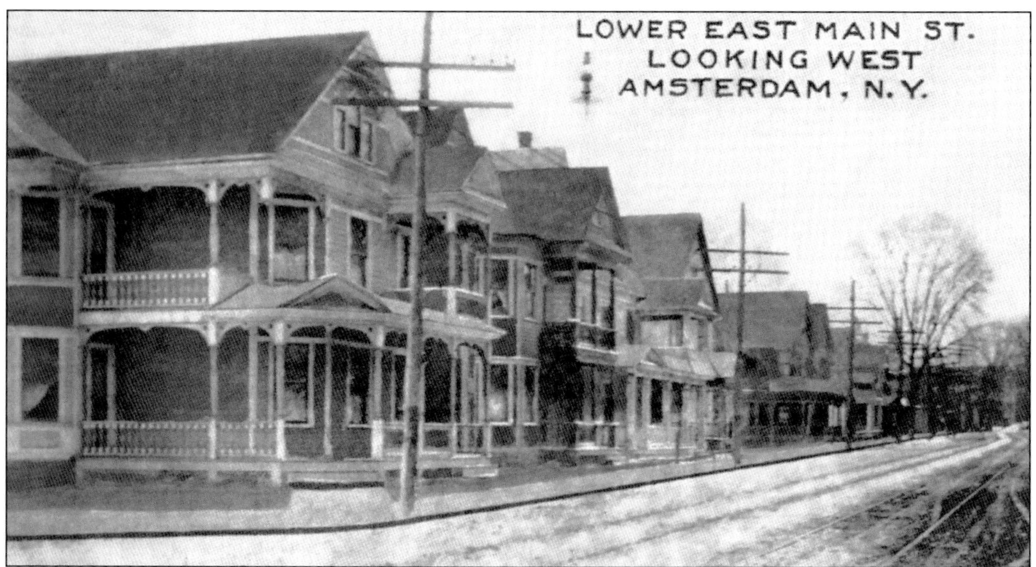


Many of these houses, minus their original ornamentation, still exist where Route 5 enters the city on the east and runs concurrent with a portion of East Main Street. Originally the homes of mill worker families, some were designed for single families, and others were two-family homes.

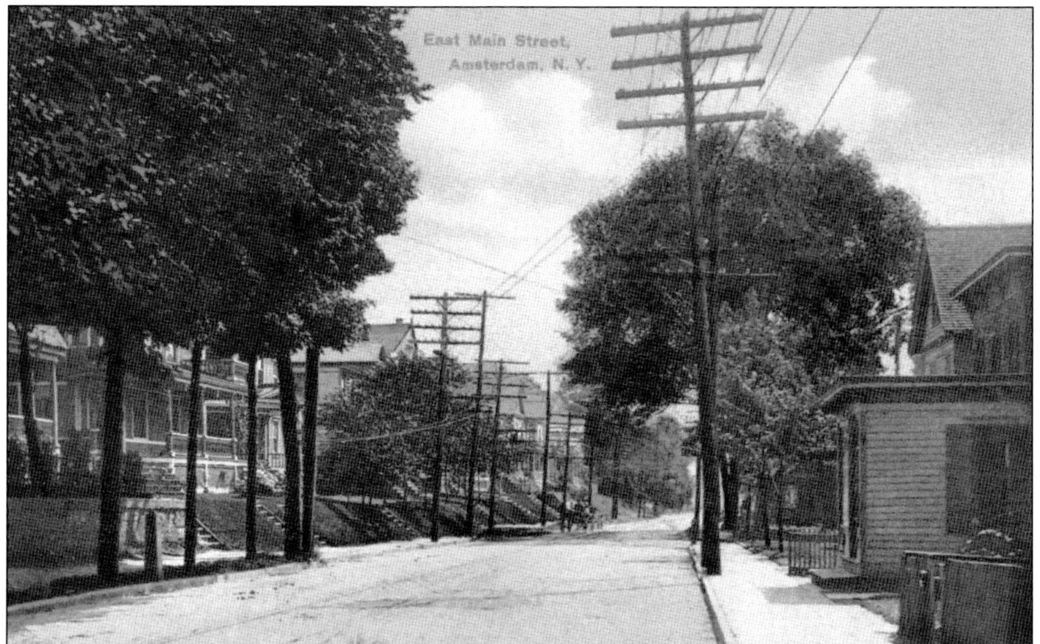


This is another view of Main Street in the east end looking east from Vrooman Avenue. The telephone poles have gone but so have many of the natural trees. Some fell victim to two waves of Dutch elm disease that swept through the city in the early decades of the 20th century. Others were removed in a misguided attempt to improve roadway safety.

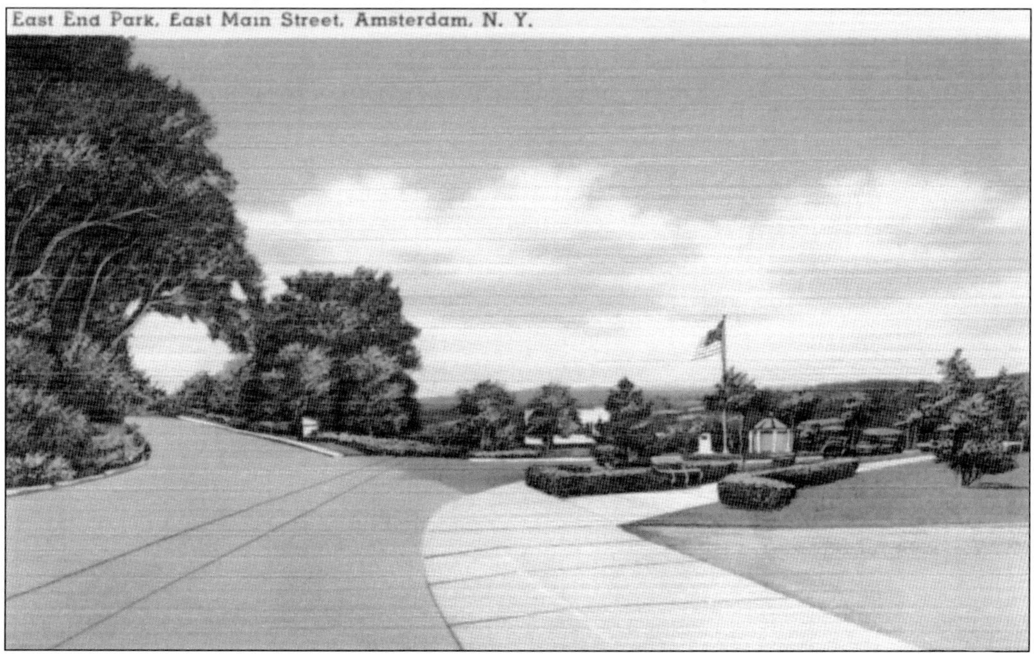


Shortly after World War I, this park was renamed Coessens Park in honor of the first Amsterdamian killed in that conflict. Popular with city children for its pool and playground equipment, the park was encroached upon first by the construction of the city's new Department of Public Works building to the west in the 1930s and later by the creation of an industrial park to the east.

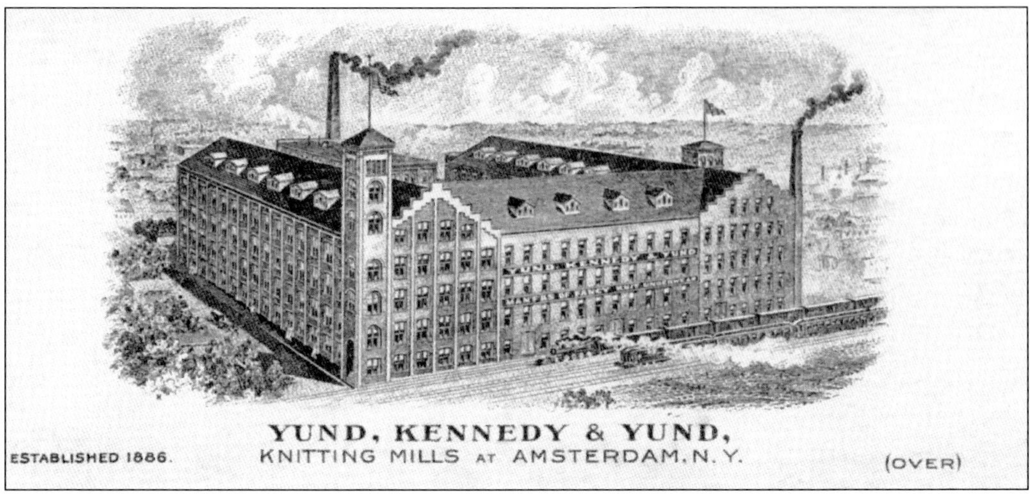


The Yund, Kennedy, and Yund Mills were established on Eagle Street in 1886 to produce knitted goods. Numerous other knitting mills were spread throughout the city, making it the second most prevalent business after carpet and rug making. Another major concern was broom making, which started early, using broom corn gown along the banks of the Mohawk River. Eventually there were at least seven firms in the city using corn stalks from the Midwest to manufacture almost all the corn floor and whisk brooms made in the United States.

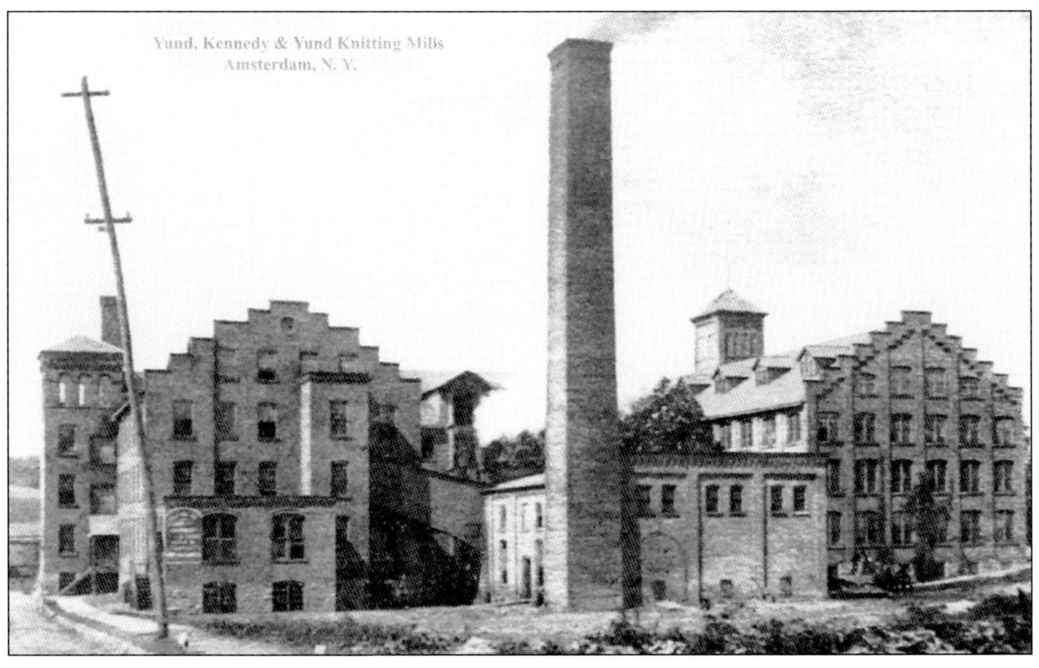

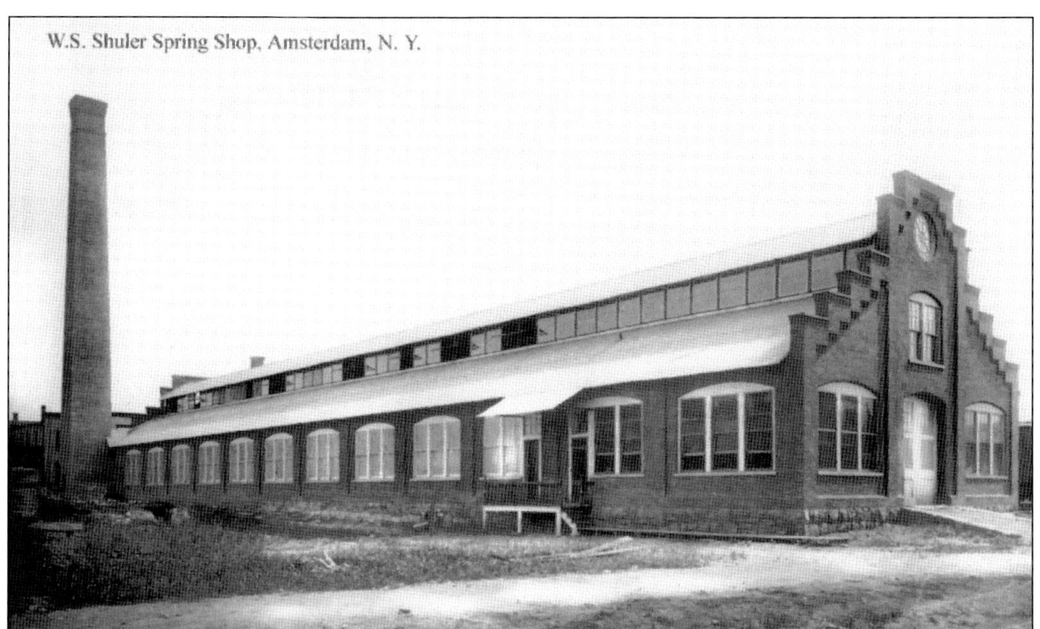


Sometime in the early 1900s, possibly due to a fire in 1903, the Shuler Spring manufacturing operation shifted from its original location on Church Street (see page 104) to this mill building on Eagle Street. The building was purchased and incorporated into the Shuttleworth holdings in 1920.

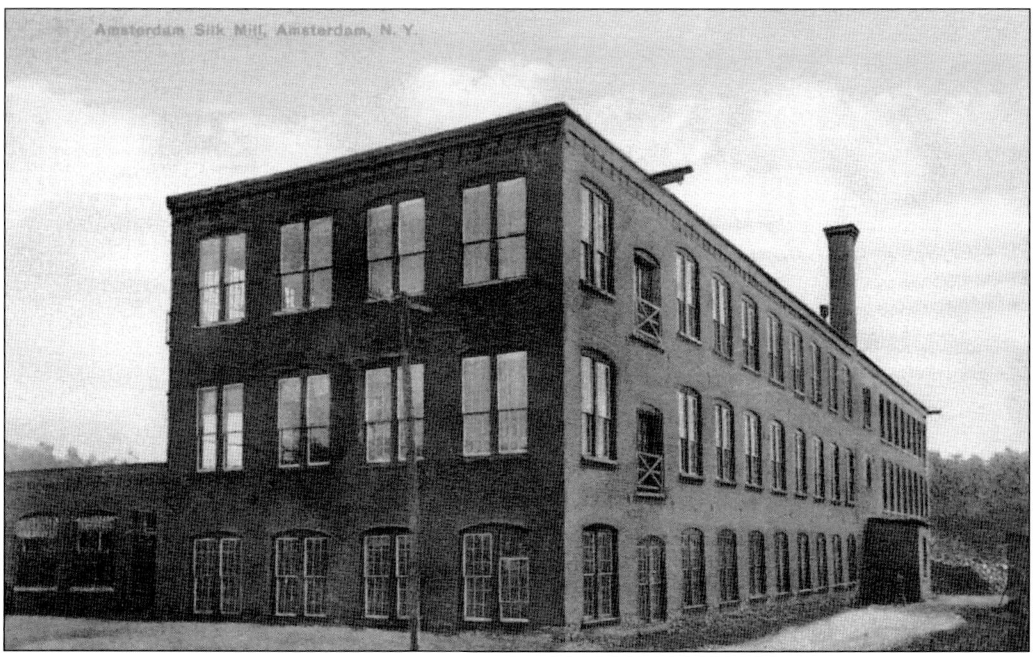


Established in 1889–1890, the Amsterdam Silk Mill manufactured gloves, hosiery, underwear, netting, and other silk products. It came under the control of Julius Kaiser and Company in 1903, part of a firm with plants in New York and Germany, and closed in 1924. In many ways, it was typical of the smaller mills and shops spread through the city that made products other than carpet, which were important to the Amsterdam economy.

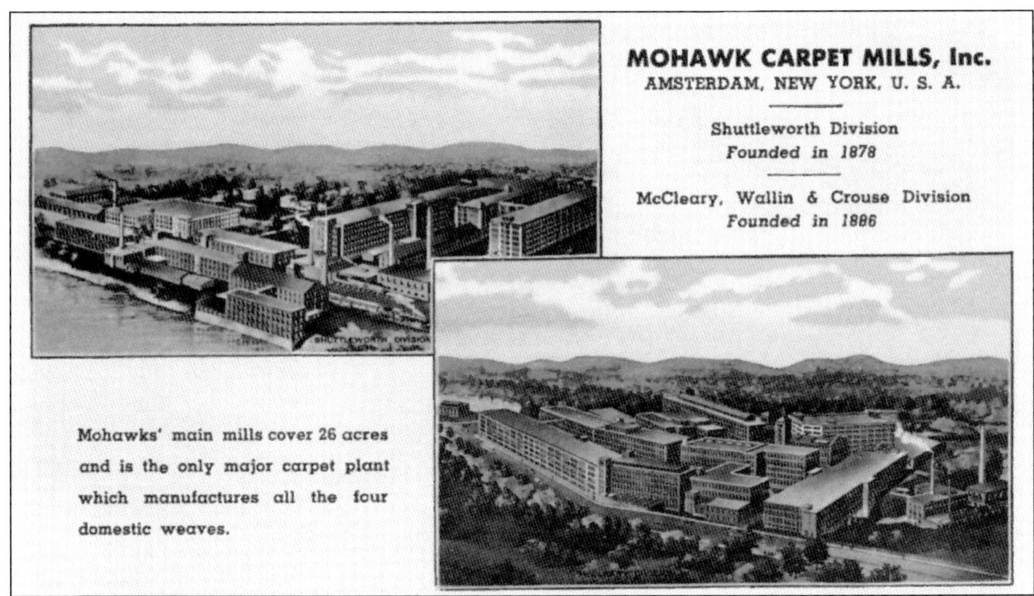


This advertising card shows the McCleary, Wallin, and Crouse plant and the Shuttleworth plant, which were combined in 1920 to form Mohawk Mills. Locals for years afterwards referred to these as the upper mills and the lower mills, respectively. The first was located on the upper Chuctanunda Creek and the latter on the Mohawk River. The "From the looms of Mohawk" and other advertising campaigns gave Amsterdam and the Mohawk Valley their greatest modern national recognition.

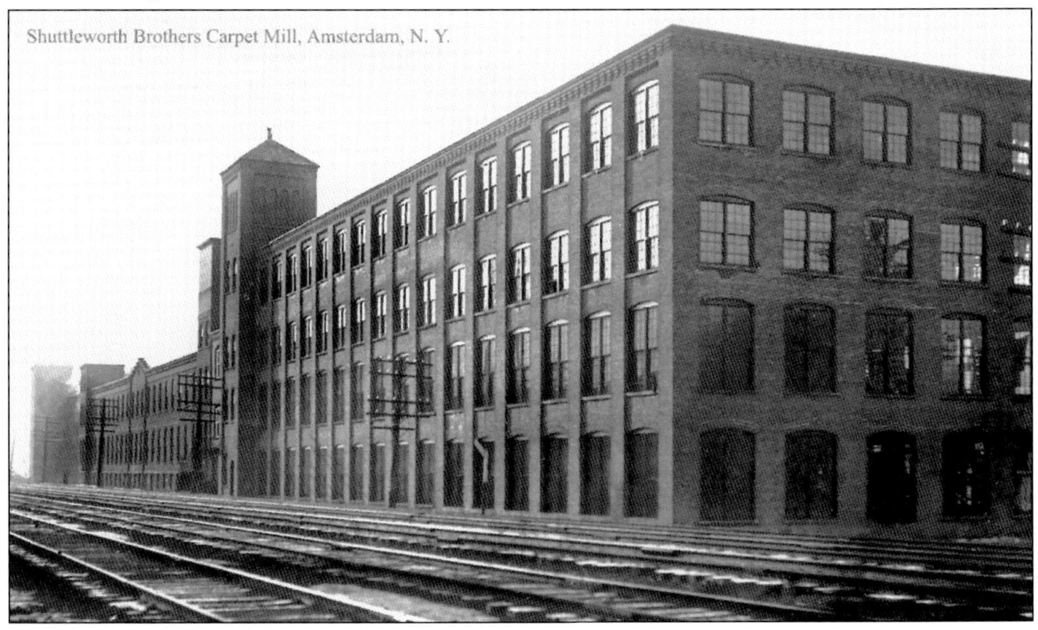


In 1872, the firm of Kline and Arnold attempted to give the Sanford Mills their first real competition but failed. Their original mill south of the New York Central Railroad tracks near the banks of the Mohawk River provided the basis for four aptly named brothers from England with carpet experience to establish their own company in 1878. In this view, the original Shuttleworth Mill is the three-story structure to the right.

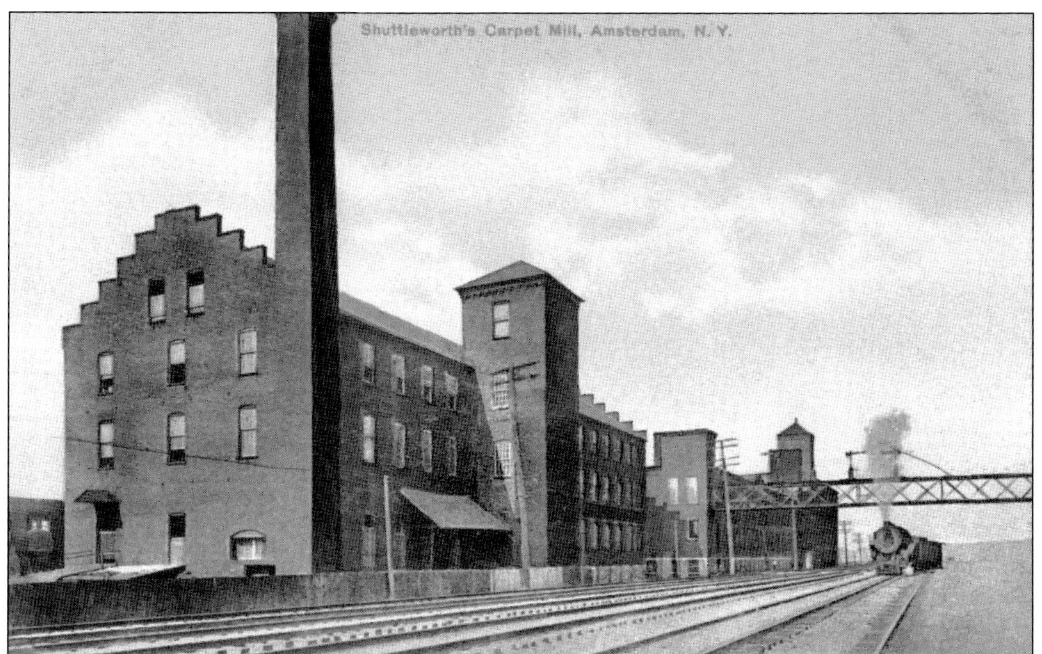


Expansion was rapid during the first decade of operation, and additional buildings were constructed south of the train tracks. This view is similar to the previous but looks from east to west. As expansion continued north of the tracks, overhead connections were made over the train tracks to the more modern buildings on the north side.

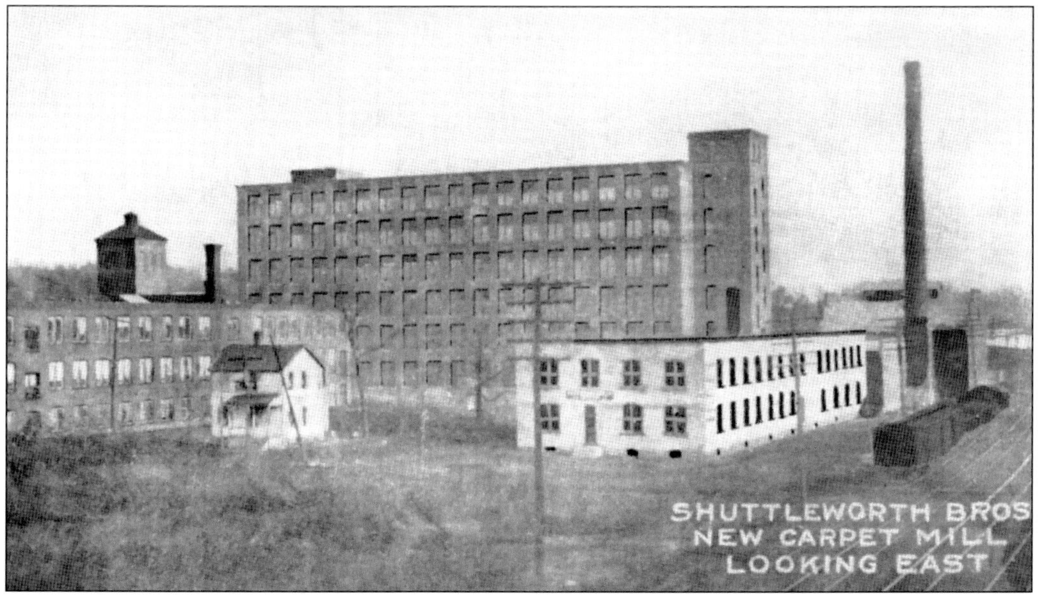


As business expanded so did the plants north of the rails. Operations in older buildings to the south were phased out, and a power plant was erected to reduce costs. Never having been dependant on waterpower permitted locating away from the Chuctanunda and closer to the New York Central Rail tracks. This allowed the firm to bring in coal and raw materials and ship product without reliance on the Amsterdam, Chuctanunda, and Northern Railroad. This view looks to the east, with the Amsterdam Silk Mill to the left.

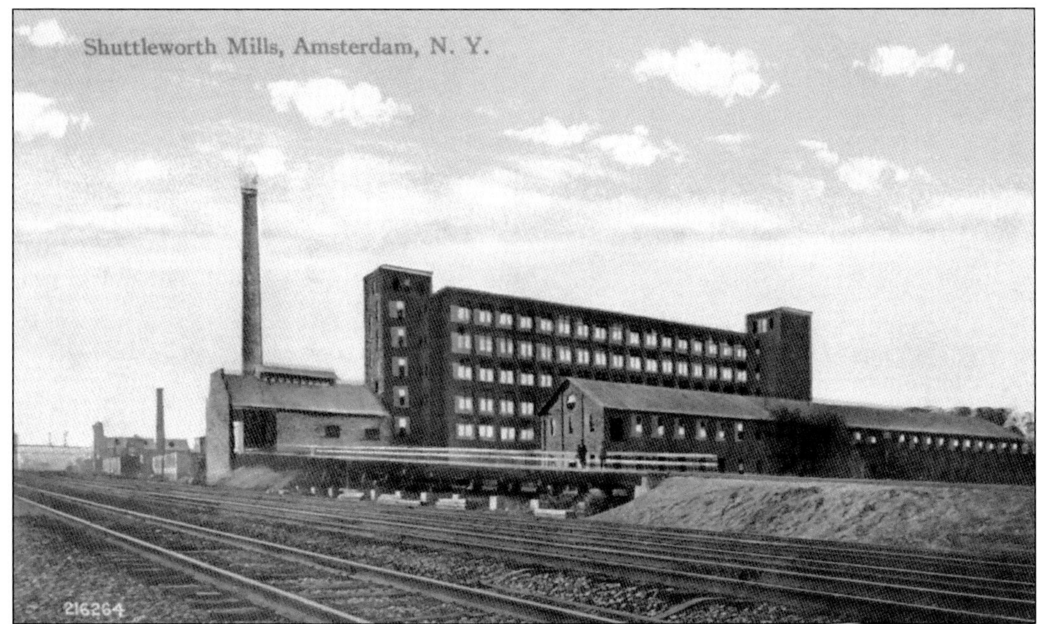

The same buildings as the previous image are seen looking west, and the power plant's coaling trestle and door are visible. Mohawk Mills survived the Depression and prospered in World War II, as did the Sanford Mills. In 1955, Mohawk merged with the Alexander Smith Company of Yonkers to become the ambiguous-sounding Mohasco (short for Mohawk Alexander Smith Company).

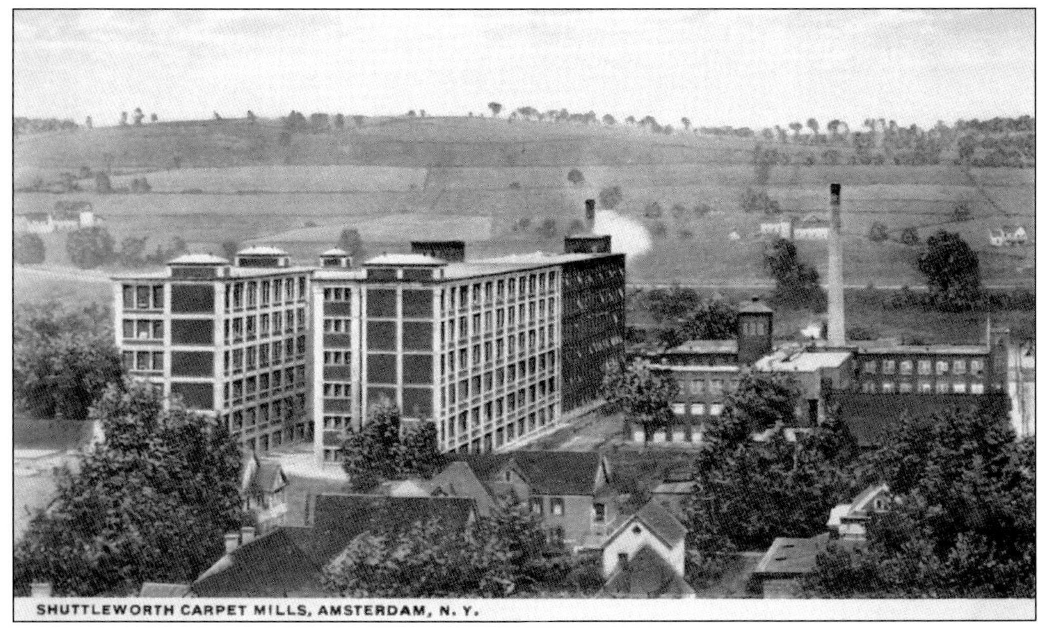

Herbert L. Shuttleworth II became president of the new firm. Shuttleworth regarded himself as an Amsterdamian and was noted for civic works, particularly with St. Mary's Hospital, local baseball, and Shuttleworth Park. Corporate control remained in Amsterdam for a number of years. However, with over 17,000 employees worldwide and sales of $650 million annually, the pressure was soon on to move out of Amsterdam. All manufacturing operations ceased by 1968.

# *Four*

# THE SOUTH SIDE

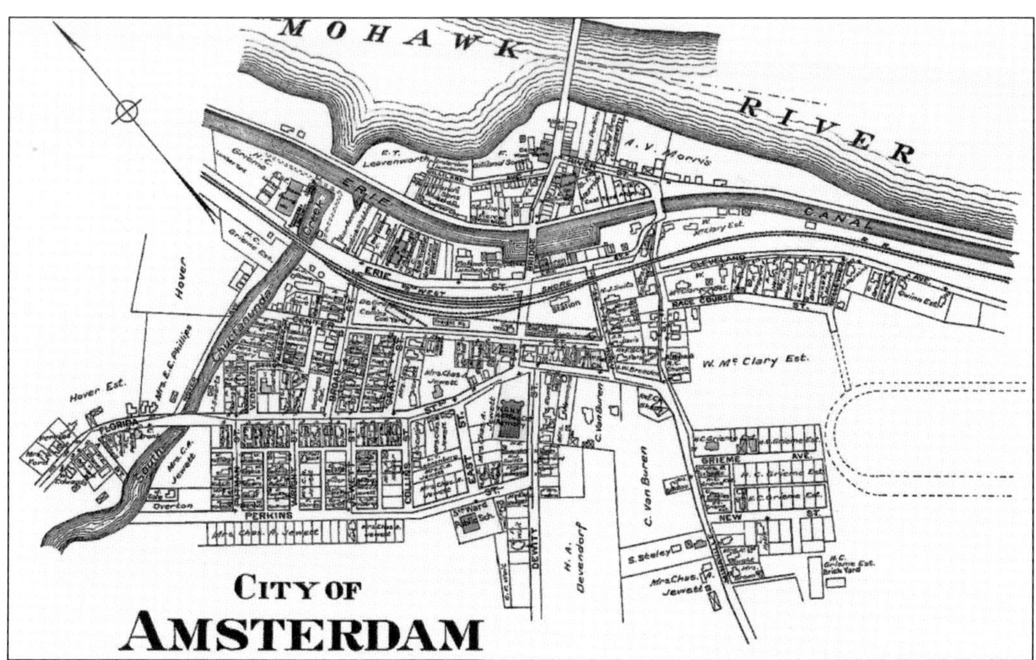


Once known as Stillwell and composed of only several homes, the south side grew rapidly after the completion of the Erie Canal in 1825. It changed its name to Port Jackson in 1835 to reflect its significance as the first major stop west of Schenectady on the canal. On April 15, 1888, Port Jackson was annexed to the City of Amsterdam and became its fifth ward. (Courtesy of Montgomery County Department of History and Archives.)

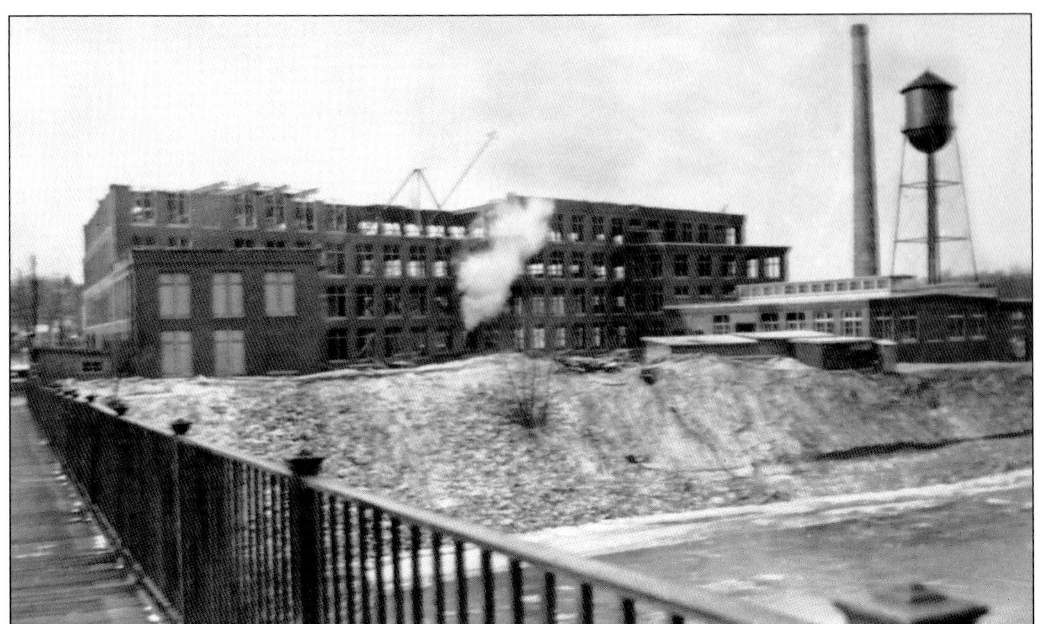

The Chalmers Knitting Company Mill of David W. Chalmers is seen under construction in 1913 from the bridge over the Mohawk River. This modern factory generated its own power and was the only large mill permanently located on the south side. The pearl button factory of Harvey Chalmers and Son on the opposite side of the river made buttons from shells (many were applied to underwear knitted in this building). For years, shells with holes drilled in them could be found on the riverbank.

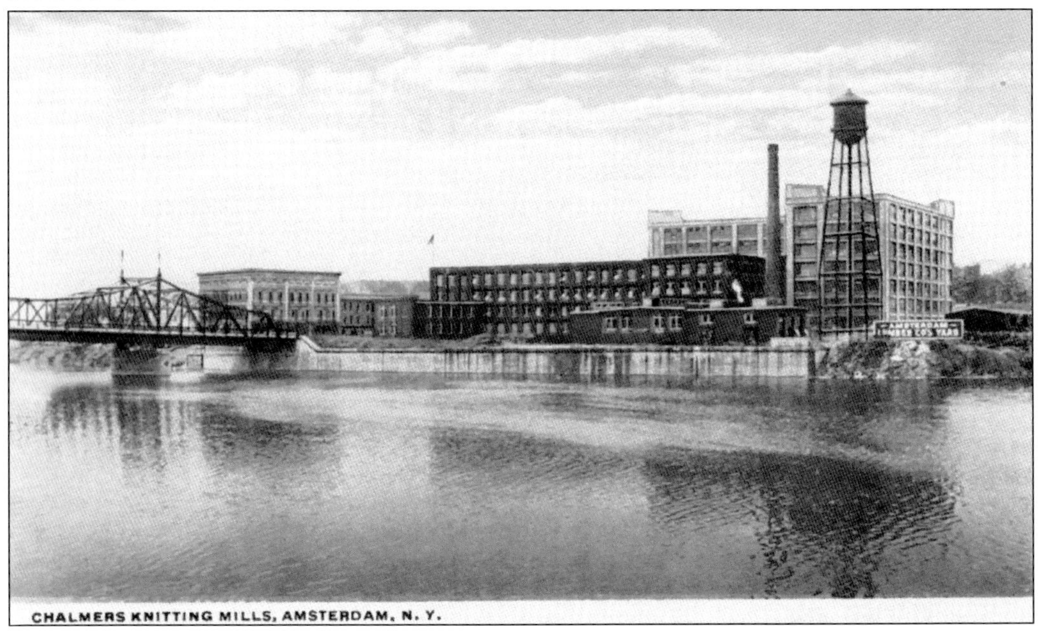

CHALMERS KNITTING MILLS, AMSTERDAM, N. Y.

An expansion of the Chalmers Knitting Company Mill was completed in 1916. Its plain, undressed walls and wide windows typify the "American Daylight Factory," a building style that inspired European modernist architects. Abandoned for years, the city recently has been unable to decide whether to save it or tear it down. The building fate's remains unclear.

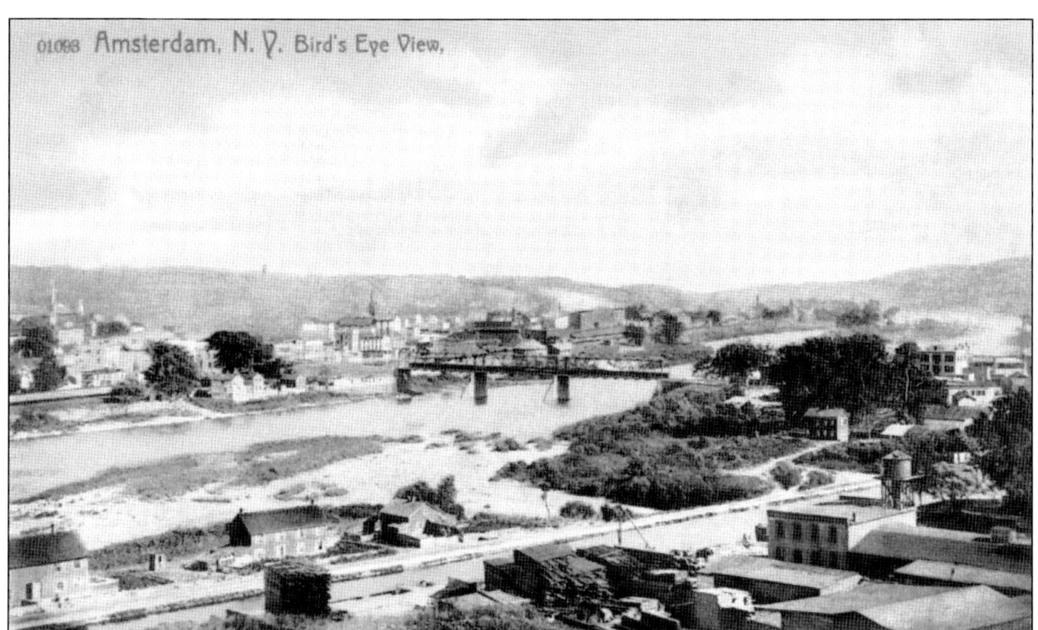


This view, looking northeast, can be dated as prior to 1912 because of the intact 1876 span over the river, the absence of the Chalmers buildings, and the water in the Erie Canal that runs through the lower portion of the image. The canal was drained at the close of its 1915 operating season in preparation for the construction of the New York Barge Canal in the Mohawk River, which opened in 1918.

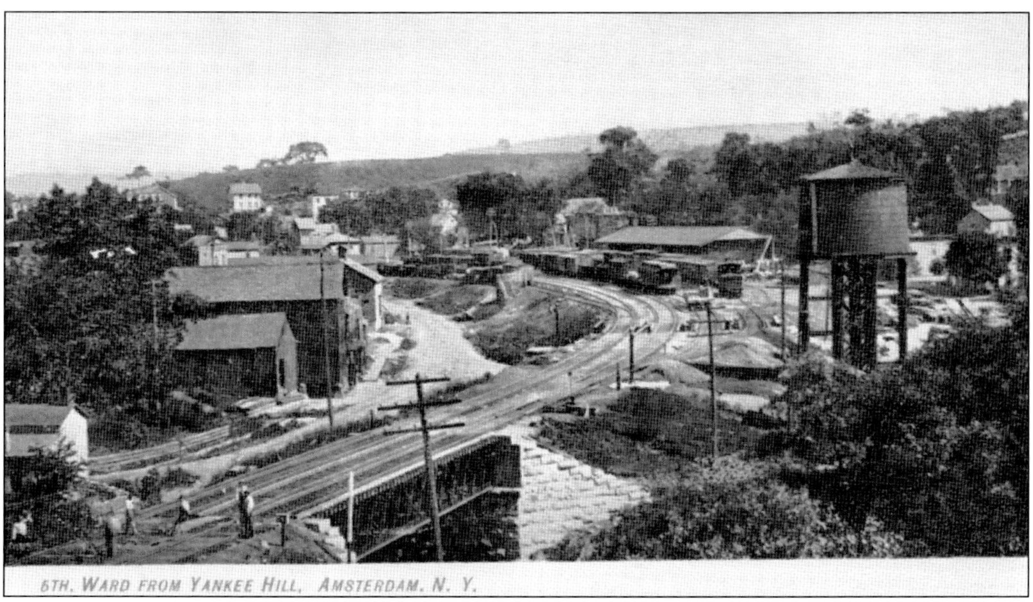


The New York, West Shore and Buffalo Railway yards are seen in this view. The railroad was established in 1883 as a competitor to the New York Central Railroad empire. Poor routing, bad engineering, and a ruthless rate war ensured that the road came under New York Central Railroad control within a few years.

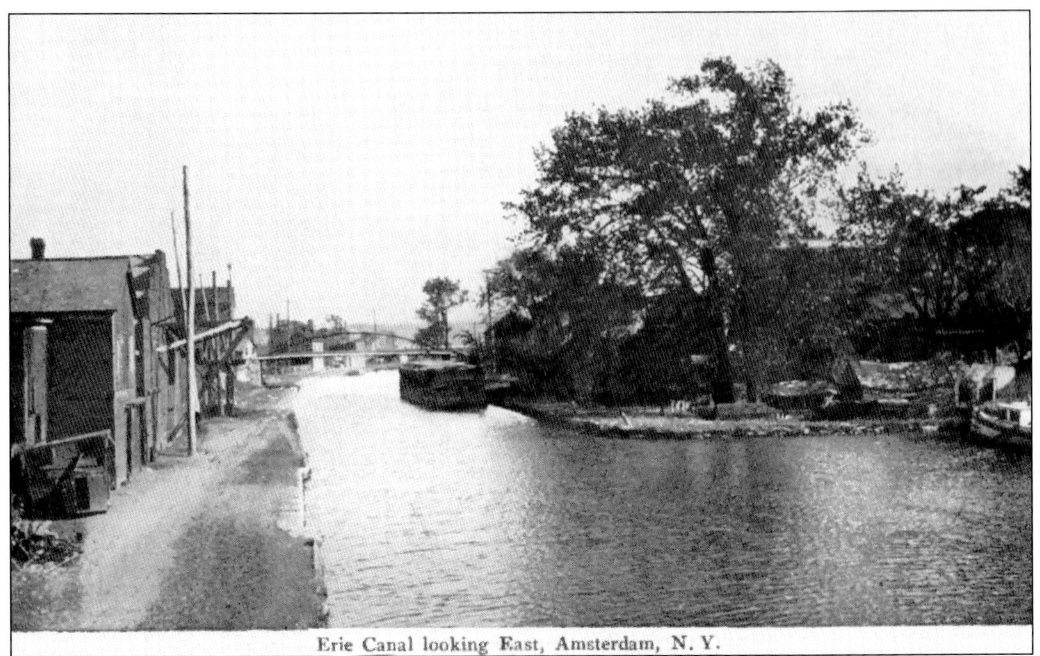
Erie Canal looking East, Amsterdam, N. Y.

This view looking eastward was taken from the Bridge Street overpass shown in the image below. On the right is Brockway's Basin, a point where canal boats could turn in or around for loading, unloading, provisioning, or repair. To the left is the towpath and a building rigged with booms and a block and tackle for handling heavy cargo.

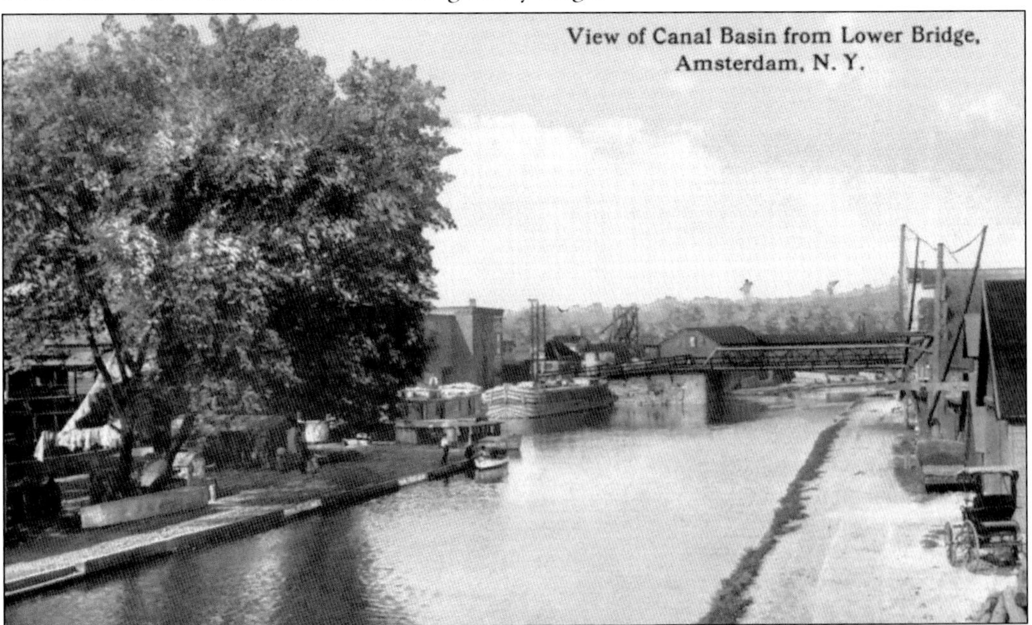
View of Canal Basin from Lower Bridge, Amsterdam, N. Y.

This is the reverse view of the above, probably taken from the Minaville Street bridge. The large building adjoining the basin is the canal-era warehouse that is now Altieri's Motors. Beyond the bridge is the Sweet Canal Store, still standing and listed on the National Register of Historic Places. When the old canal was filled in, the boat basin became the land on which today's Fifth Ward Memorial Park was built.

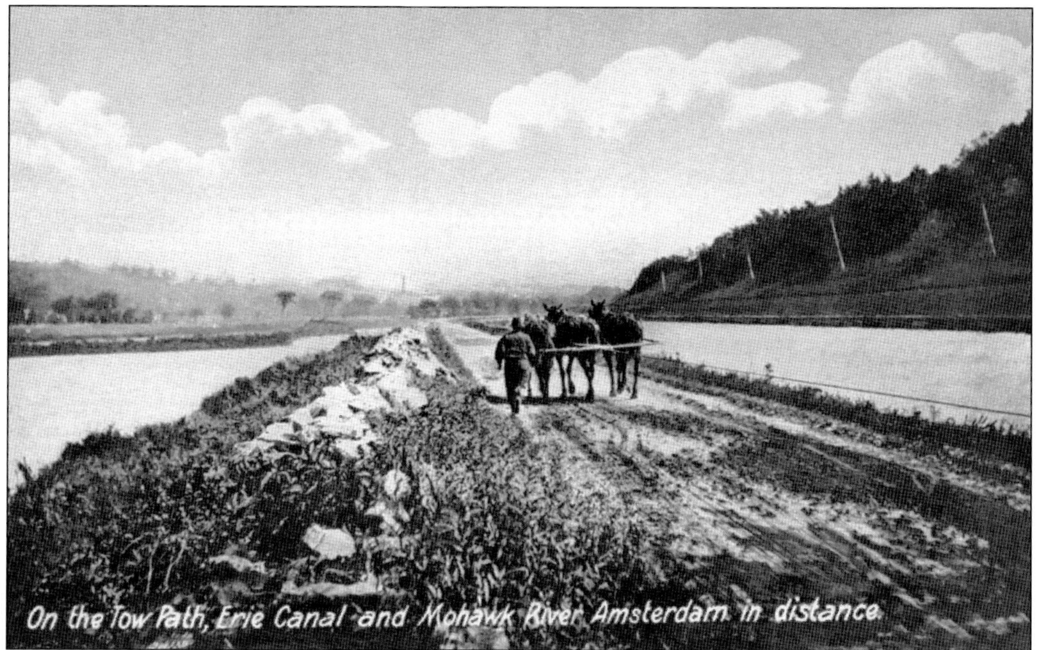


With the Mohawk River to the left and the Erie Canal to the right, a three-team hitch (probably indicating a double boat in tow) plods its way east towards the spires of Amsterdam in the background. During the winter when the canal was closed, farmers along its path made additional money by housing the mules and horses used along the towpath.

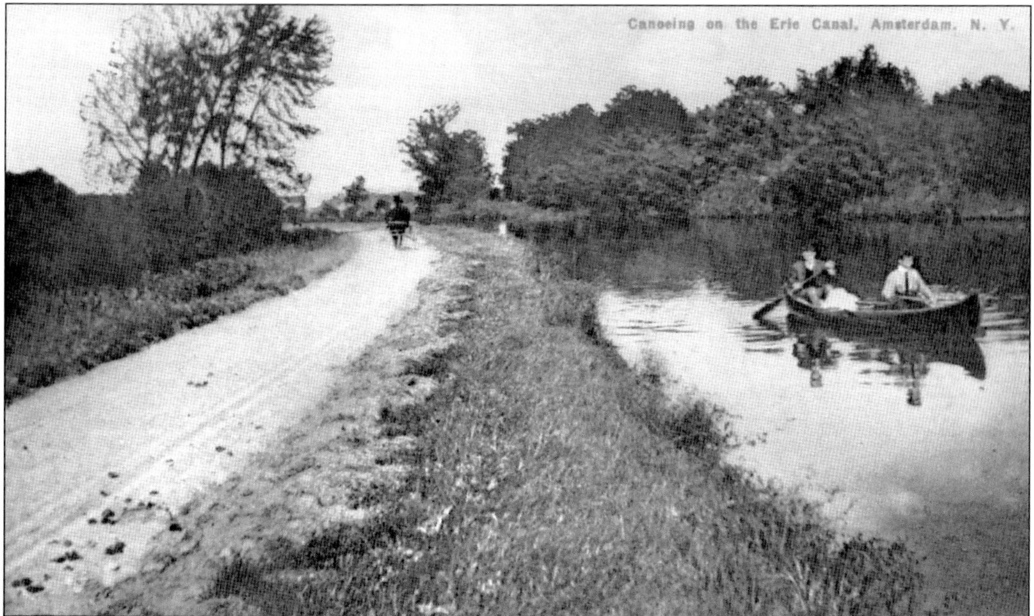


Recreational use of the canal began soon after its opening in 1825 and continues to this day. Recreational boaters are the most prevalent users on the modern canal, now collocated with the Mohawk River. Hikers and bikers today enjoy a pathway that incorporates portions of both the original canal and the West Shore Railroad. Both the original canal bed and iron rails are visible along its route.

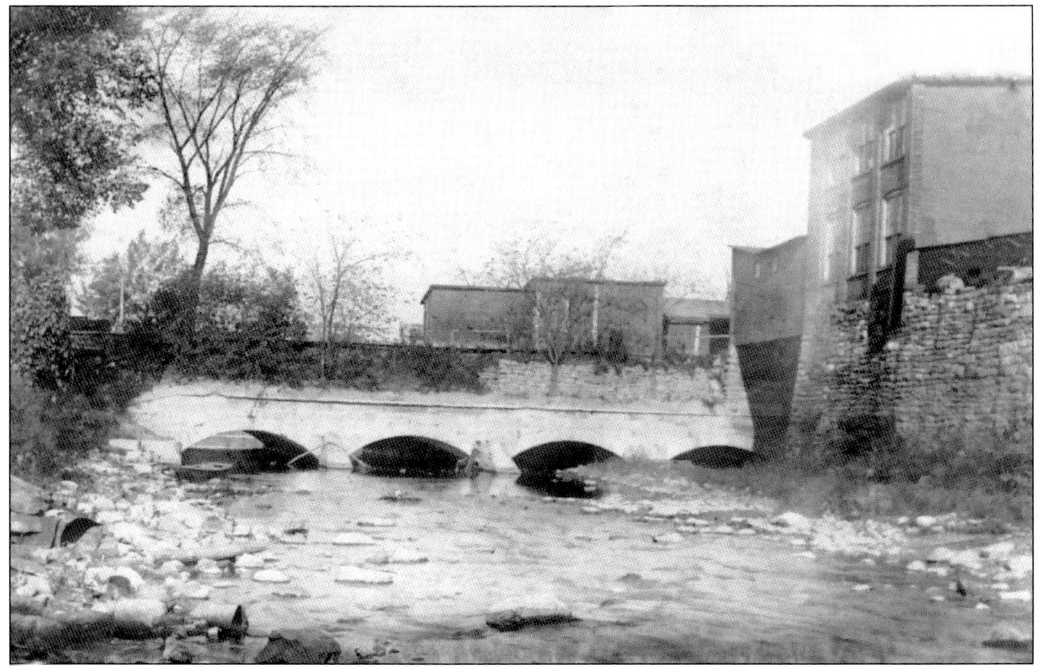

These views looking downstream toward the Mohawk River show the Erie Canal viaduct crossing the South Chuctanunda Creek. The viaduct's low stone arches were covered with several feet of dirt, and the canal dug through the dirt as if on regular land. The canal had to pass above creeks and streams so that its water level would not be affected by variations in their flows. (The image above appears to have been erroneously flipped horizontally when made into a postcard.)

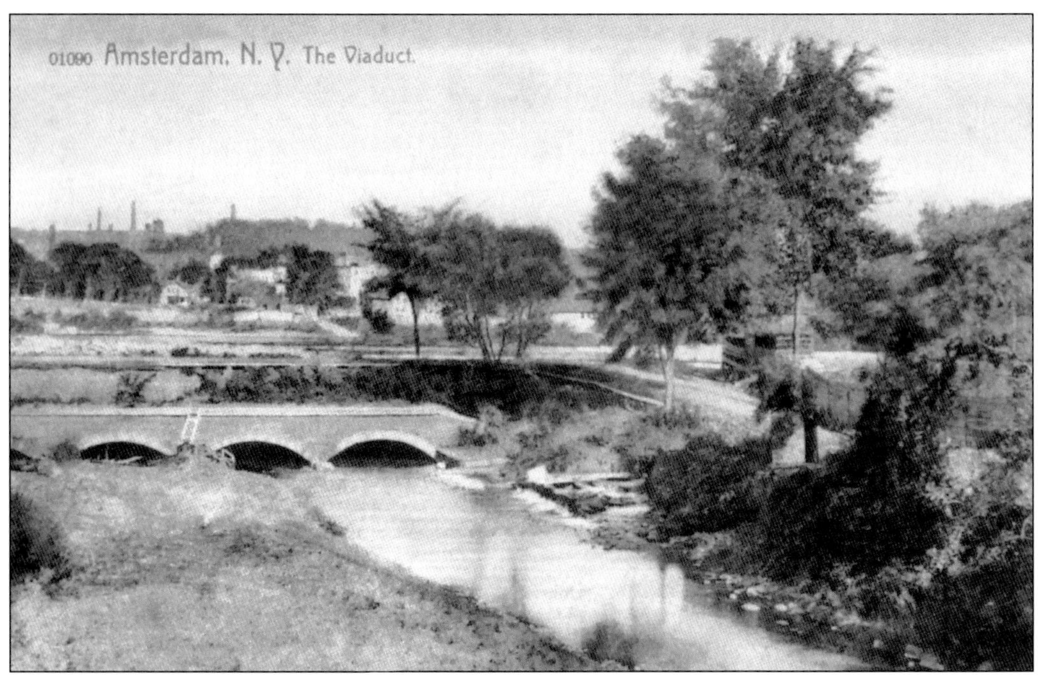

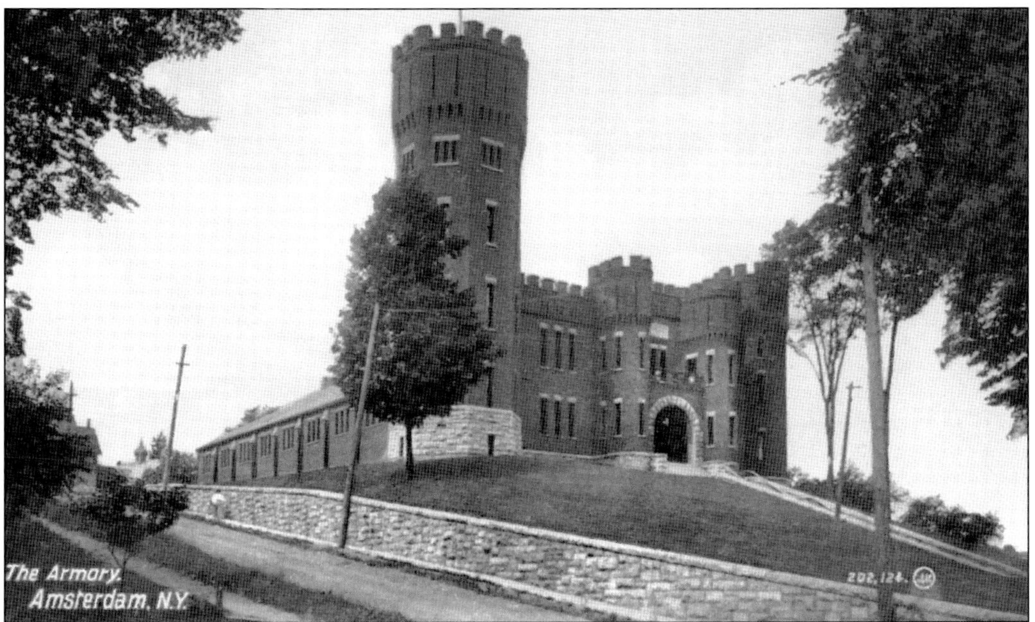


The armory was built in 1895 to house the 46th Separate Company of the New York National Guard (established in 1887). The unit changed names several times over the next century until the armory was closed and sold in 1993. Armory soldiers served in the Spanish-American War, the Mexican border emergency of 1916, both world wars, and many state emergencies. The building is now a private residence and a bed and breakfast.

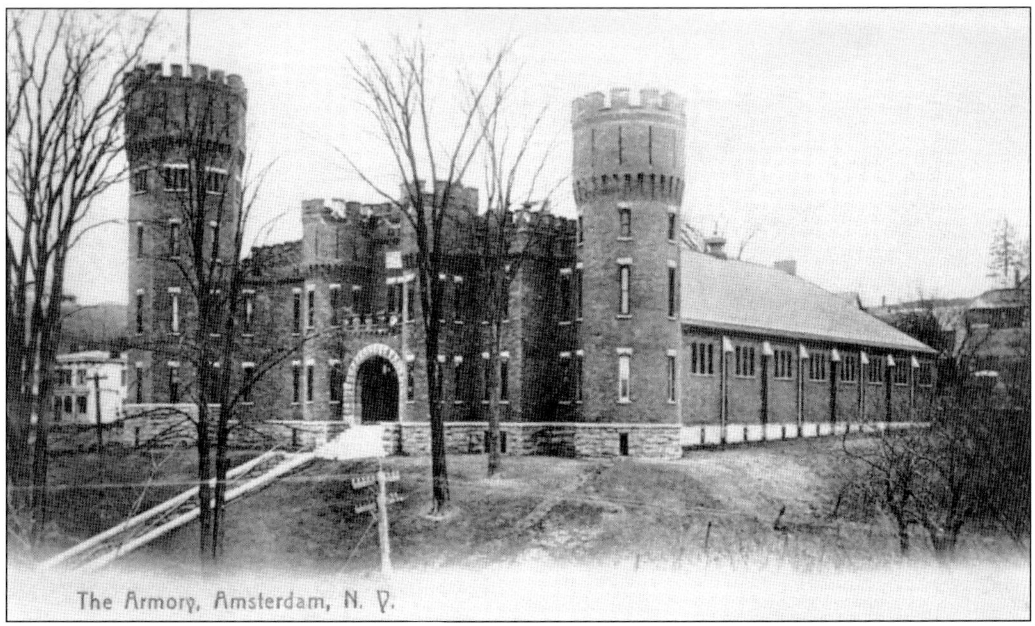


The dramatic placement and castle-like appearance of the armory was not just architecturally fancy. Within living memory of the attacks on armories during the Civil War and at the height of industrial unrest, the building was intended to be defensible if necessary. The design, which splits functions between a head shed that houses administrative and social functions and a drill shed for troop practice, is uniquely American.

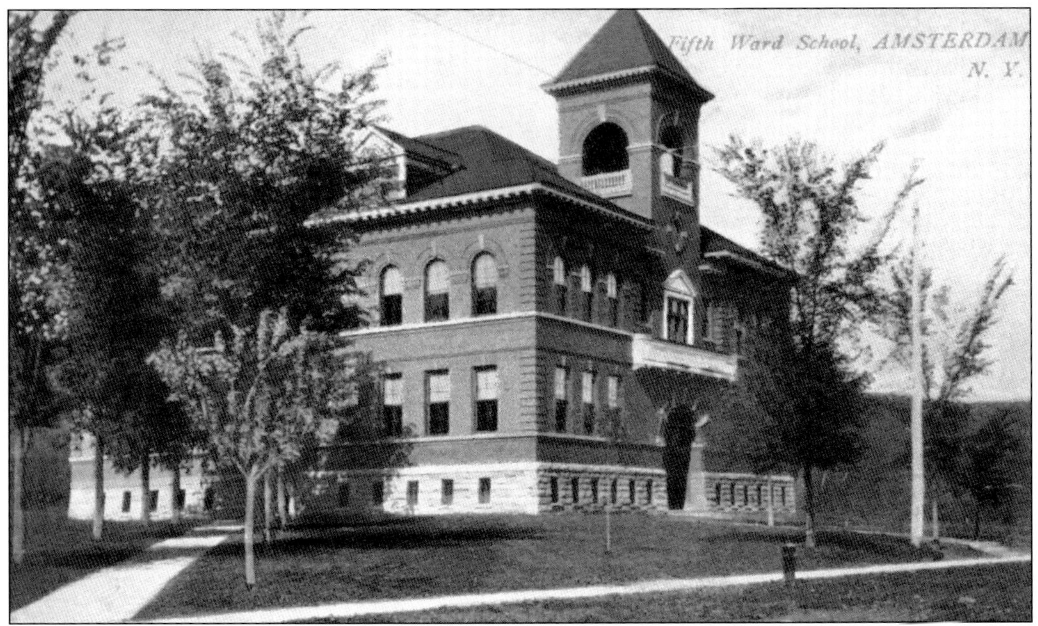


The Fifth Ward School was built in 1906 on Perkins Street and enlarged in 1916 and 1926. When Port Jackson was annexed by the city in 1888, its school was comprised of 210 students and 3 teachers. This building was the first home of the Walter E. Elwood Museum prior to its relocation to the Guy Park Avenue School in 1968. (In 2009, the Elwood moved again to Guy Park Manor.)

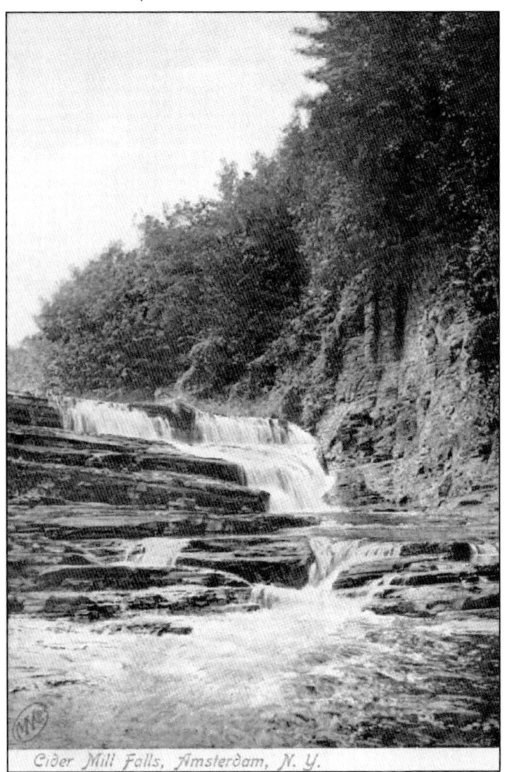


The South Chuctanunda Creek flows from Mariaville Lake into the Mohawk River approximately opposite the mouth of the North Chuctanunda Creek. Although gristmills, sawmills, a cider mill, and a tannery were established on the South Chuctanunda Creek during the initial settlement, these were destined to be eclipsed by the mills on the more powerful North Chuctanunda Creek once good contact was established across the Mohawk River.

A small tributary makes a dramatic entrance to the South Chuctanunda Creek, cascading over the sedimentary rocks that make up the gorge at the entrance to Mudge Hollow. Many such falls that graced the banks of the Mohawk River disappeared with the construction of the barge canal, the railroads, and the ever-expanding highway systems.

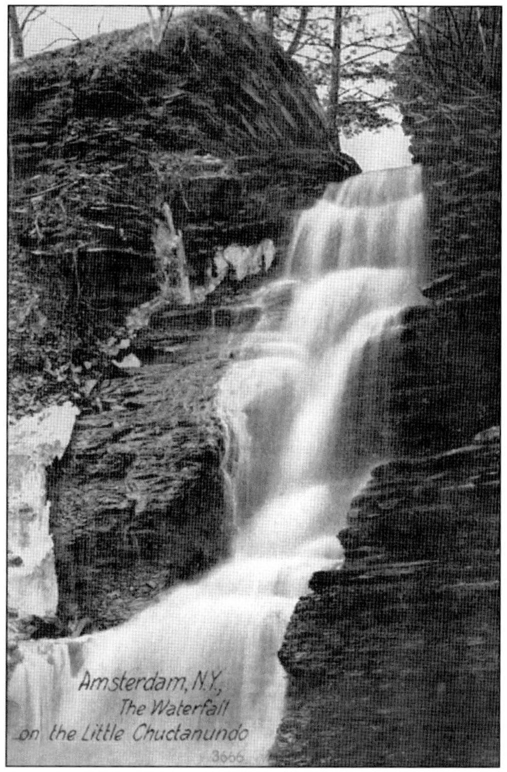


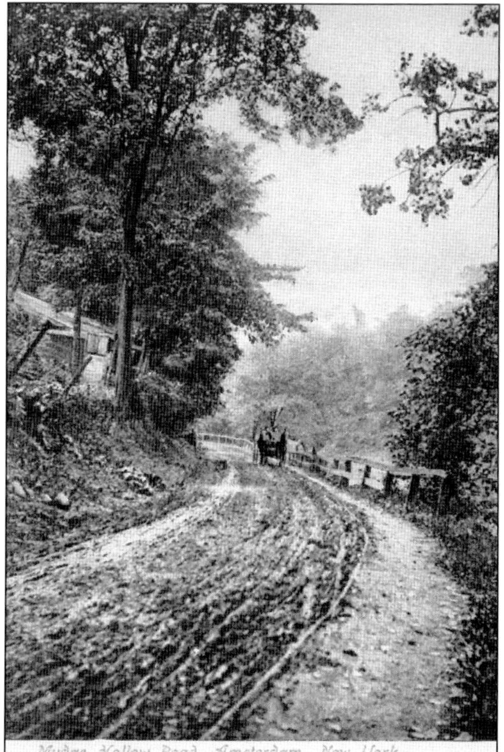


Mudge was the name of an early Town of Florida family. As commercial and residential development in Port Jackson concentrated on the canal, the Town of Florida from which it was annexed remained mainly agricultural. Thus, longer portions of the South Chuctanunda Creek have remained open and pristine than in the case of its northern counterpart.

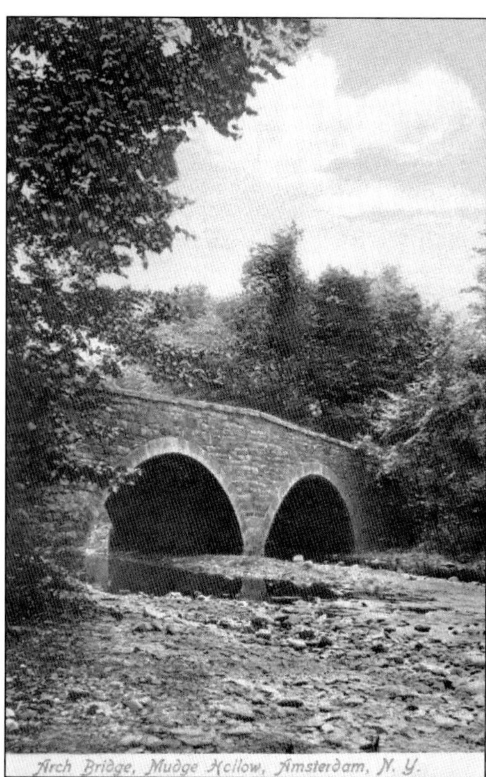


The Mudge Hollow Bridge carries Mudge Hollow Road over the South Chuctanunda Creek near the southern limits of the city. It is the only access for a small grouping of homes south of the creek since the abandonment of the portion of the road previously connecting it with Snooks Corners Road.

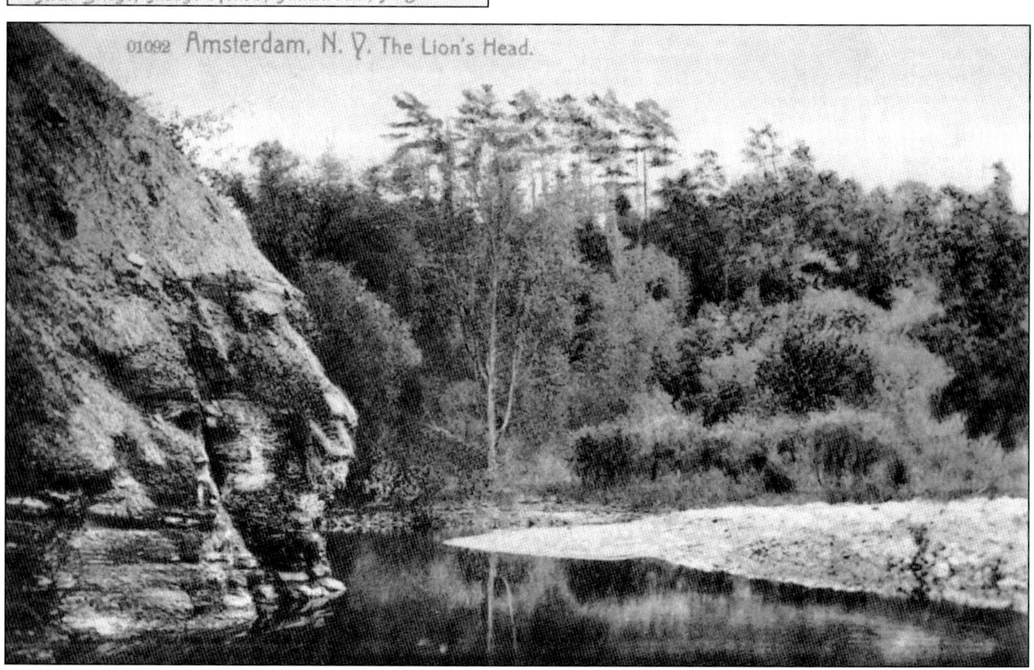


Given the quantity and age of the sedimentary rock that encompasses the river and creek bottoms, it was inevitable that some would take shapes that the human mind would find patterns in. This formation, "the Lion's Head," is just upstream from the Mudge Hollow Bridge, and although much weathered since first photographed, it is still recognizable.

*Five*

# THE WEST END

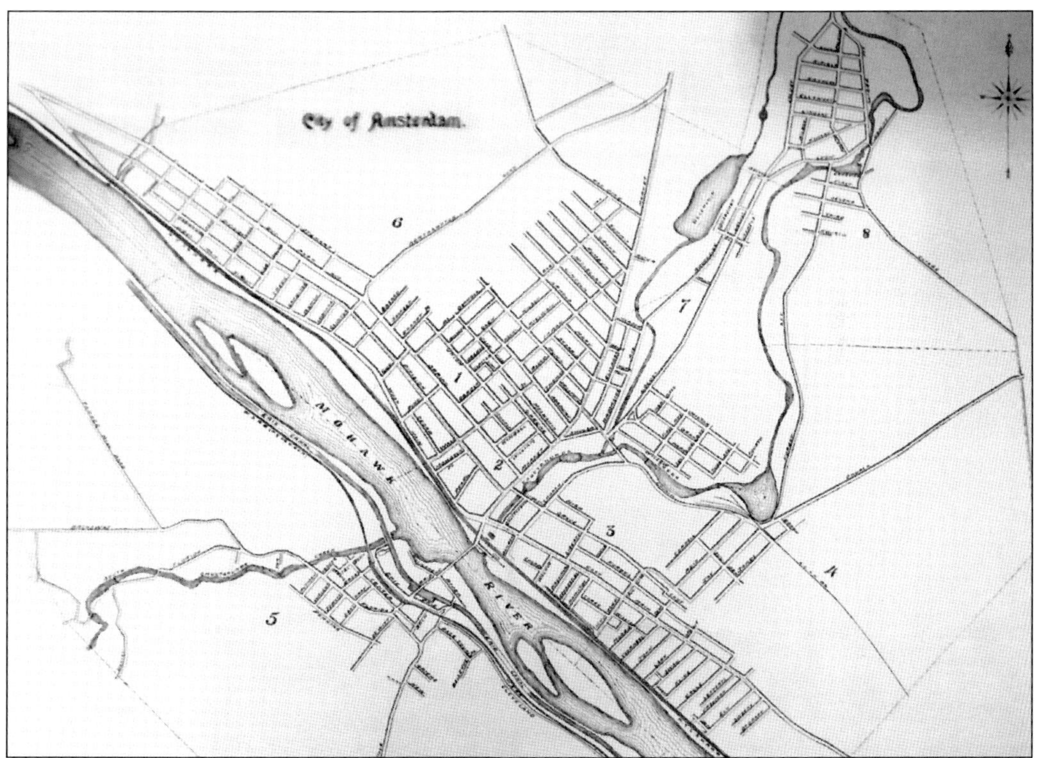


By the time of this 1908 map, Amsterdam had annexed Port Jackson to the south and Rockton to the north and had grown on both the east and west ends. Surging industrial development increased the demand for housing and drove up land values to the point where development became feasible, and streetcar service was extended as development moved west. (Courtesy of Montgomery County Department of History and Archives.)

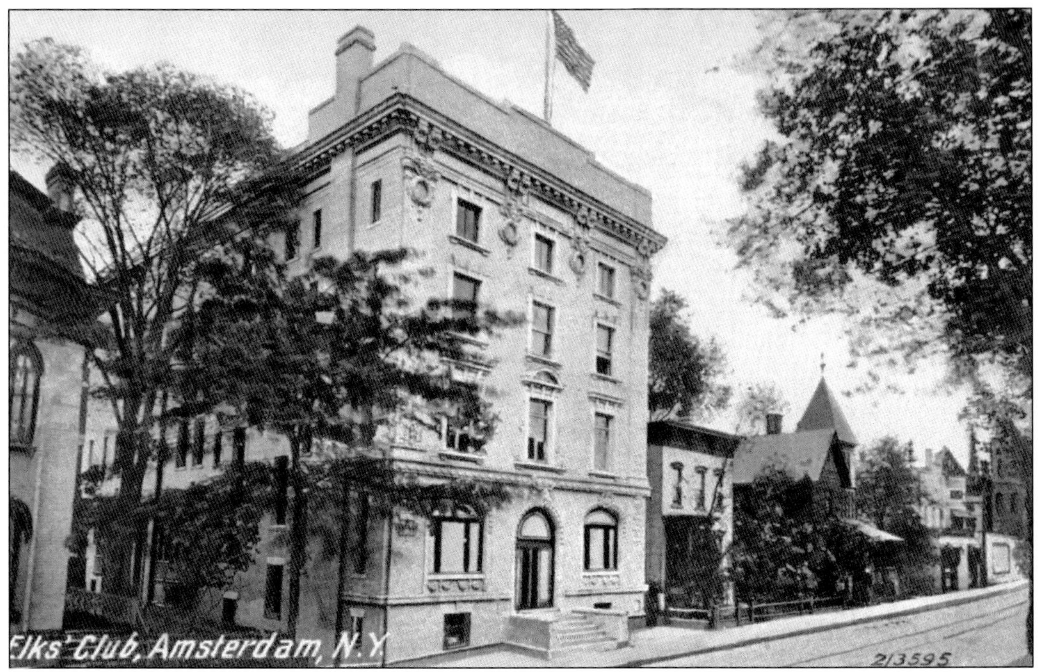


The Benevolent and Protective Order of Elks was one of many fraternal organizations that grew up in Amsterdam after the Civil War, as salaries and leisure time began to increase. This building on the north side of Division Street west of Market Street was built in 1910 and was a popular location for holding large social events.

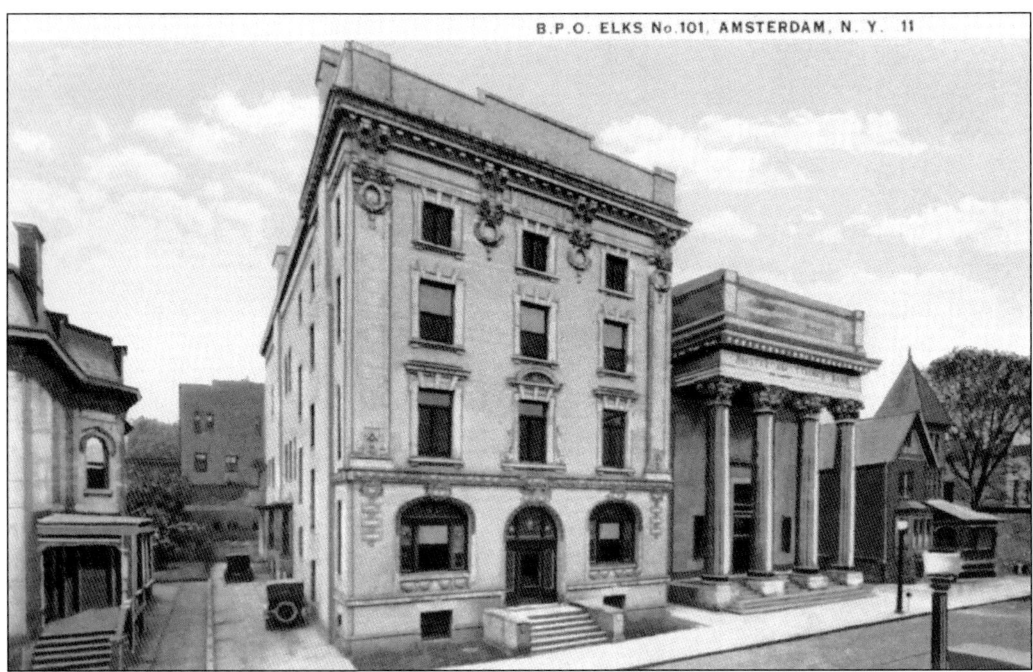

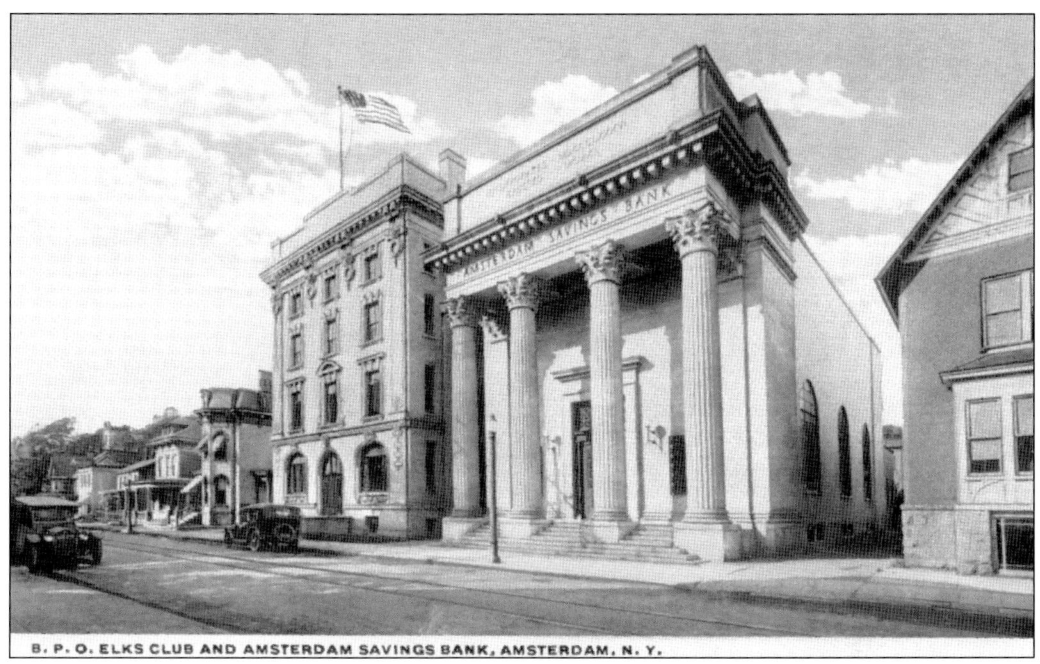


The Amsterdam Savings Bank was established in 1887 and was originally located on the east side of Market Street by Division Street. This new building was constructed for the bank on the north side of Division Street in 1913. In 1974, it was significantly remodeled and expanded onto the former location of the Elks building. Long gone is the massive green marble teller's counter.

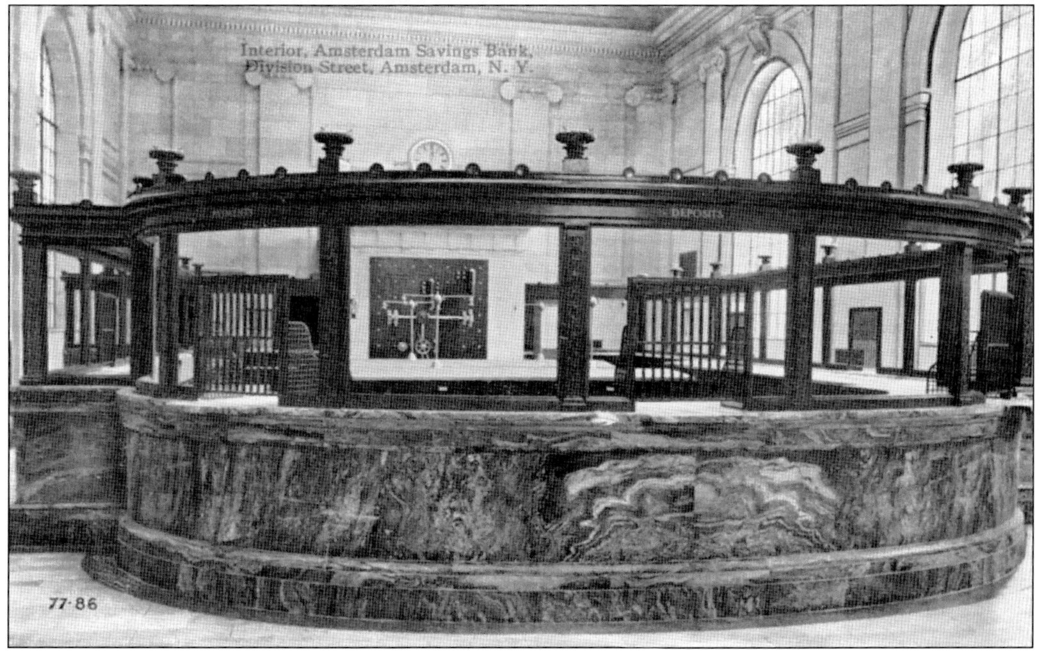

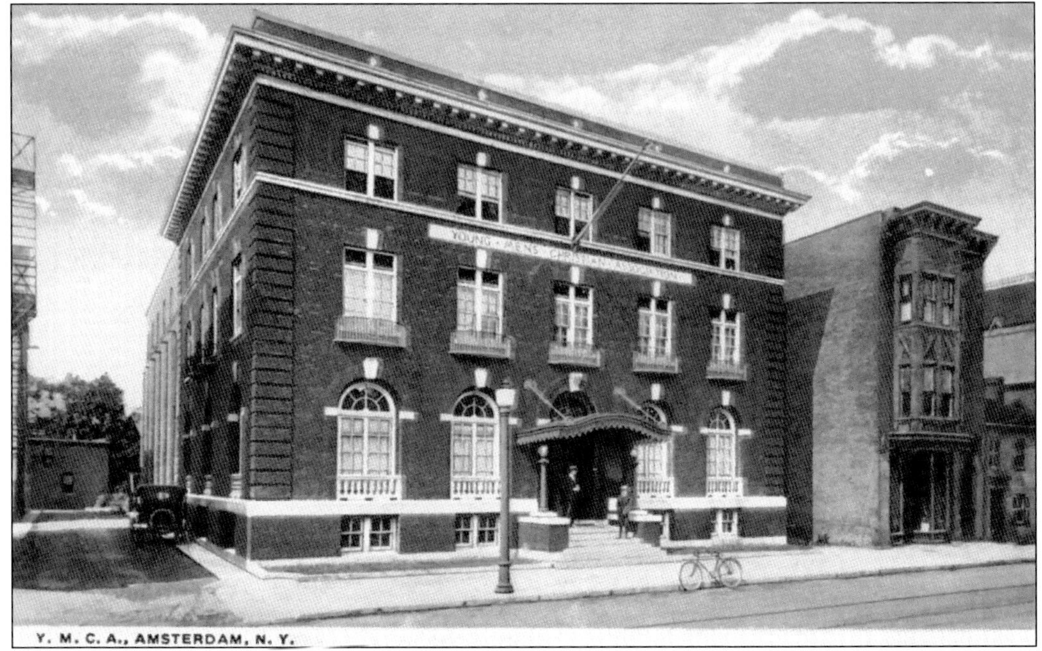


Established in 1854, the Amsterdam YMCA offered little more than housing until it secured space downtown in 1884. This building was erected in 1914 to provide permanency and expand recreational services. The building to the right was replaced by a pool annex constructed in 1961. Early in the 21st century, the organization relocated outside the city to Hagaman, and the former YMCA currently houses interfaith charities. Demolition of the pool annex has been suggested to improve downtown traffic.

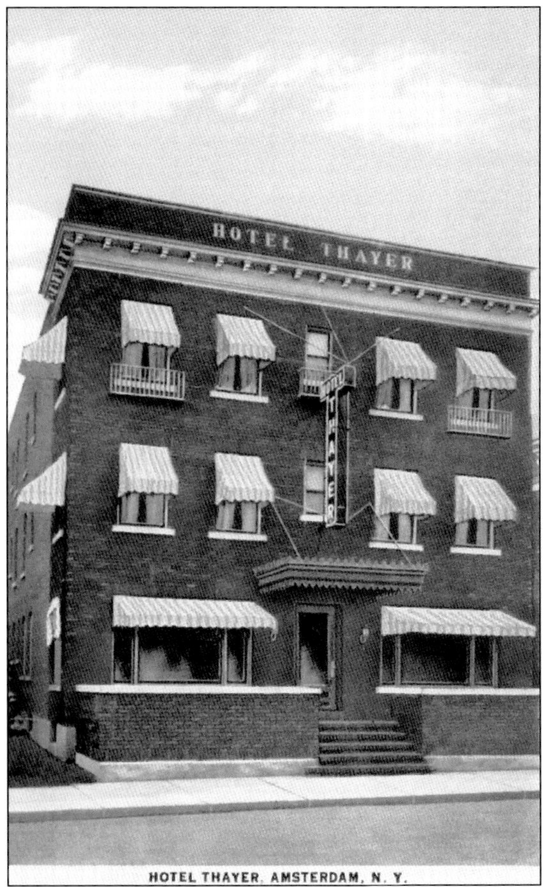


The original Thayer House was near the eastern city limits. This hotel just west of the Amsterdam Savings Bank was built on Division Street in 1924. As with the larger hotels closer to the city center, its clientele were businessmen and salesmen in town to work with the commercial and manufacturing firms.

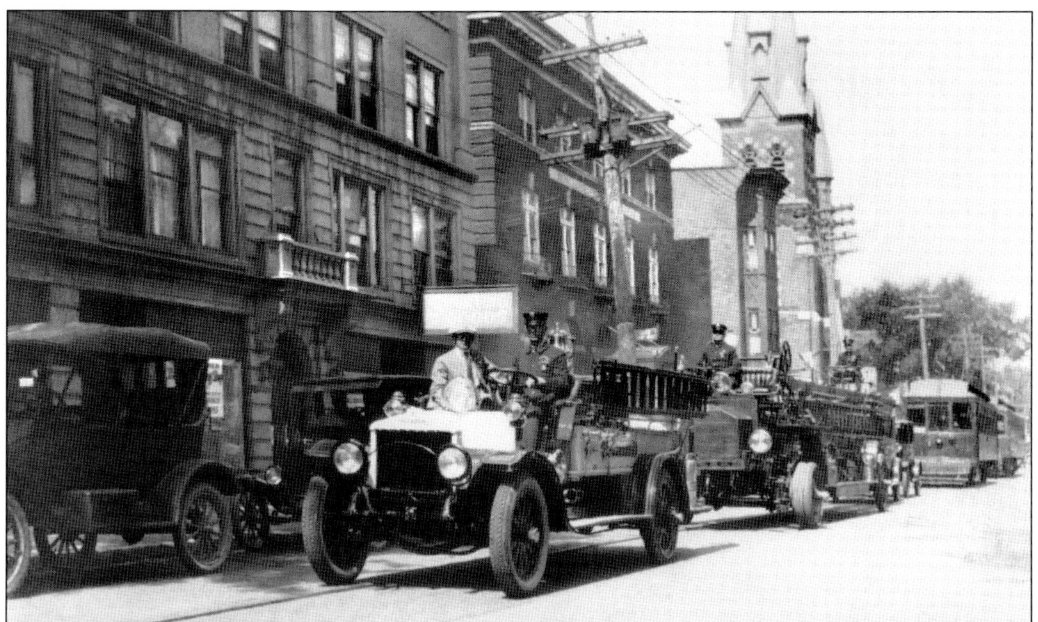

Two of the first motorized pieces of fire equipment, *c.* 1913, purchased by the Amsterdam Fire Department roll past the YMCA. The ladder unit to the rear is riding on double solid tires. The first volunteer fire company in Amsterdam was the Mohawk Engine Company, founded in 1839. The force was professionalized in 1907.

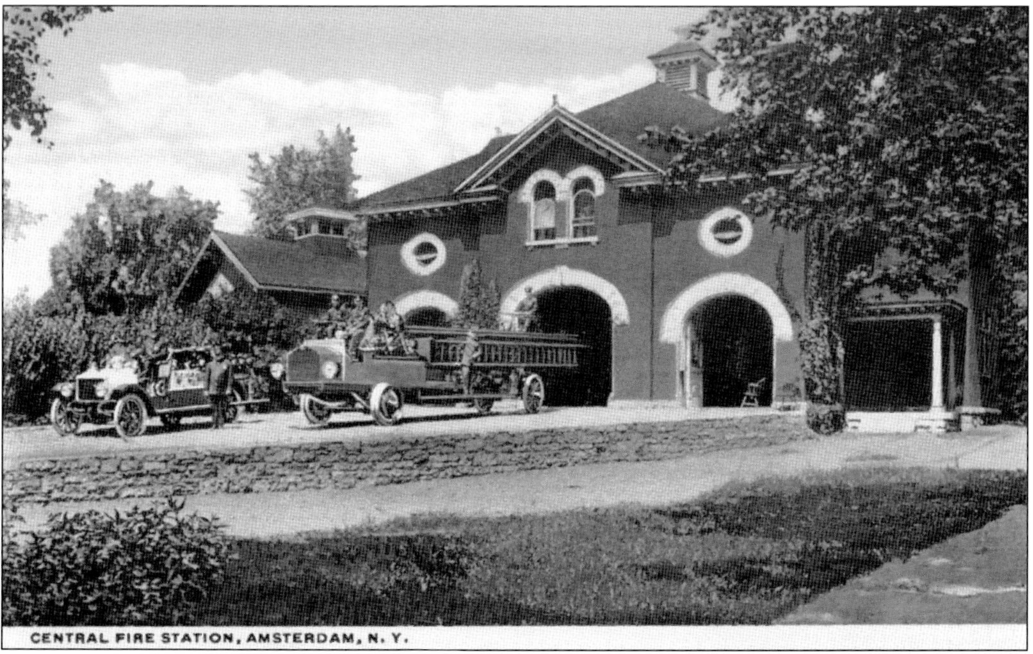

CENTRAL FIRE STATION, AMSTERDAM, N. Y.

The Central Fire Station was established 1920 in the repurposed Kellogg stables at West Main and Pearl Streets. The opening of this station not only permitted the housing and maintenance of faster motorized equipment, but it also allowed the closing or other city reuse of earlier fire stations. In a similar fashion, the establishment of the new public safety building in 1974 made this and several outlying stations obsolete.

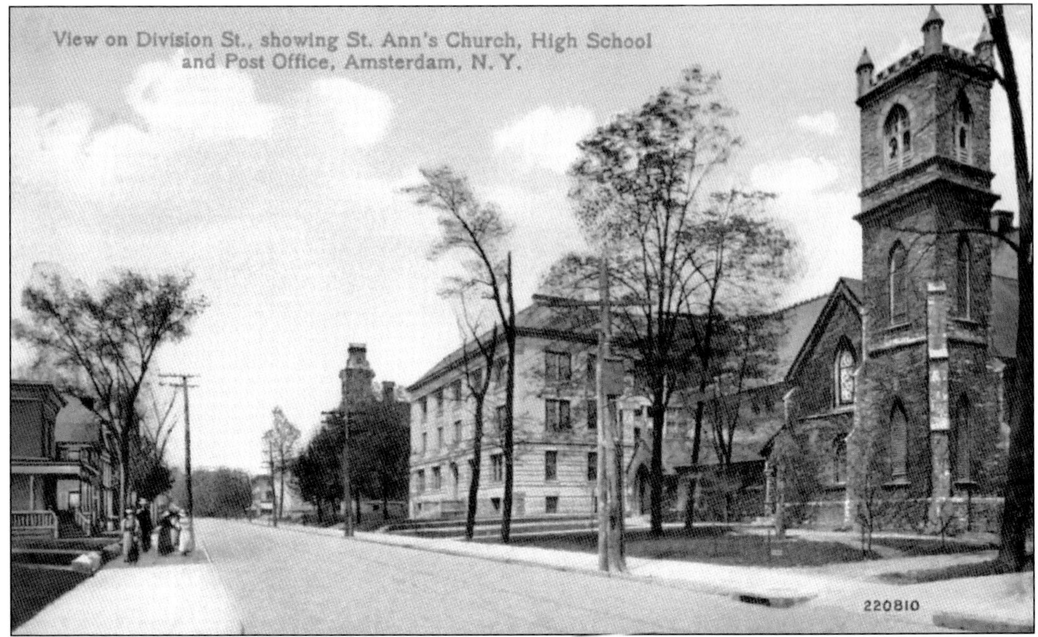


St. Anne's Episcopal Church is the lineal descendant of the chapel endowed in 1712 by Queen Anne of Great Britain to bring Christianity to the Mohawk Indians at Fort Hunter. The original chapel was lost to canal construction in 1820, and the parish was reconstituted in Port Jackson in 1835. After the American Revolution, the Anglican Church (Church of England) in America changed its name to the Protestant Episcopal Church of the United States.

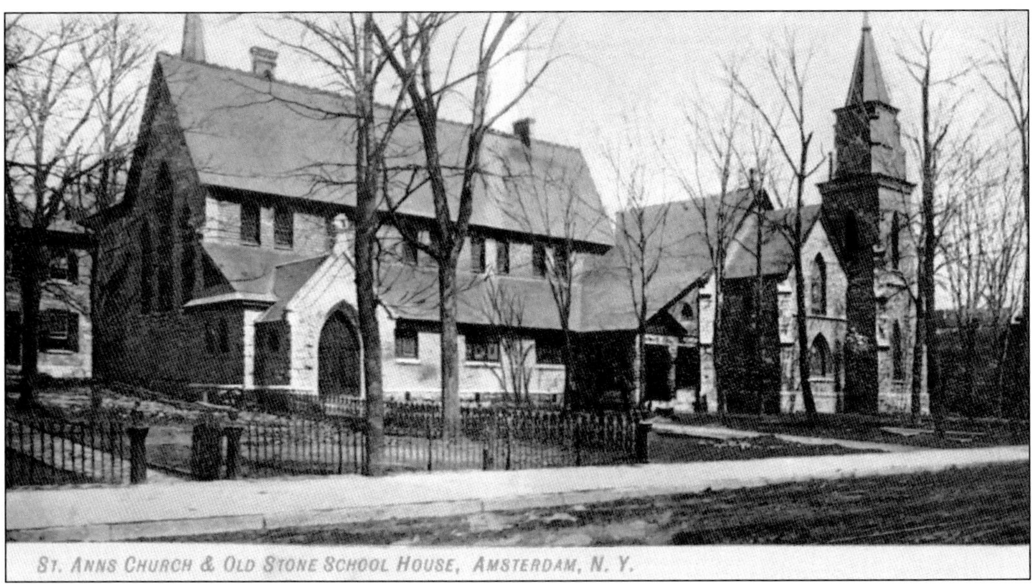


Consecrated in 1851, St. Anne's Episcopal Church was expanded in 1888 with the addition of the main body of the church, which runs parallel to the street. This may have been the same time at which the steeple was lowered and remodeled. It was probably accomplished before the new high school was constructed in 1904, as seen immediately to the left in the top image.

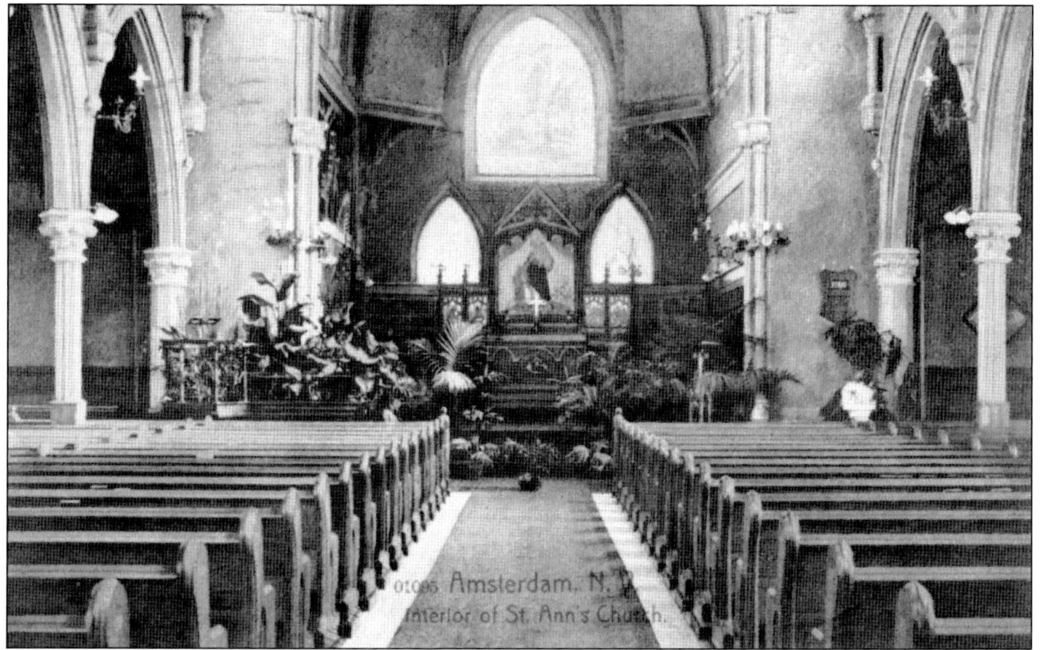


The Gothic-style St. Anne's church was completed inside in classic high Anglican style, with fittings and communion service items that were the gifts of Queen Anne and other notables. The church is still an active parish, standing at what is now the beginning of Division Street surrounded by arterial highways and urban renewal.

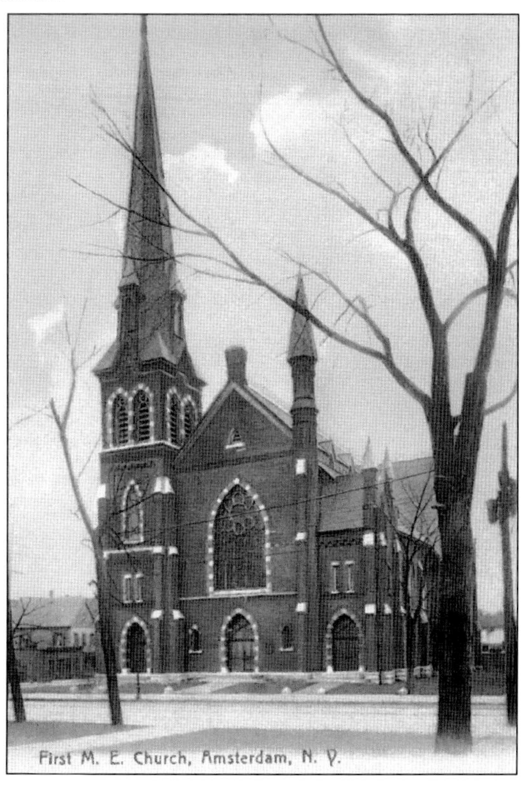


The First Methodist Church on the southwest corner of Division and Pearl Streets was built in 1883 during Amsterdam's peak church-building period (1880–1910). Later congregations from Fort Johnson and Forrest Avenue and east end churches were consolidated into this location. Still later, the Methodist church resited itself outside of the city limits in a new facility in the Town of Amsterdam. Today the site is occupied by a modern Masonic temple.

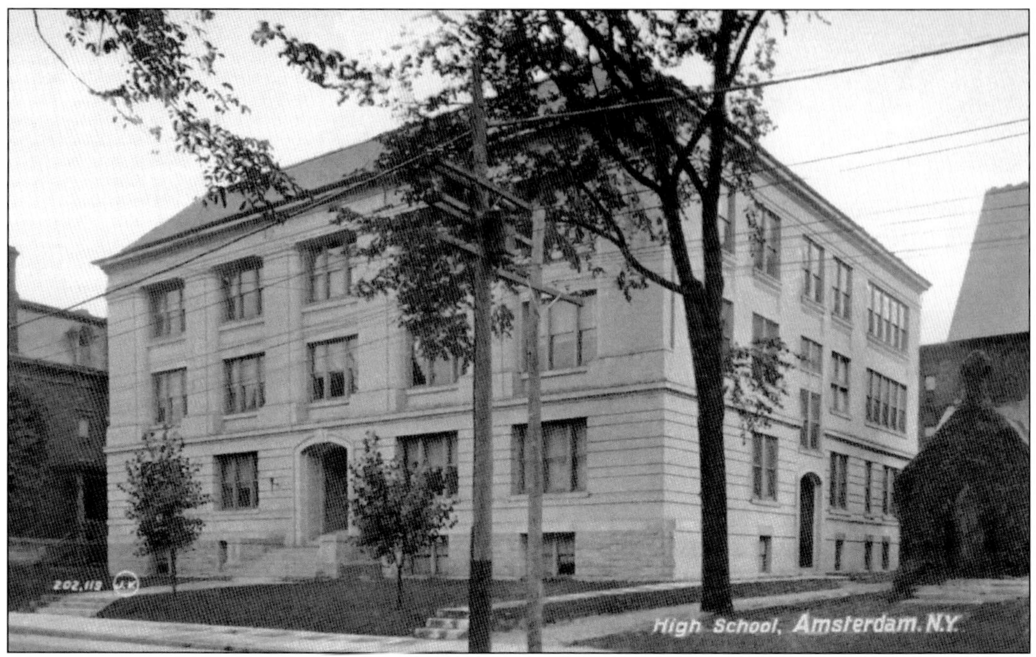


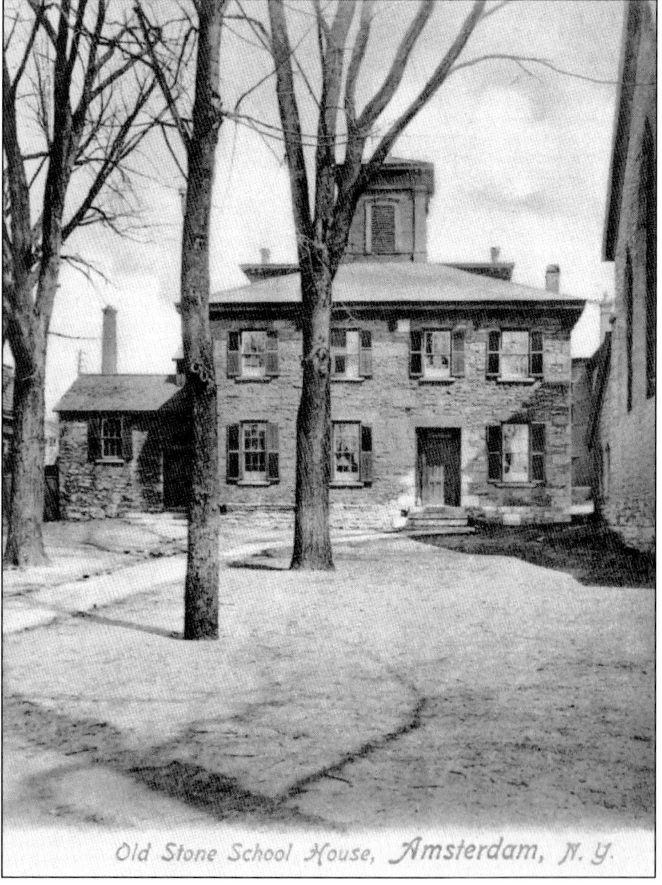


The city's first purpose-built high school was constructed on the north side of Division Street immediately west of St. Anne's Episcopal Church. After the completion of the Wilbur H. Lynch High School in 1930, it served as an annex to the junior high school before being razed for urban renewal. The 1904 high school was built on the site of the 1838 Old Stone School House, which was torn down to make room for it. The stone building was the second public school constructed in the original village, the first being a wooden structure on East Main Street in either 1802 or 1808.

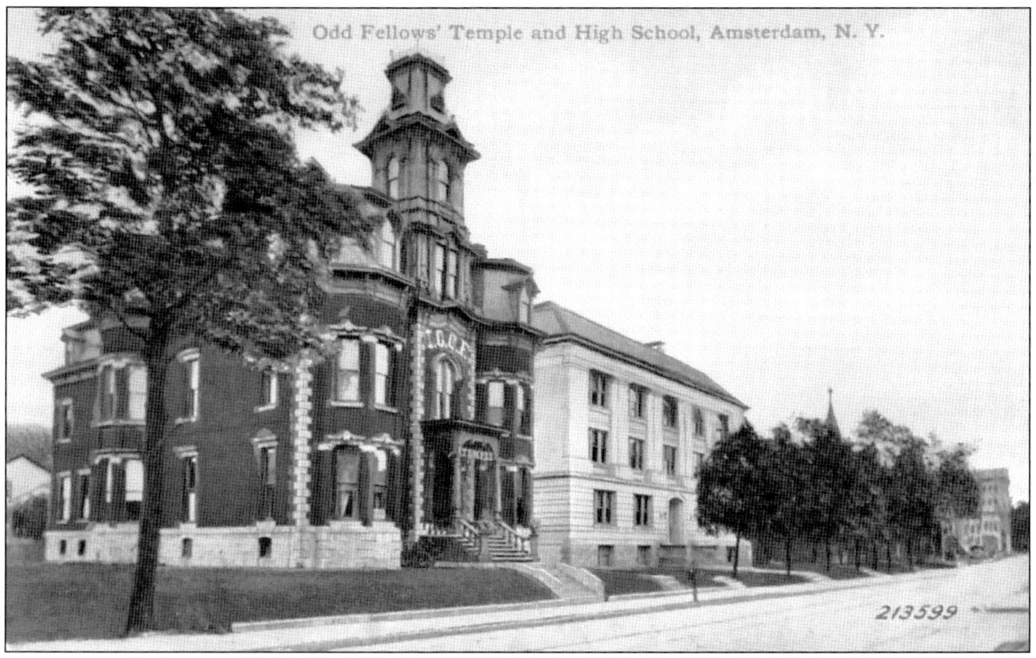


The Independent Order of Odd Fellows was a fraternal organization that opened its first chapter in the city before the Civil War. In 1898, several chapters banded together to purchase the McDonald house on Division Street opposite Mohawk Place for use as a meeting hall. The postcard above shows its original appearance; in the one below, its belvedere has been removed and the roofline lowered. The 1904 high school is to the right. The building was eventually used as school administrative offices before it was torn down around 1970.

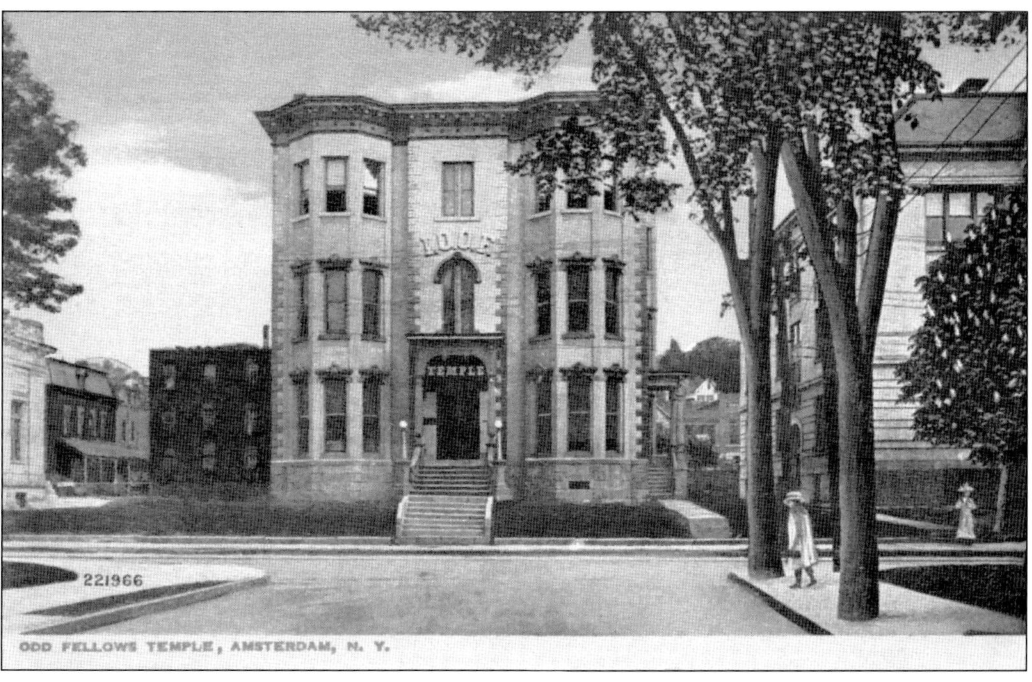

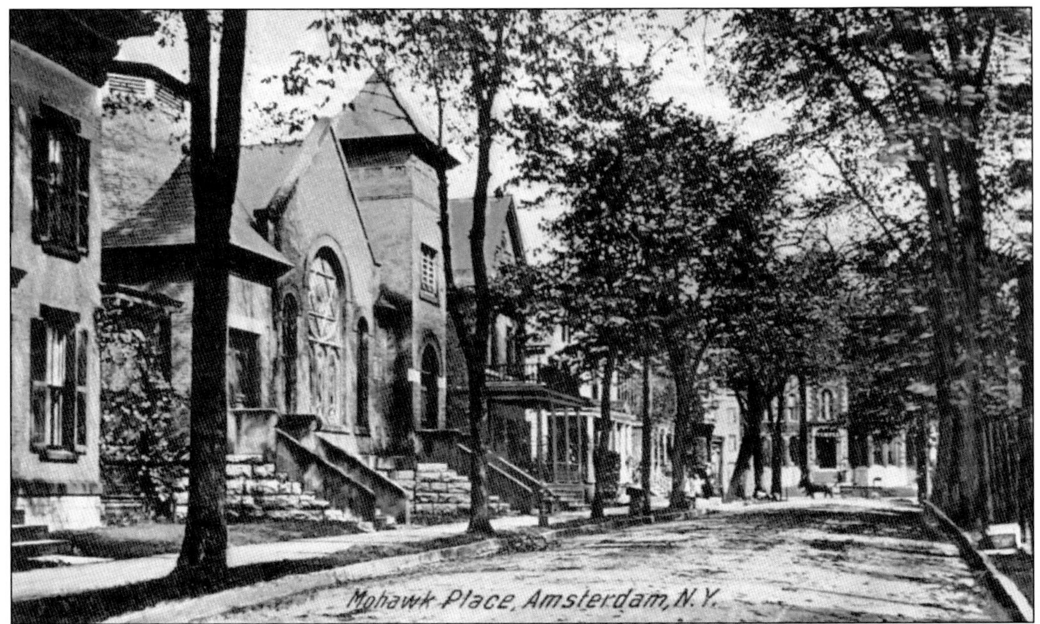


At center left is the Temple of Israel, a reform synagogue built in 1902 and now listed on the National Register of Historic Places. Amsterdam had a rabbi as early as 1875. Conservative Jews congregated at Germania Hall, which they obtained in 1914 for use as a synagogue. Germania Hall was lost to arterial construction, and the congregation built a new temple on Guy Park Avenue in 1976.

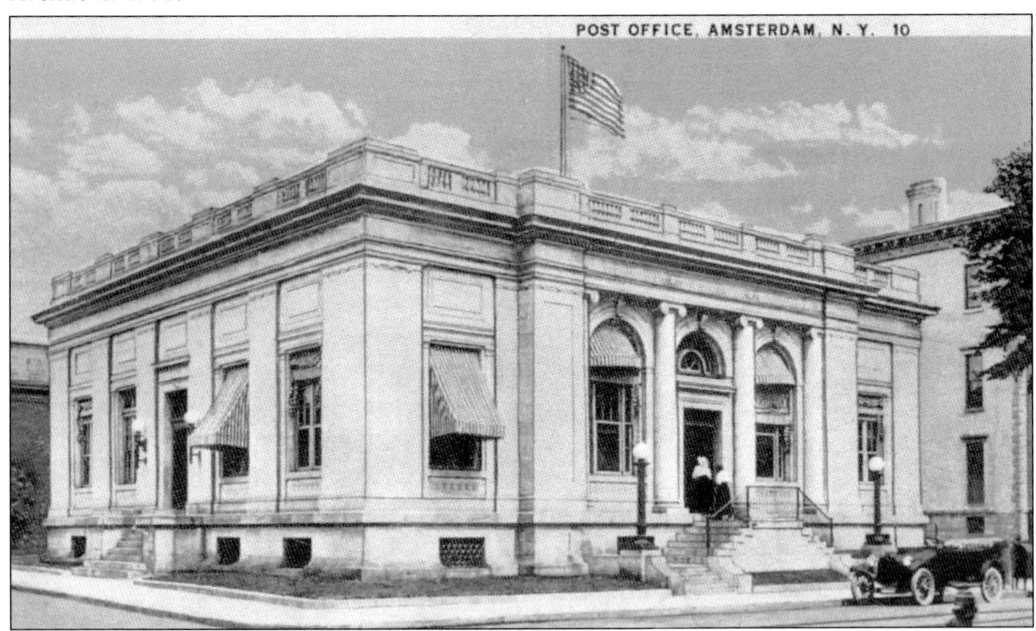


Amsterdam's first postmaster was appointed in 1804. The post office was located in various places downtown before Amsterdam's first federal building was erected in 1912 at the corner of Division and Wall Streets. Dissatisfaction at how far it was removed from the center of downtown helped create the momentum to build a new post office on Church Street in 1936 (see page 27). This building was torn down in 1979.

The Baptist church in Amsterdam was organized in 1800. This church building was erected in 1891 on the south side of Division Street between Wall and Pine Streets. The 1842 church it replaced (see page 23) was sold off when the new one opened. The last service here was conducted in 1968 prior to the move to a modern church on Guy Park Avenue. The building was razed to make room for the Amsterdam Housing Authority (AHA) high-rise.

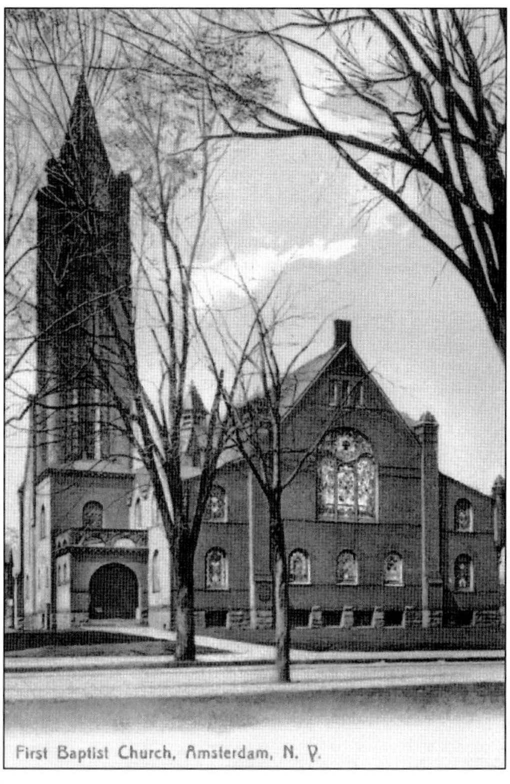
First Baptist Church, Amsterdam, N. Y.

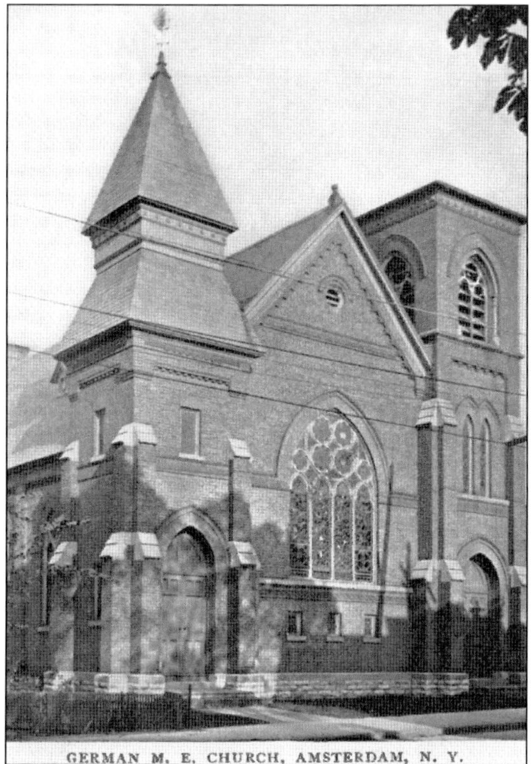
GERMAN M. E. CHURCH, AMSTERDAM, N. Y.

The German Methodist Episcopal Church was located just to the west of the Baptist church seen above but on the north side of Division Street. It was built in 1886 and later, as its congregation diminished, it was used by Christian Scientists. A small commercial building and parking lot now occupies this space.

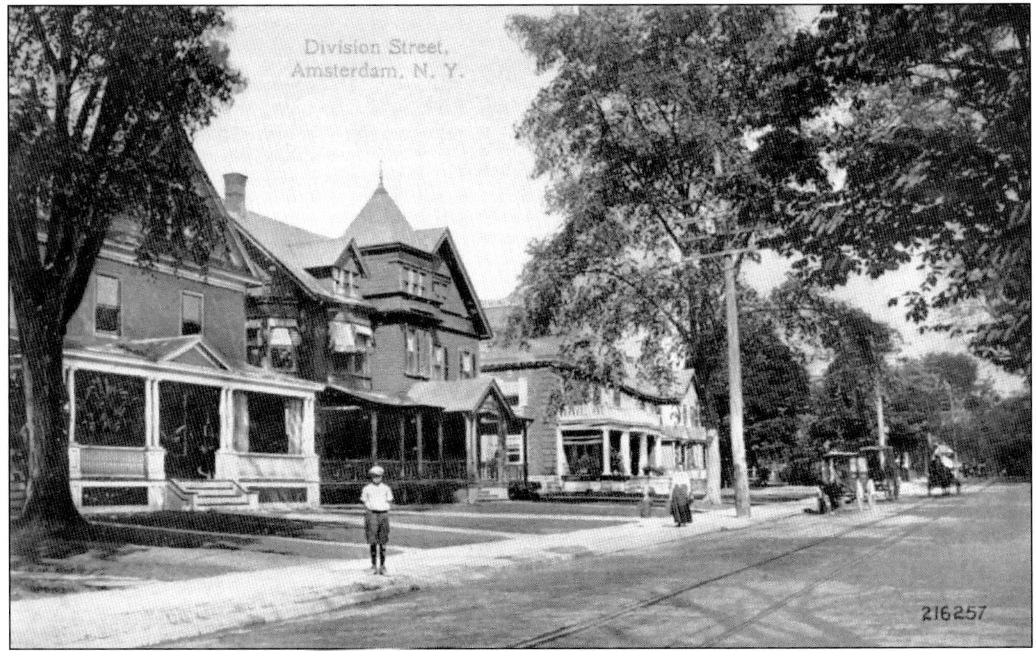


Moving out from downtown, Division Street became more residential as it went west. These two cards provide both east and west views of a portion of the south side between Pine and Guy Streets. It was a favored location for middle- and working-class homes because there was direct access to the trolley line. It was also regarded for the small mom-and-pop–type stores that clustered on its corners.

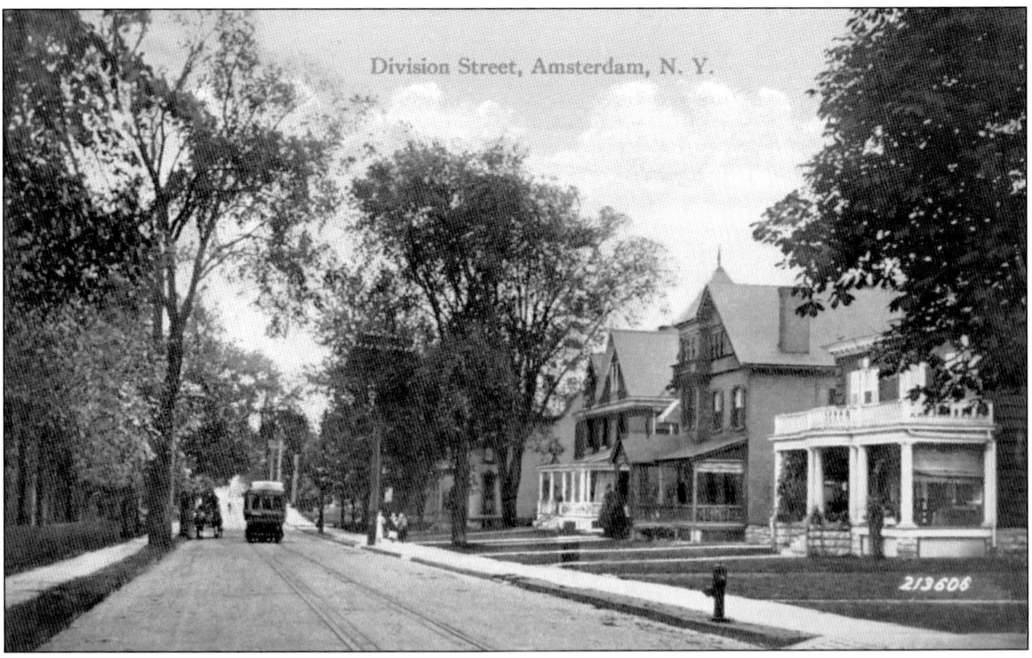

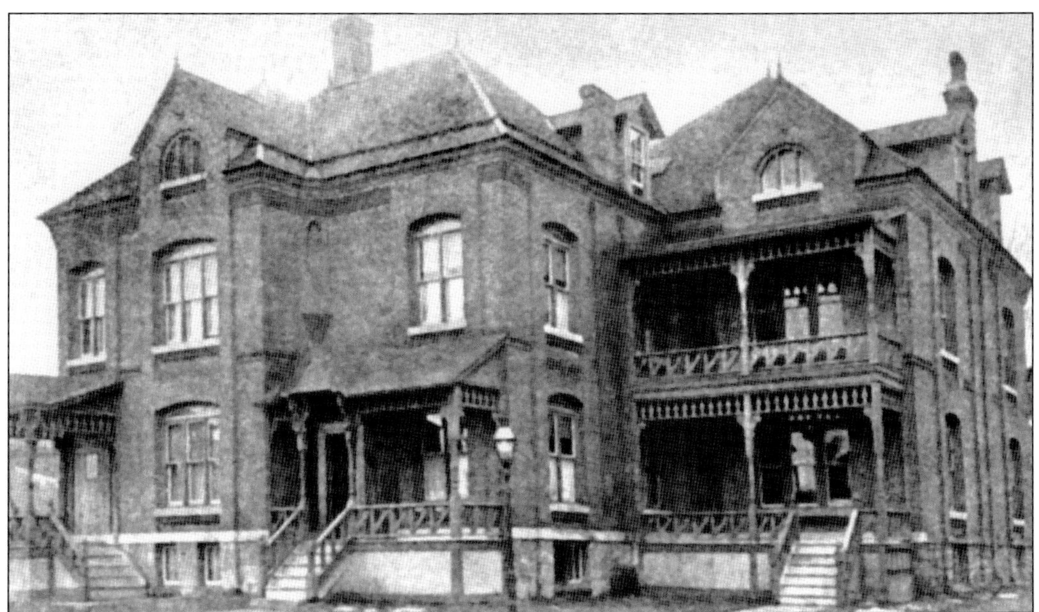

Established in a house in 1889 at 201 Division Street as a cottage-style hospital, Amsterdam City Hospital sought to meet the growing needs of the city. The original hospital had seven beds. It was expanded with an addition on the east side in 1890. In 1892, the hospital started a two-year training course for nurses, who worked in exchange for room, board, training, and a $2 a week allowance.

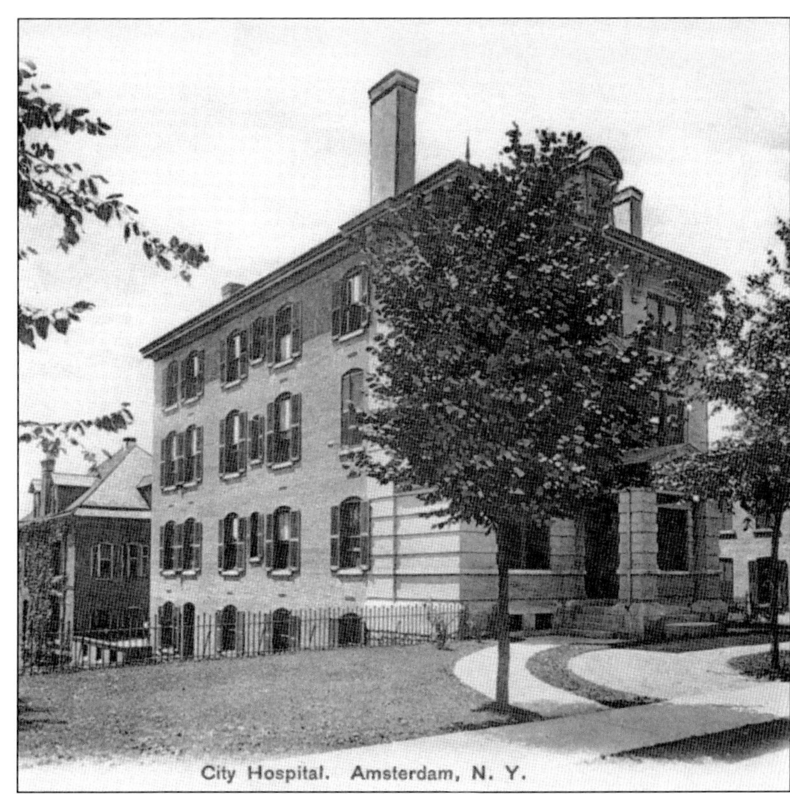
City Hospital. Amsterdam, N. Y.

In 1894, Stephen Sanford bought the lot behind the city hospital on Spring Street to provide for future expansion. In 1900, two more lots on the west side on Division Street were bought and donated. The East Pavilion on Guy Park Avenue (formerly Spring Street) was opened in 1904. The new facility had a surgical department, x-ray department, laboratory, men's ward, children's ward, two dining rooms, private rooms, and a telephone system.

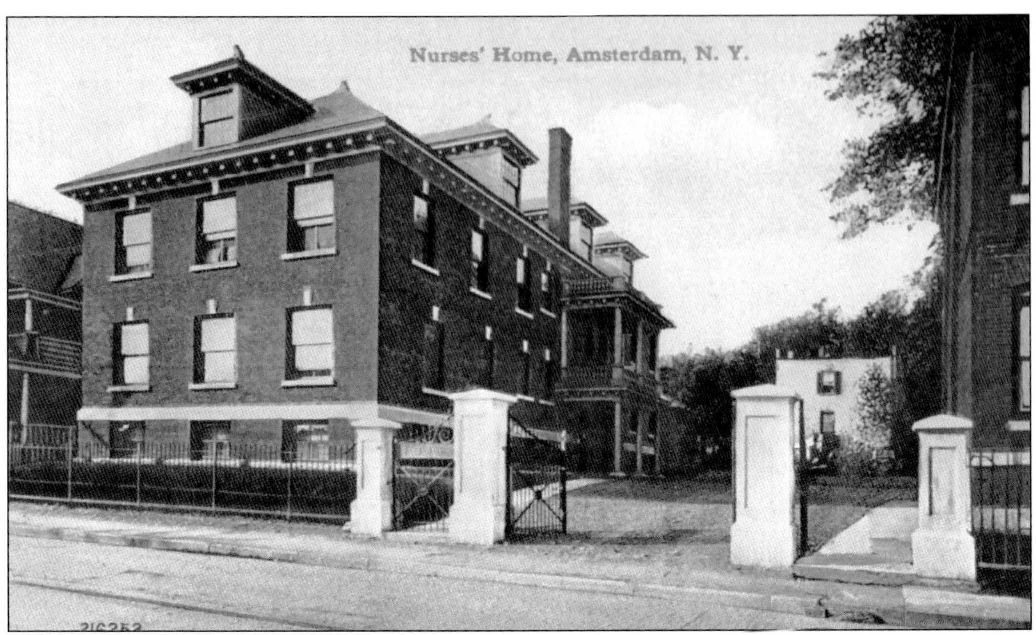


This addition to the city hospital was built in 1911 and unofficially called Sloan Hall after donor William Sloan. Sloan's grandfather had come to the Amsterdam area in 1818 and practiced medicine for nine years. Built on the two lots to the west of the hospital on Division Street, it contained 19 bedrooms, a living room, a matron's suite, a classroom, a kitchen, a dining room, a laundry, and a sleeping porch. It was used for nursing instruction.

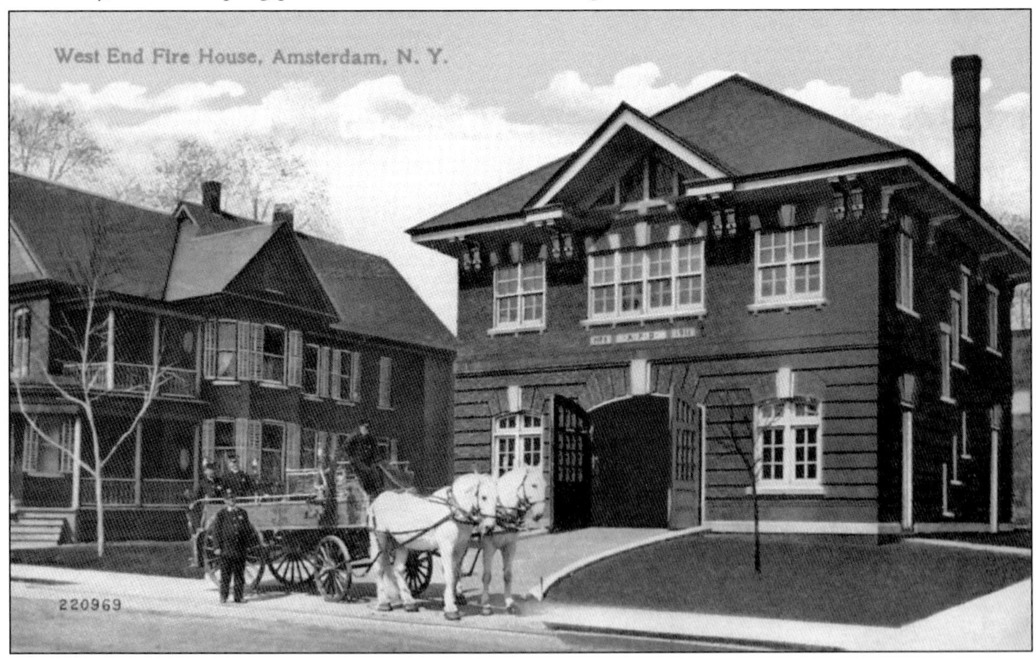


This firehouse was built on Division Street at the intersection of Hennrietta Boulevard in 1911 to provide quick response for the rapidly expanding west end. It closed in the 1970s, as modern technology and the new public safety building rendered it superfluous. Now a private home, the owners are restoring the first floor to its original firehouse appearance.

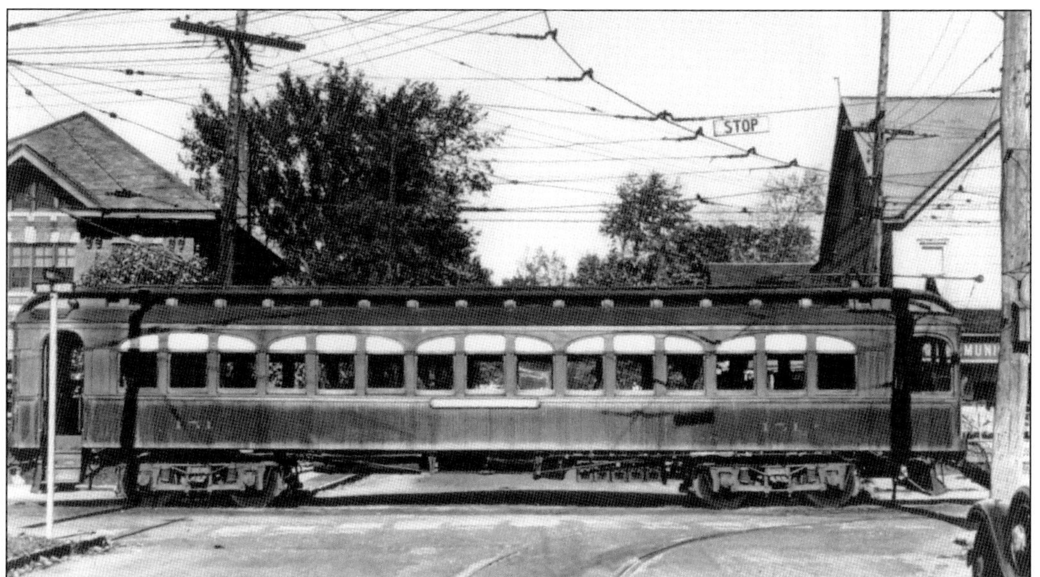


The Fonda, Johnstown and Gloversville interurban car No. 151 heads eastbound on Division Street across Henrietta Street. The interurban cars were long haul top-of-the-line streetcars, with plush interiors, toilets, heat, and hot and cold water. Interurban service to Schenectady started in 1903 and ended in 1938. The carbarn for local trolleys was located on the southeast corner of this intersection and at one time had a dance hall on the roof above the maintenance facilities.

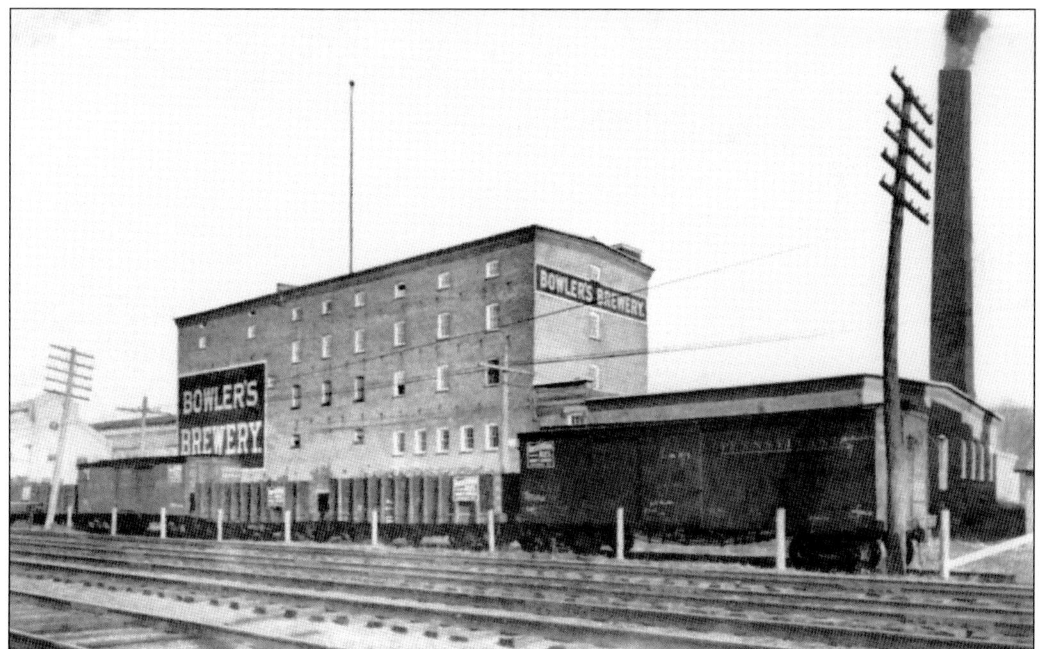


Bowler's Brewery, established in the 1880s, at first made only Amsterdam Ale but soon added a lager line to its production. After a major fire in 1895, the brewery was rebuilt, and production quickly rose again to 50,000 barrels a year. In addition to having its own well and brewing facilities, the plant had a power plant and a stable for draught horses. Production ceased during Prohibition.

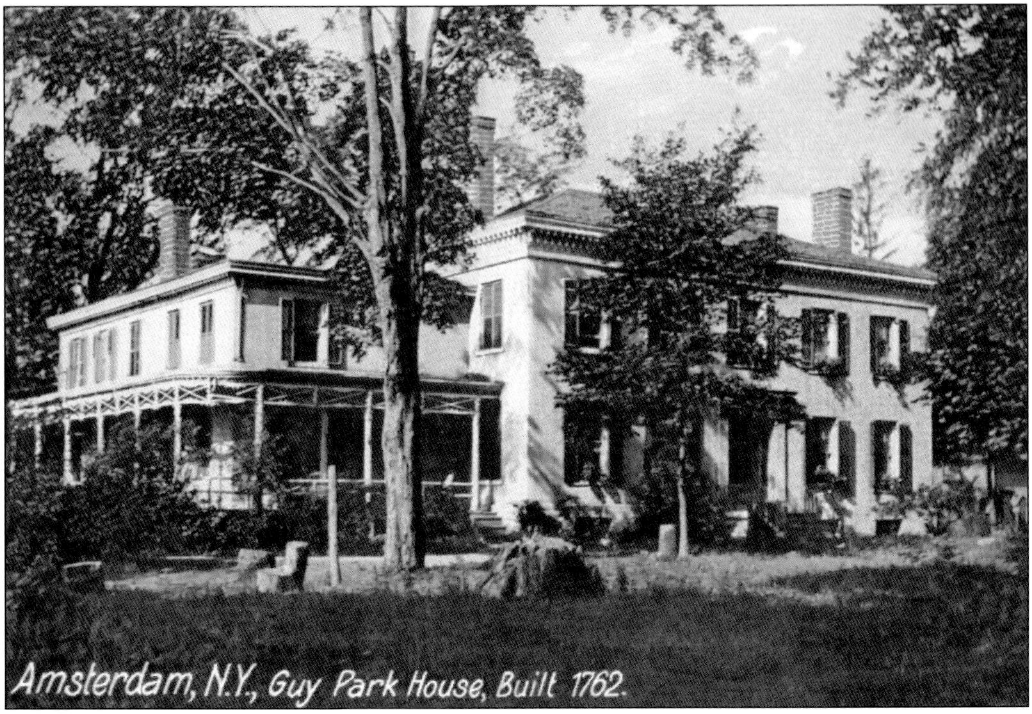

Amsterdam, N.Y., Guy Park House, Built 1762.

Guy Park Manor is the oldest building in Amsterdam and was originally constructed by Sir William Johnson for his nephew Guy Johnson and his wife, Sir William's daughter Polly. As loyalists who fled to Canada (Polly died en route), the Johnson family home was confiscated by the state government and sold off to become, at various times, a residence, a tavern, and offices for the chamber of commerce and the local state assemblyman. Now it is the home of the Walter Elwood Museum.

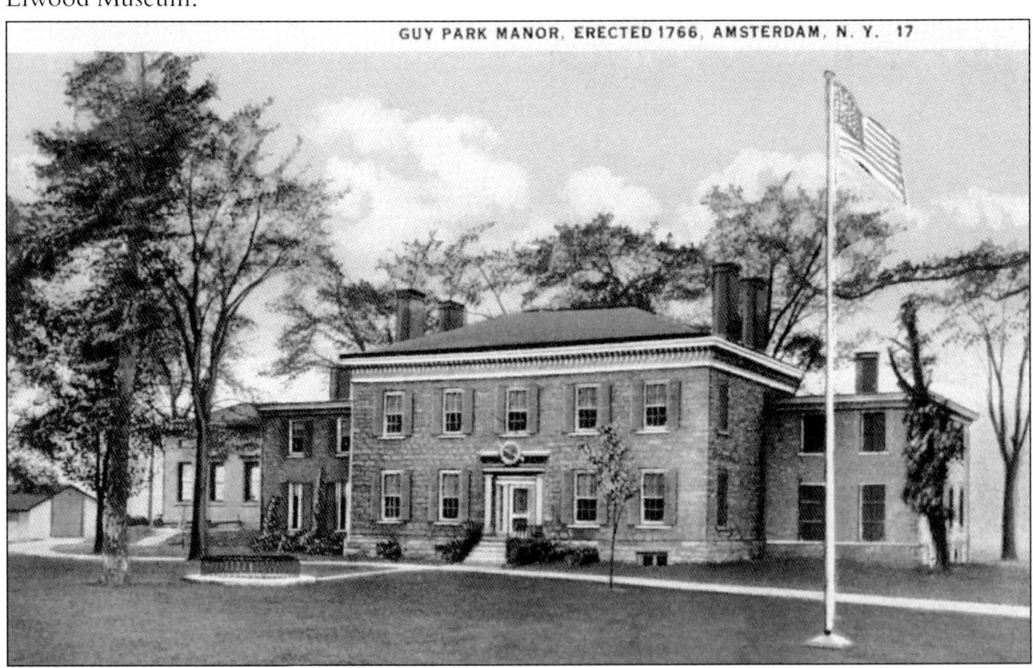

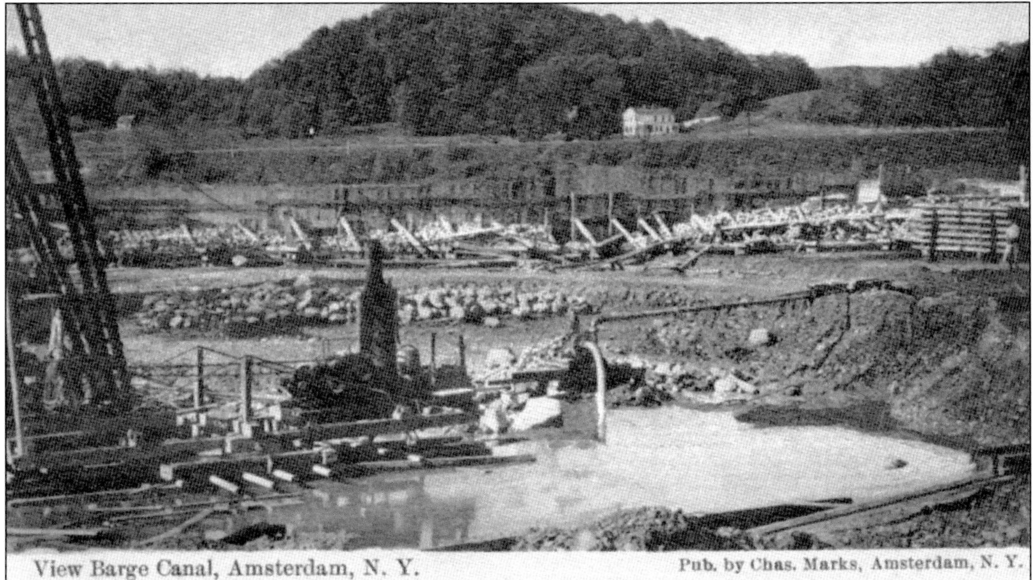
View Barge Canal, Amsterdam, N. Y. Pub. by Chas. Marks, Amsterdam, N. Y.

Seen here are the derricks and steam-powered equipment emplaced for the building of a cofferdam to allow the construction of Lock 11 of the New York Barge Canal in the Mohawk River, between 1916 and 1918. The original Erie Canal was built with picks and shovels to parallel the Mohawk River because the technology did not yet exist to place it in the river. After several expansions and improvements in the middle and later 19th century, the decision was made that it was now feasible and desirable to put the canal in a dredged and improved river.

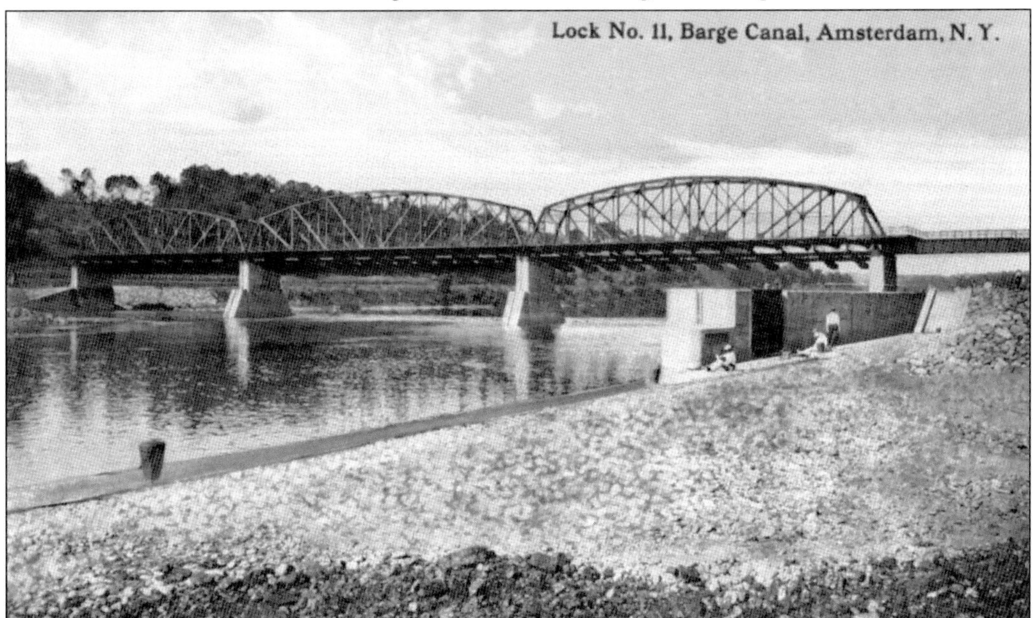
Lock No. 11, Barge Canal, Amsterdam, N. Y.

While the locks on the new barge canal continued to function fundamentally in the same way as the old canal, it was necessary to throw a series of dams across the river to control the level of water on either side of the lock; in essence, the river was turned into a stepped sequence of different level lakes. The superstructure across the river is not a bridge but the framework for a series of moveable metal plates that can be raised or lowered to control the flow of the river.

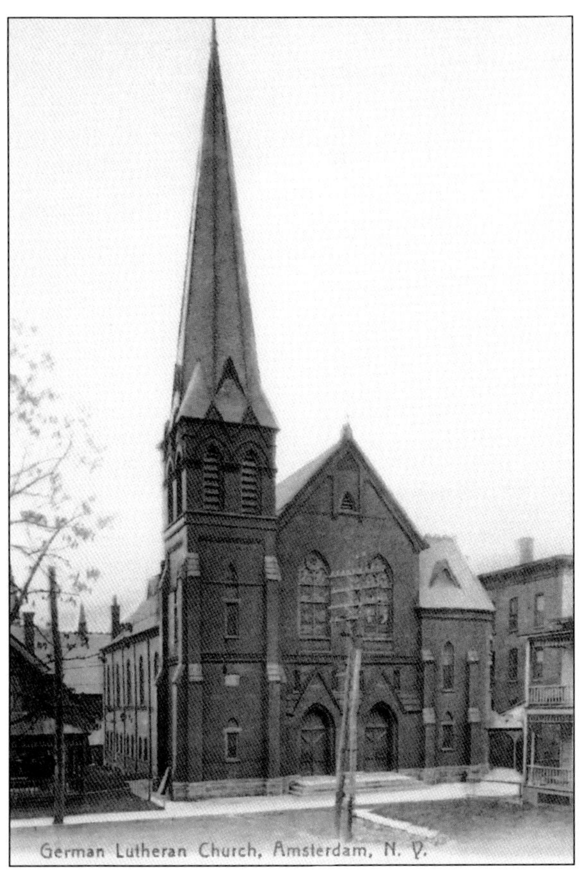
German Lutheran Church, Amsterdam, N. Y.

Originally known as the German Lutheran Church, Trinity Lutheran Church still stands on the south side of lower Guy Park Avenue. The Lutheran congregation that eventually erected this church was founded in 1863 and held its first prayer meetings in the Old Stone Schoolhouse on Division Street before seeking other quarters, leadership, and funding elsewhere. After assistance from the New York Synod, a first church was erected in 1869. The church pictured replaced the first one in 1888.

The Theodore Roosevelt Junior High School, built in 1924 between Guy Park Avenue and Division Street, became excess to the Greater Amsterdam School District's needs when a new high school was constructed north of the city and the former Wilbur H. Lynch High School was converted into a middle school. The junior high building was demolished to make way for a fixed-income high-rise bearing the same president's name.

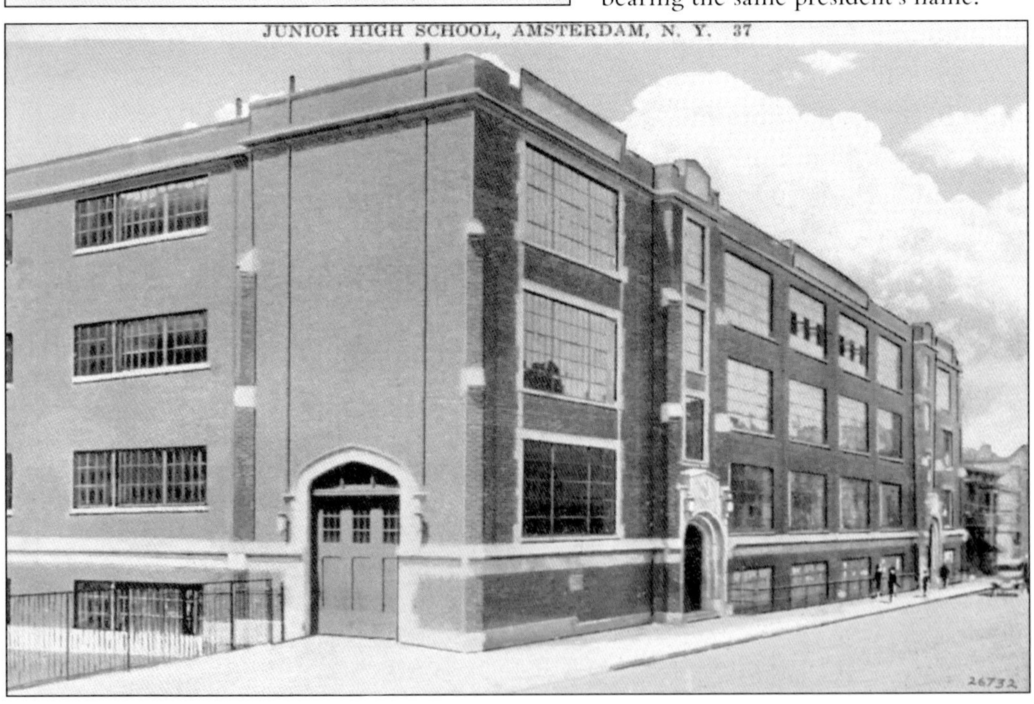
JUNIOR HIGH SCHOOL, AMSTERDAM, N. Y. 37

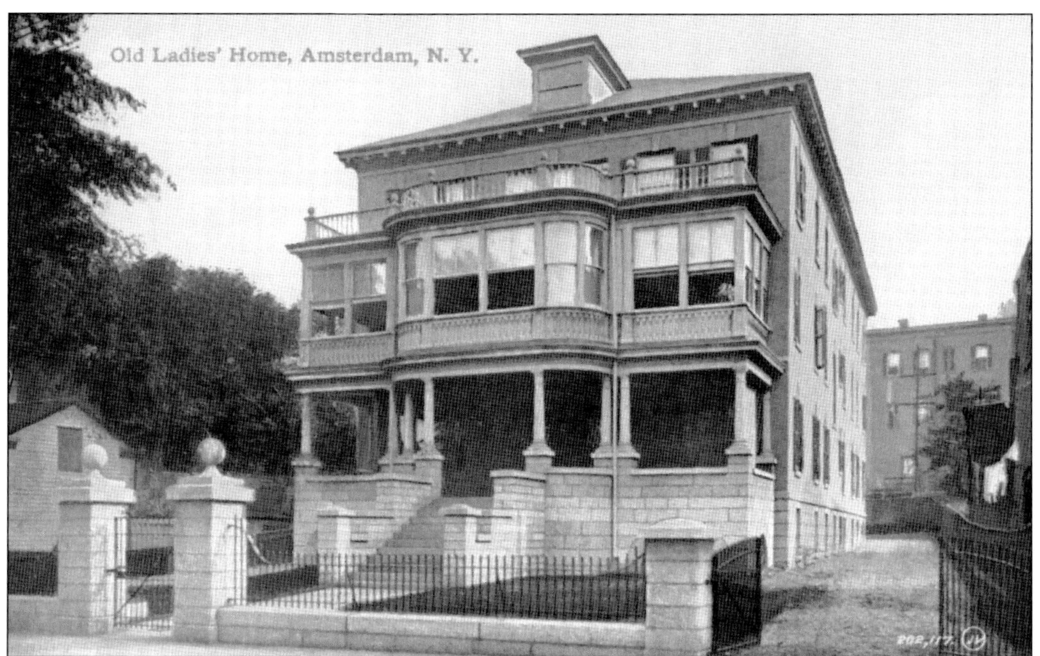


The Sarah Jane Sanford Home for Women was opened in 1906 as a philanthropic endowment of Stephen Sanford and named for his wife. The home still exists on Division Street and in 2009 added a modern addition, expanding the structure farther west down the street.

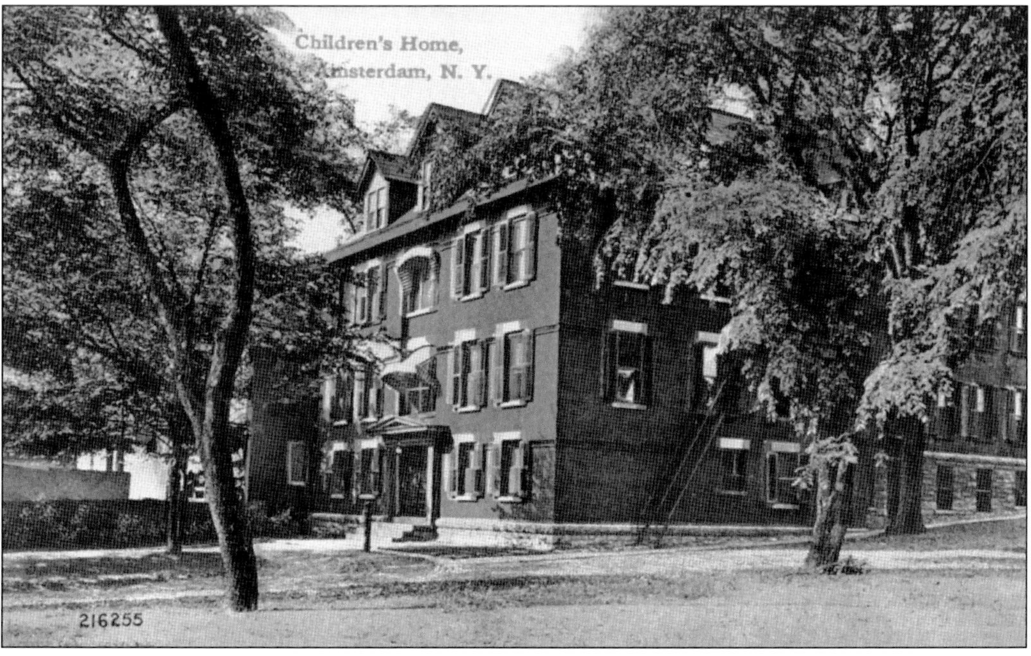


Another charitable action of Stephen Sanford was the establishment of the children's home, donated in honor of his son William. This orphanage existed from 1896 to the 1940s, when the placement of children in foster homes and other programs diminished its original purpose. It was razed to make room for a New York State unemployment office.

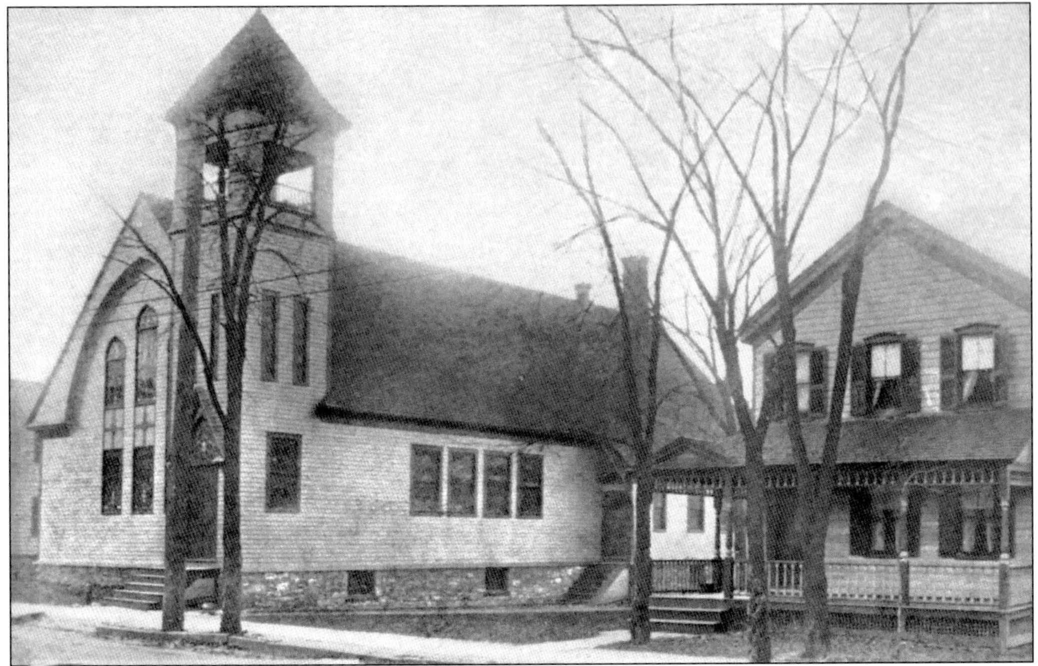

Erected on the corner of Guy Park Avenue (originally Spring Street) and Pine Street, St. Luke's English Lutheran Church was torn down to make room for a new brick church of the same denomination facing Pine Street. The *English* in its title reflects a growing disagreement between older and younger German Lutherans in the 1890s. The immigrants wanted the sermons and services to continue in the language of the old country, while their sons and daughters thought this a hardship and barrier to assimilation.

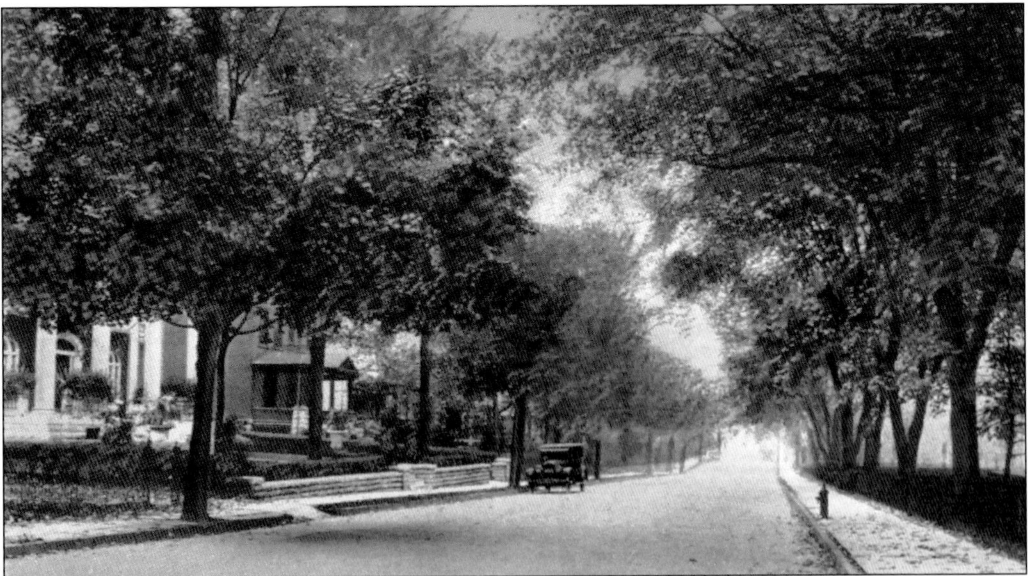

Originally known as Spring Street for the drinking-quality water that flowed out of the rise that paralleled the street to the north, when it was extended westward its new portion was named Guy Park Avenue, while the older part remained Spring Street. Soon the new name was applied to the entire street.

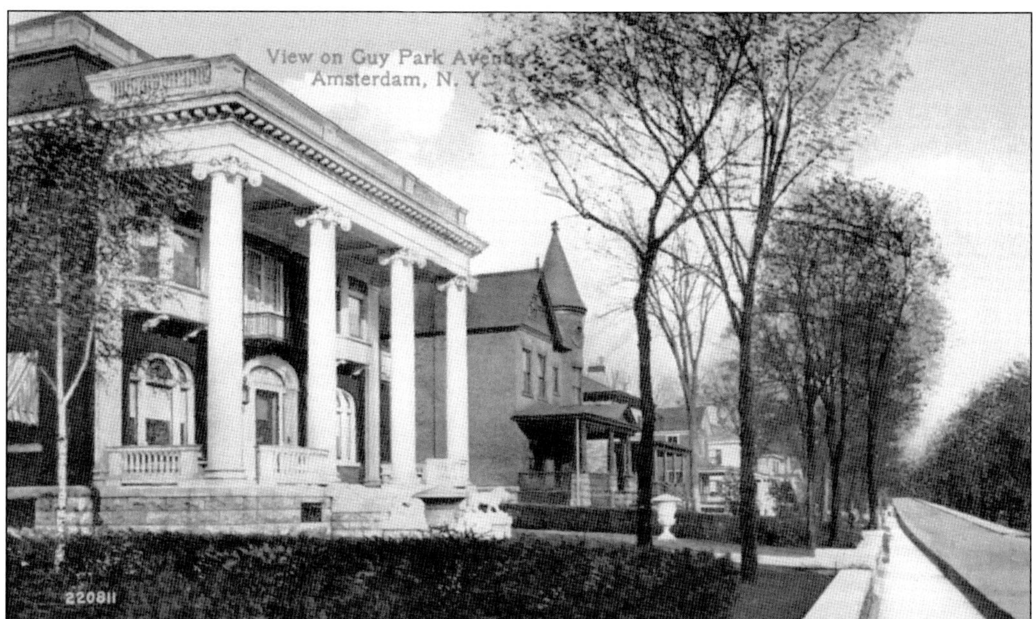


Upper Guy Park Avenue became the place for the social elite to build their homes after the sale of farms on the western edge of the city at the dawn of the 20th century. At left around 1913 is 125 Guy Park Avenue, the home of Theodore J. Yund, an owner of the knitwear mill of the same name. Today the mansion is an office building. A portion of this home is visible on the previous card.

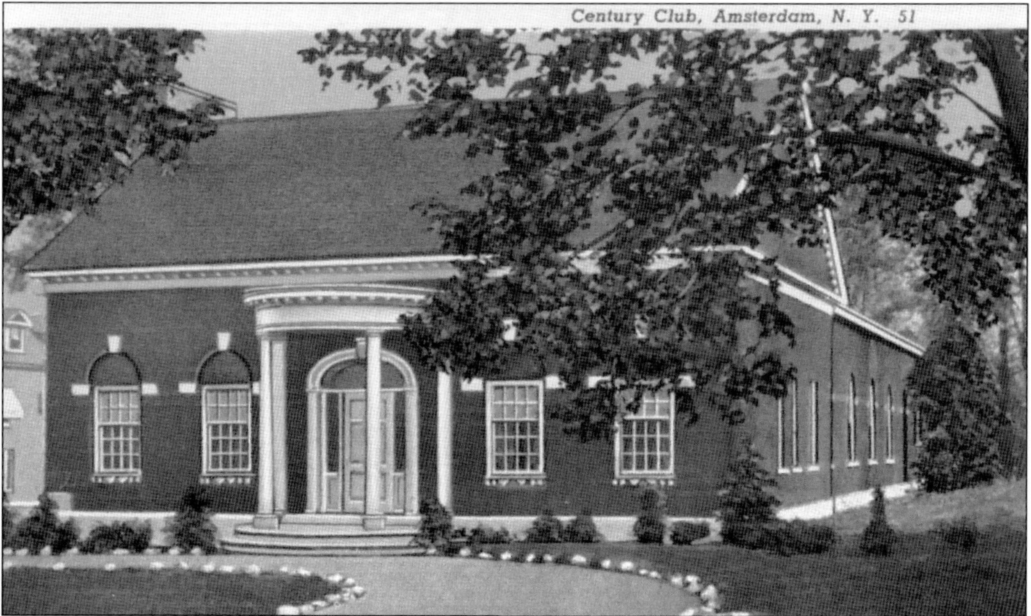


The Century Club was founded in 1895 as a cultural and charitable organization, with membership limited to 100 (soon raised to 200) of the leading women of Amsterdam. Meetings were held in the Sanford Homestead building (Mrs. Stephen Sanford was a founding officer) until the construction of this facility on Guy Park Avenue in 1933. The organization today is affiliated with the General Federation of Woman's Clubs and has recently remodeled the building interior.

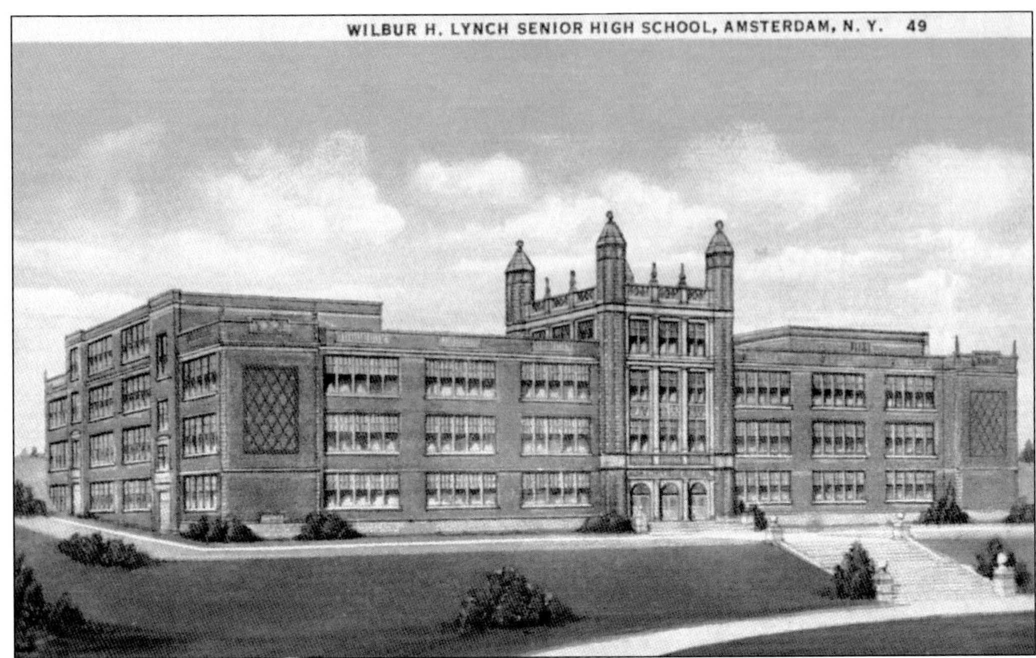


Built in 1930 on an extensive property that curtailed development in the area, additions and improvements have occurred to Wilbur H. Lynch High School over the decades since. When a new high school outside city limits was finished in 1977, this building was converted to a middle school. After World War II, temporary veterans' housing was erected behind the school. The auditorium is where the actor Kirk Douglas first performed while he was a student, and *The Amsterdam Oratorio* premiered there in 2001.

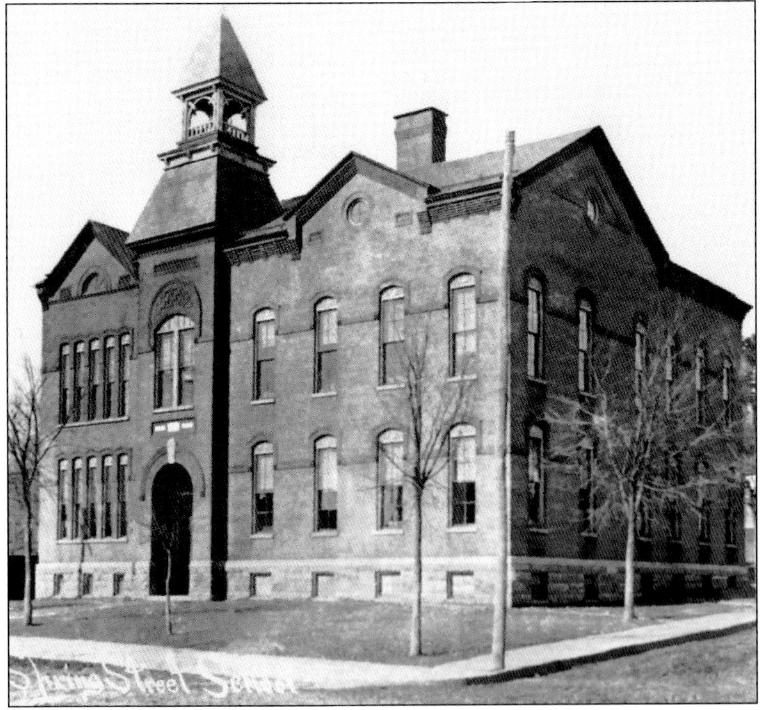

West Spring Street School, so called to differentiate it from an earlier school closer to downtown on Spring Street, was built in 1885 to serve the increasing needs of the west side. With the completion of other more modern schools in the mid-1960s, it was razed to make room for a professional building.

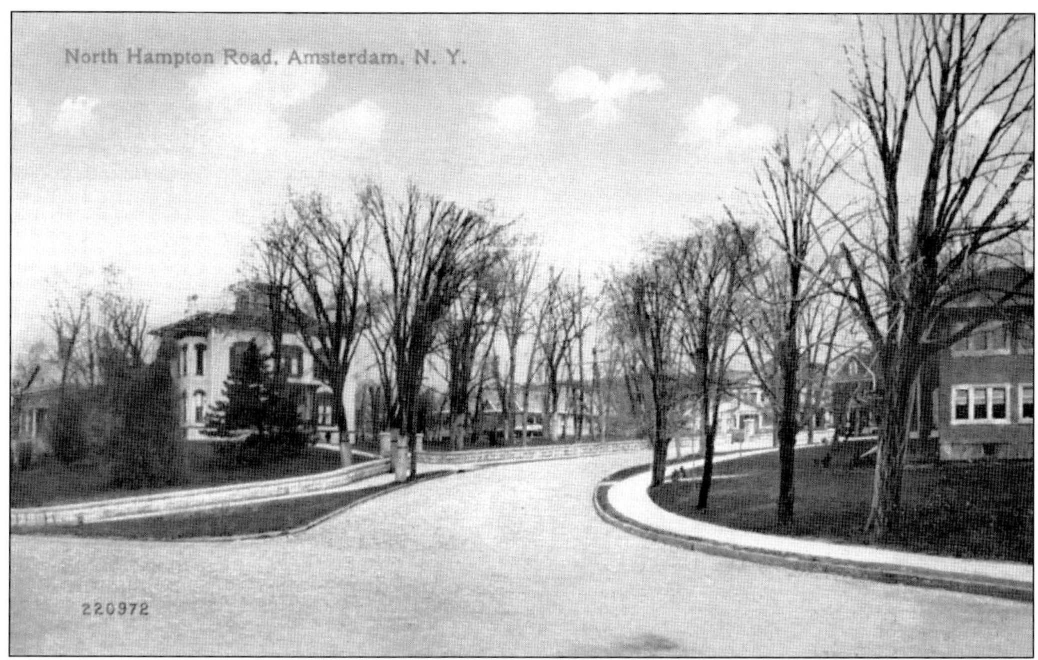


The mansion to the left was the home of Lewis E. Harrower, owner of the Rural Hosiery Mill in Harrower's in 1890. It was later a home for the aged and then a medical office. The triangle at the intersection of Guy Park Avenue and Northampton Road once had a flagpole and ornamental plantings. Northampton Road was called the Amsterdam and Fish House Plank Road in the 1850s, a toll road running through Perth to Northampton.

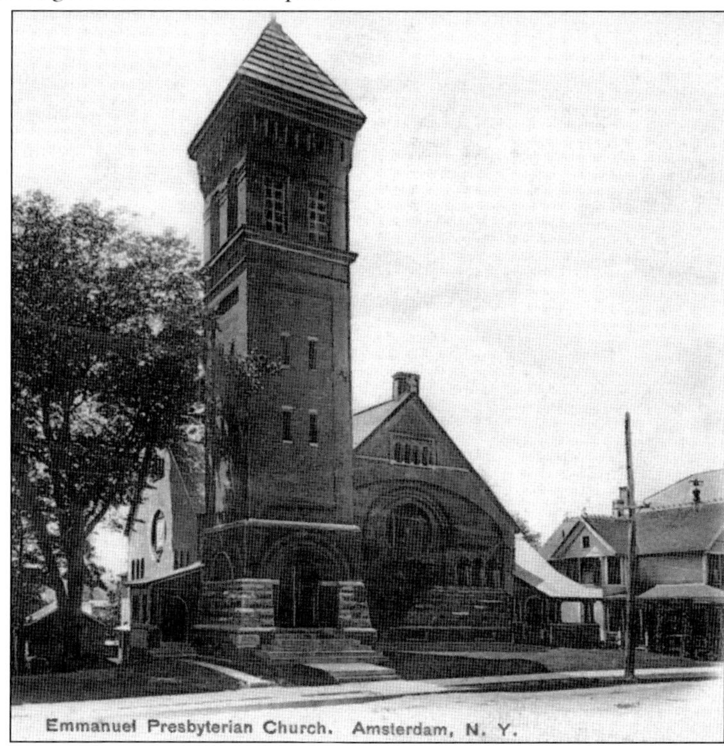


Emmanuel Presbyterian Church was consecrated in 1888 by members of the Second Presbyterian Church to meet the needs of the west side. Today the building is home to a Hispanic Seventh Day Adventist Church. The 1900 house to the right was originally the pastor's home, and after that, it was the home of Maria Riccio Bryce, who composed *The Amsterdam Oratorio* there in 2001. (Courtesy of Montgomery County Department of History and Archives.)

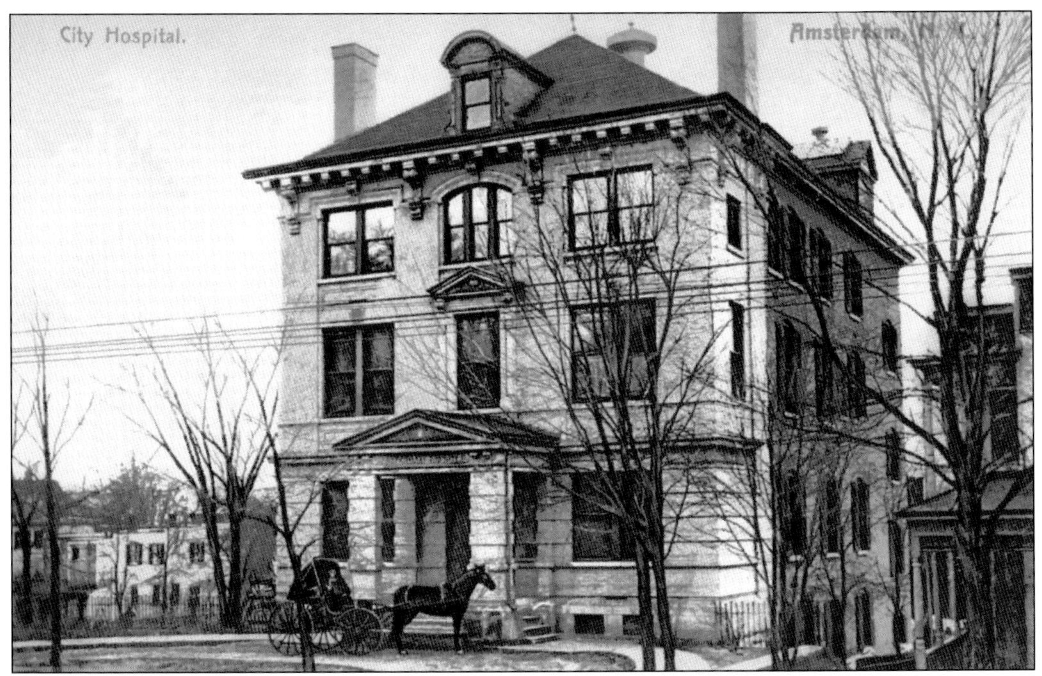


Amsterdam City Hospital was established in 1889 on Division Street. This 1904 building was an expansion facing onto Guy Park Avenue and became the east wing of a further expansion. In 1963, the hospital moved to a new 25-acre site north of the city and changed its name to Amsterdam Memorial Hospital. In 2009, it consolidated with St Mary's Hospital.

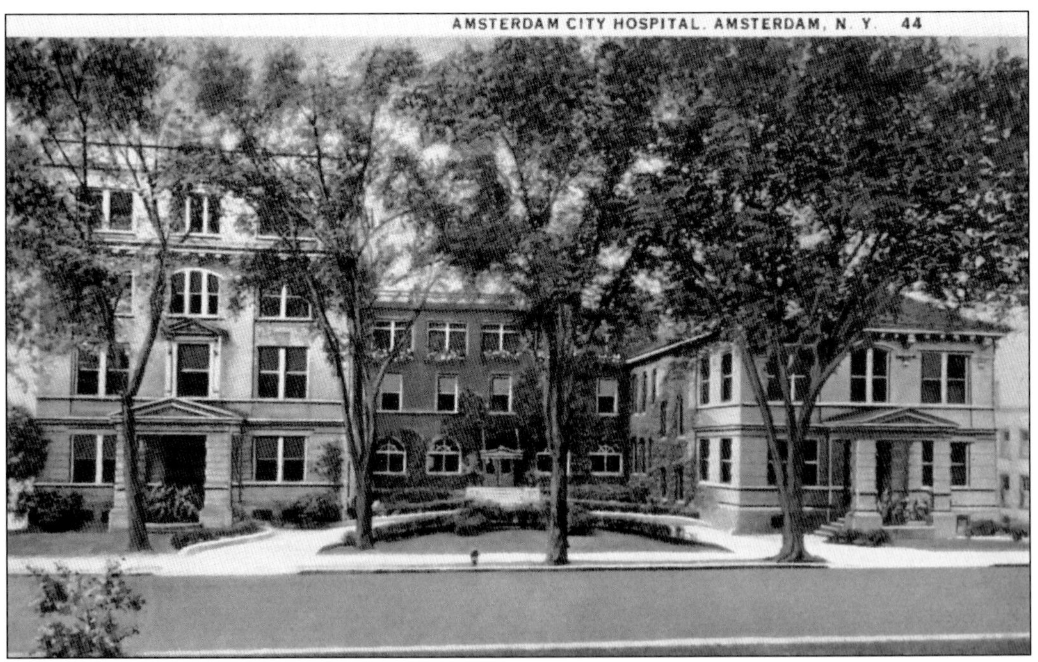


This view shows the full frontage of the expanded Amsterdam City Hospital on Guy Park Avenue, with the building shown above on the left. Today the site is Sirchia Park, named after the first Amsterdamian to be killed in France after D-day, June 6, 1944, during World War II.

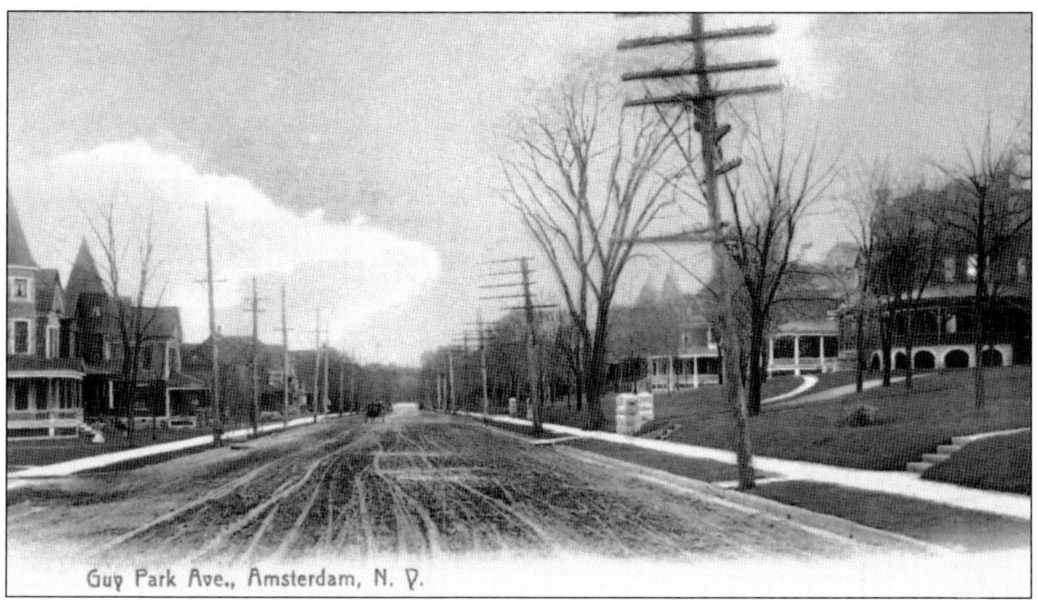


With its wide roadway and shade trees, it is no wonder that after the initial confusion about Guy Park Avenue and Spring Street (see page 84), many locals simply referred to it as "the Boulevard." The avenue does not lead to Guy Park Manor but rather farther west, however, the name was suggestive of the large manor estates the land developers wished to sell.

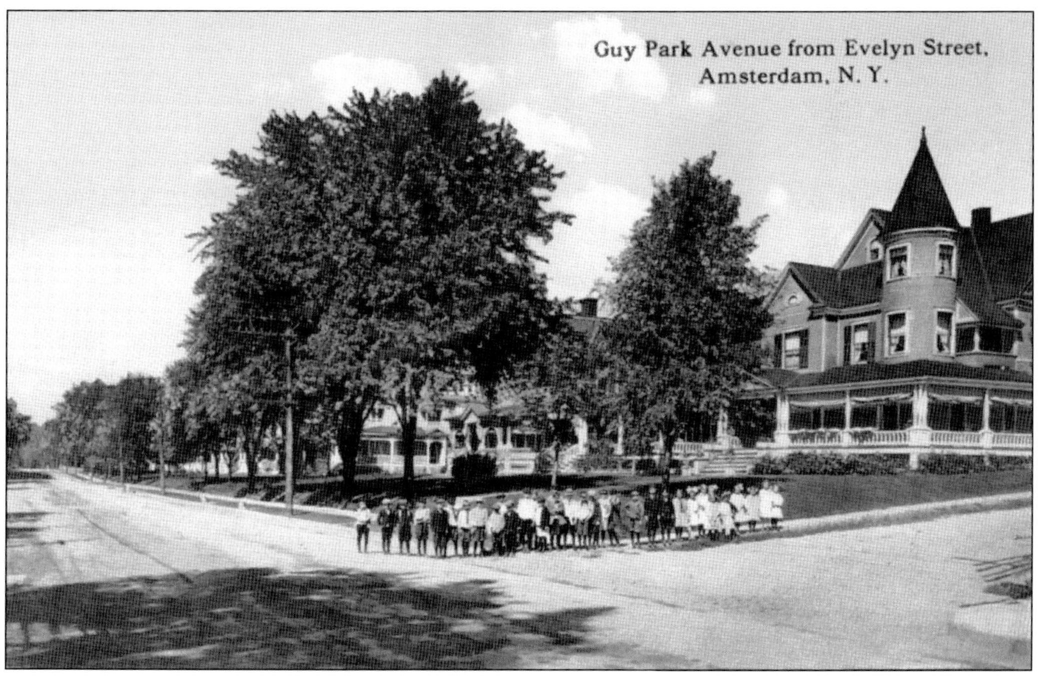

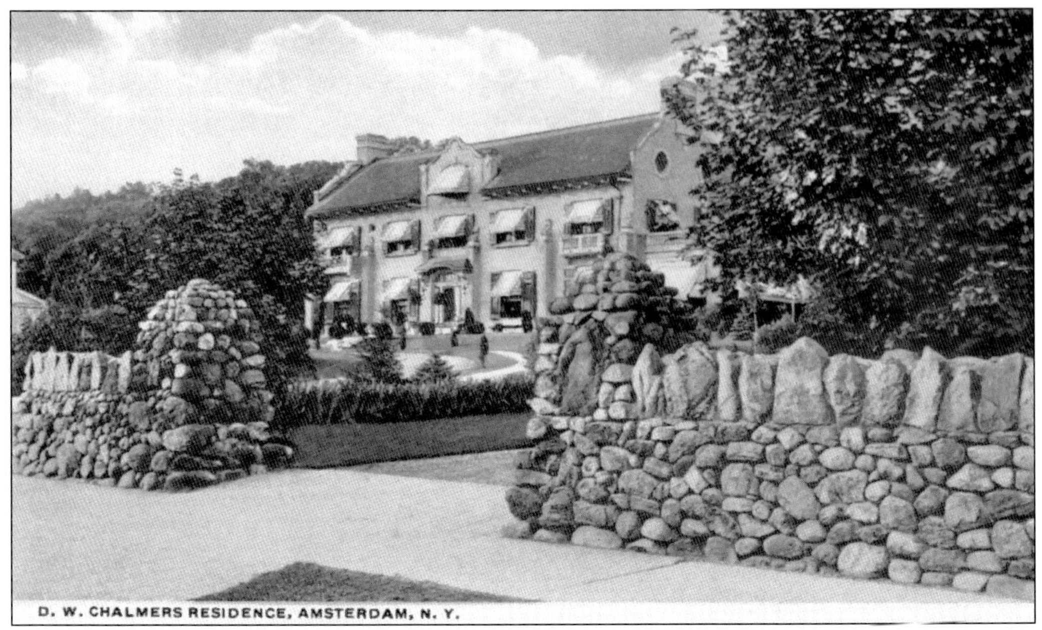


The home of David Chalmers, partner in the Chalmers Knitting Mill, was typical of the Guy Park Avenue mansion: large houses on large plots, set well back with elaborate lawns and gardens, often with pools and tennis courts. Some had separate carriage houses or garages that faced onto nearby streets. Most of these homes were on the north side of the avenue west of Northampton Road, with smaller but still substantial houses on the south.

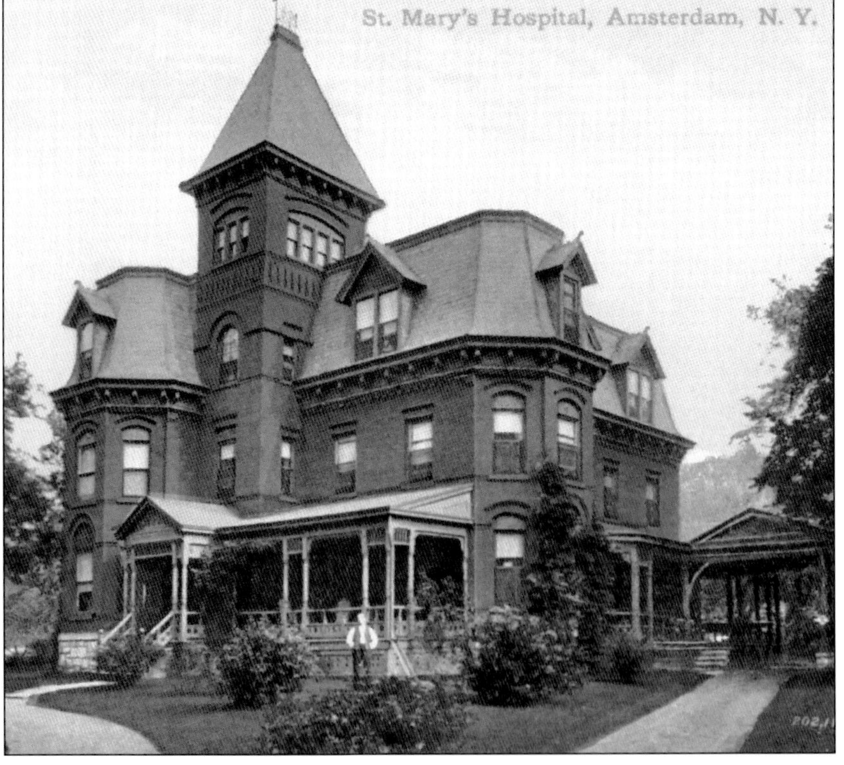


The Marcellus house, west of Steadwell Avenue on Guy Park Avenue, was purchased in 1903 with funds raised by parishioners of St. Mary's Roman Catholic Church. The Sisters of St. Joseph of Carondelet established the city's second hospital with 27 beds here in this former mansion near the western limits of the city.

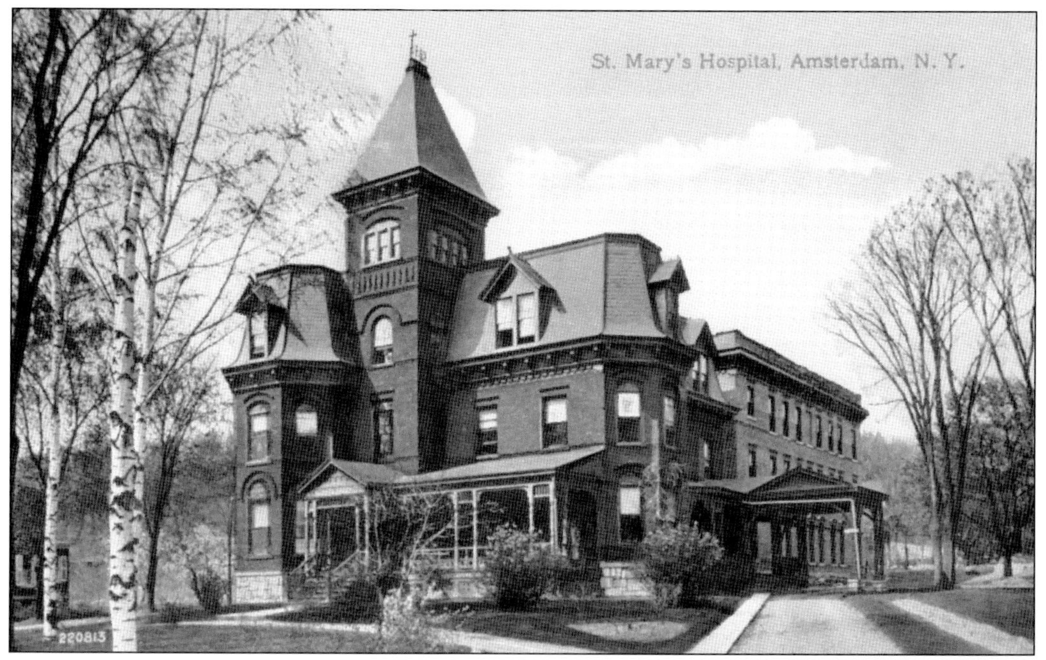


Above, the first expansion of St. Mary's Hospital occurred in 1915 when this 30-bed extension was built. Below, additional units were built in 1927 and 1948. A completely new hospital and mental health unit was built in 1974 just west of this site, and the old hospital was leveled to provide parking. Over the years, St. Mary's has come to occupy buildings on both sides of Guy Park Avenue.

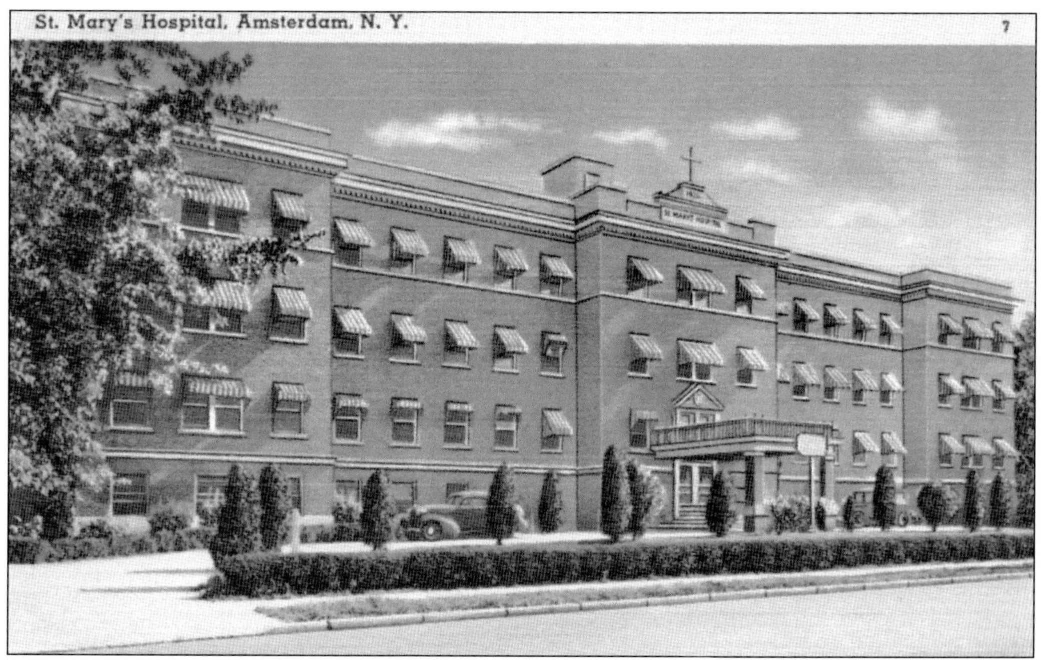

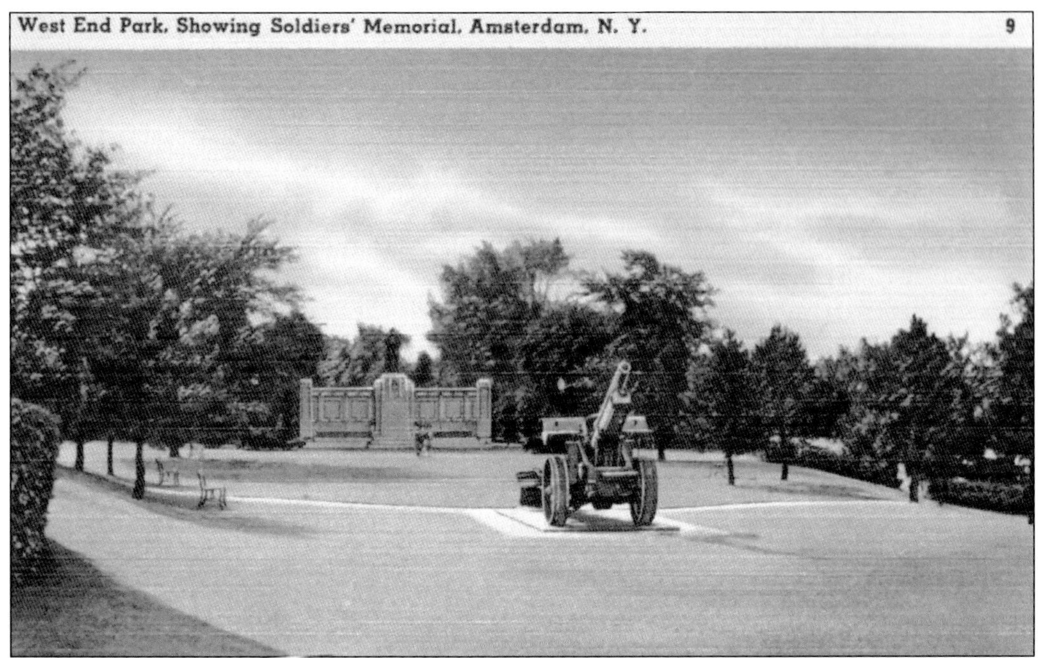


The memorial to World War I soldiers in West End Park was erected in 1923 using money that had been raised during wartime drives. The gun in the foreground is invariably described as a German Big Bertha; however, it is a smaller and more common howitzer. It was removed at some unknown point and subsequently replaced with the American field gun that is now there. A fountain was added to the park in 2009.

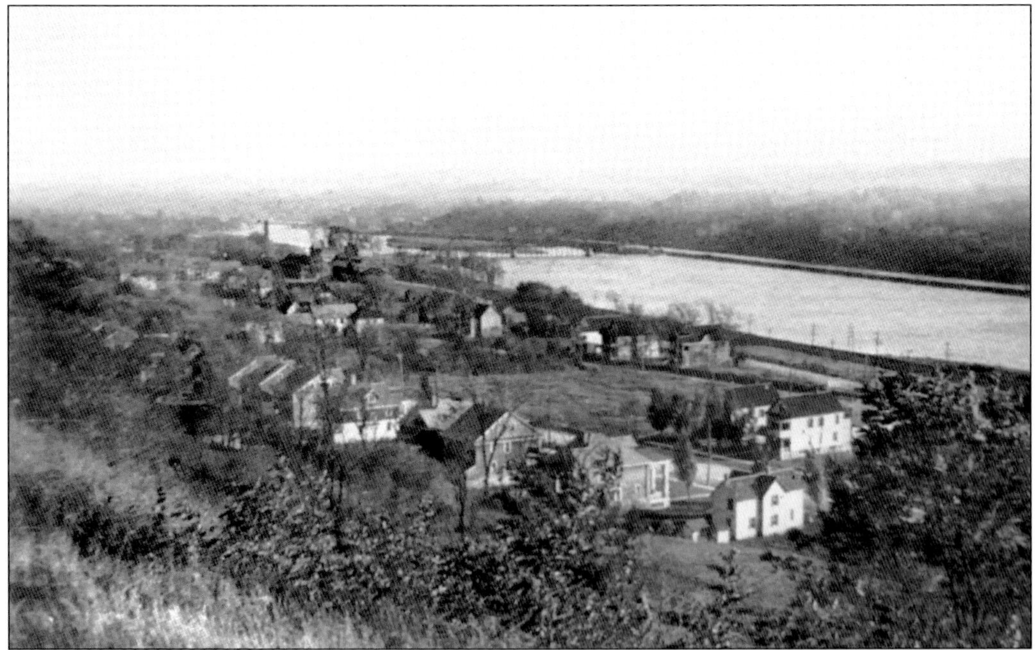

This 1915 view of the west end from Fair View Cemetery shows how this portion of the city grew rapidly in the early 20th century. To the middle right behind the tree is the intersection of Division Street and West Main Street. The smokestack in the middle of the frame is Bowler's Brewery.

*Six*

# Market Hill, Church Street, and Rockton

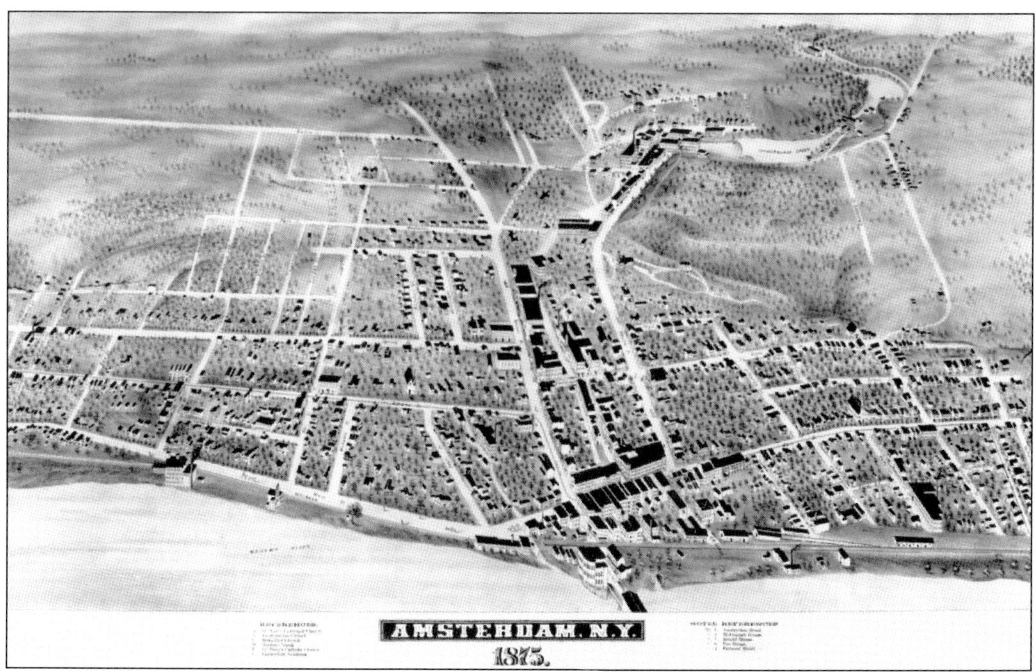


This bird's-eye view of the city shows the geography that shaped the growth of Amsterdam. The large greensward in the right center is Green Hill Cemetery. The cemetery itself is indicative of Amsterdam's growth. Eventually it was surrounded by mills and housing, as all the open areas in this view became the last expansion of the city in the late 1800s and early 1900s. (Courtesy of Montgomery County Department of History and Archives.)

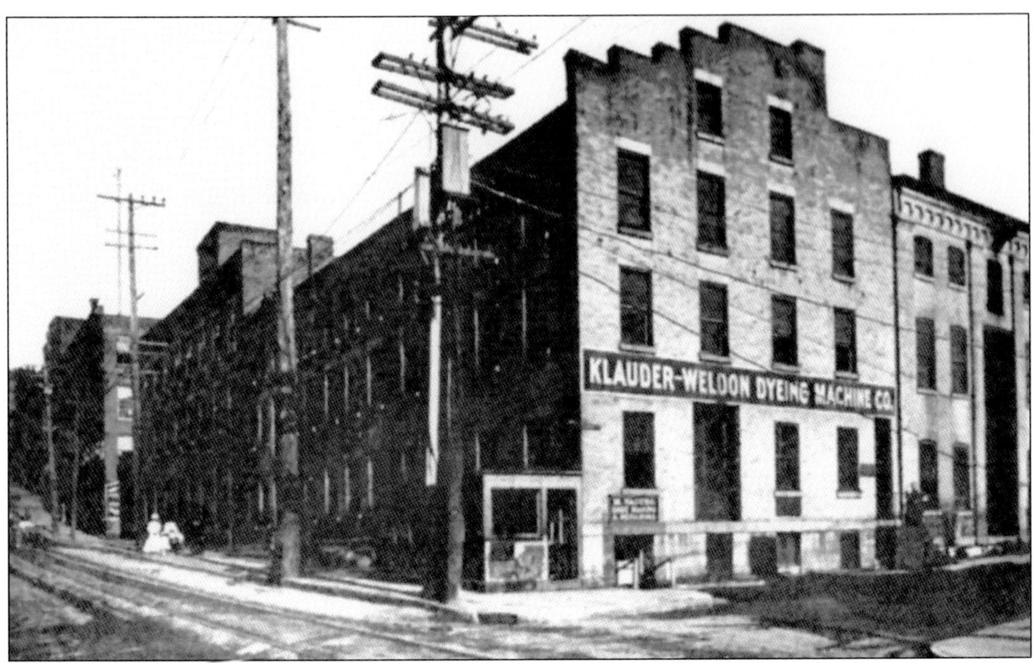


This company was one of the first to manufacture machinery for the dying of raw textiles. Located at the intersection of Livingston (later Grove) Street and Market Street, this was later the site of the Rialto Theater, one of several Amsterdam movie houses.

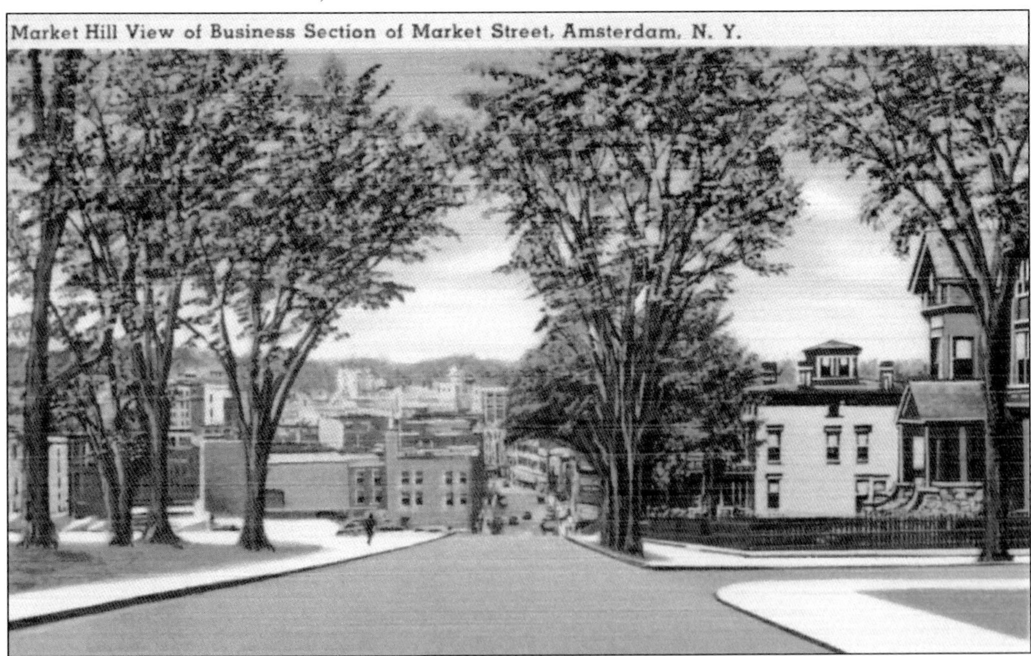


The view from Market Hill to the highlands south of the river was spectacular and the breezes were excellent, which is why many early successful business owners established their homes there. However, most of the structures to the left were destroyed by arterial roadways. The Greene house to the right displayed its Victorian "painted lady" colors for decades, much to the consternation of tourists who were told "the yellow house is the Greene House." (See page 17.)

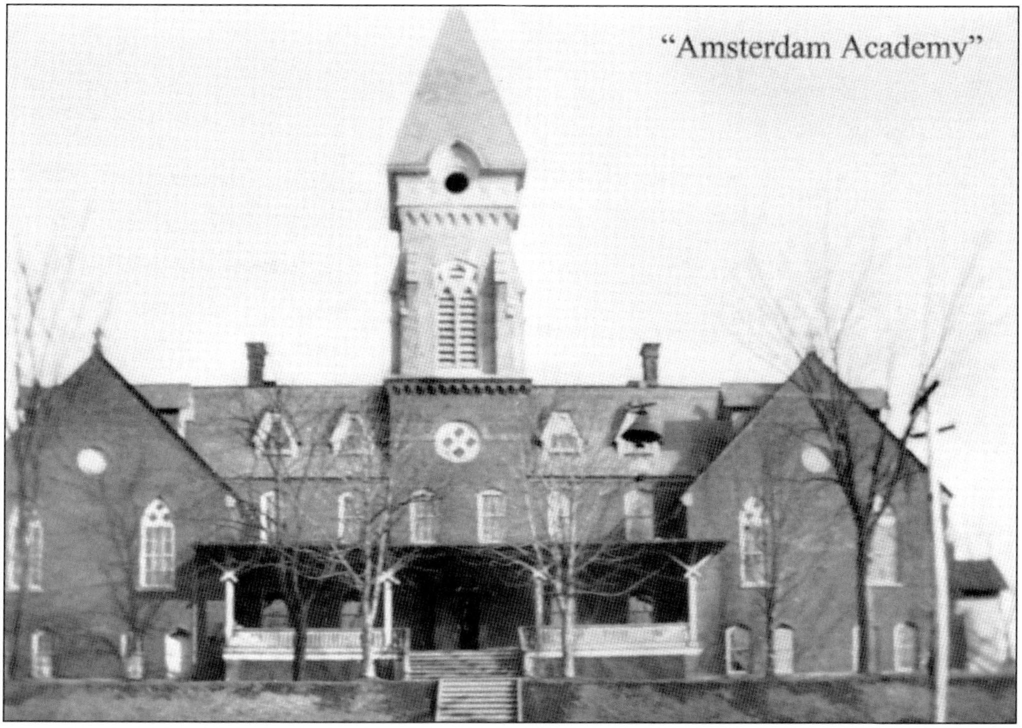

"Amsterdam Academy"

The Amsterdam Female Seminary combined with the Amsterdam Academy and obtained a new charter under the latter's name in 1865. Soon afterwards, it built a new $25,000 building at the top of Wall Street on the ridgeline just north of Amsterdam. The school was consolidated into the Amsterdam School District in 1895 and continued in use until the new building below replaced it. The district's first high school classes were organized here.

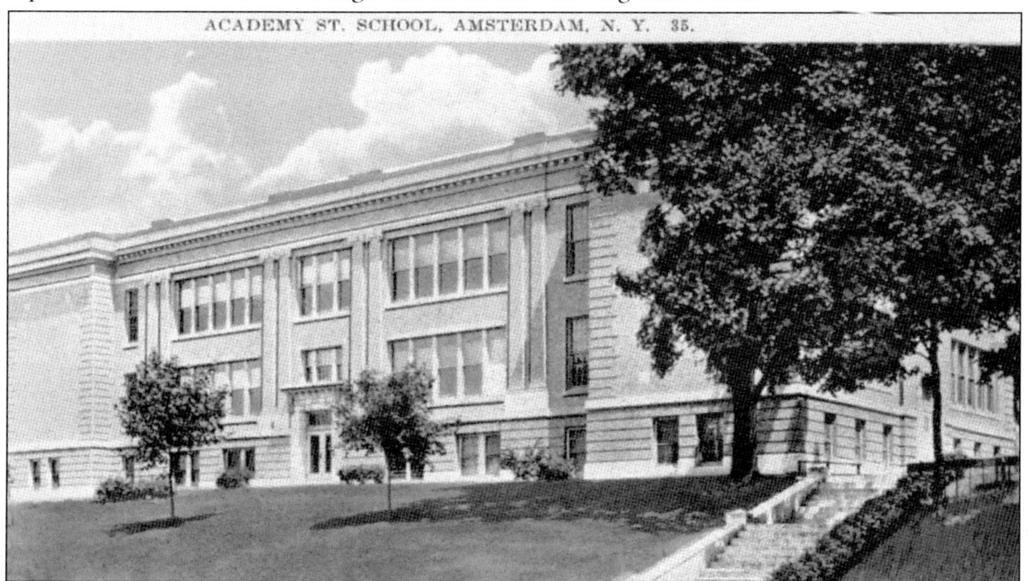


The new Academy Street School was built in 1917 on the site of the former Amsterdam Academy. The access from Market Street built for the Amsterdam Academy is now Academy Street, for which the school is named.

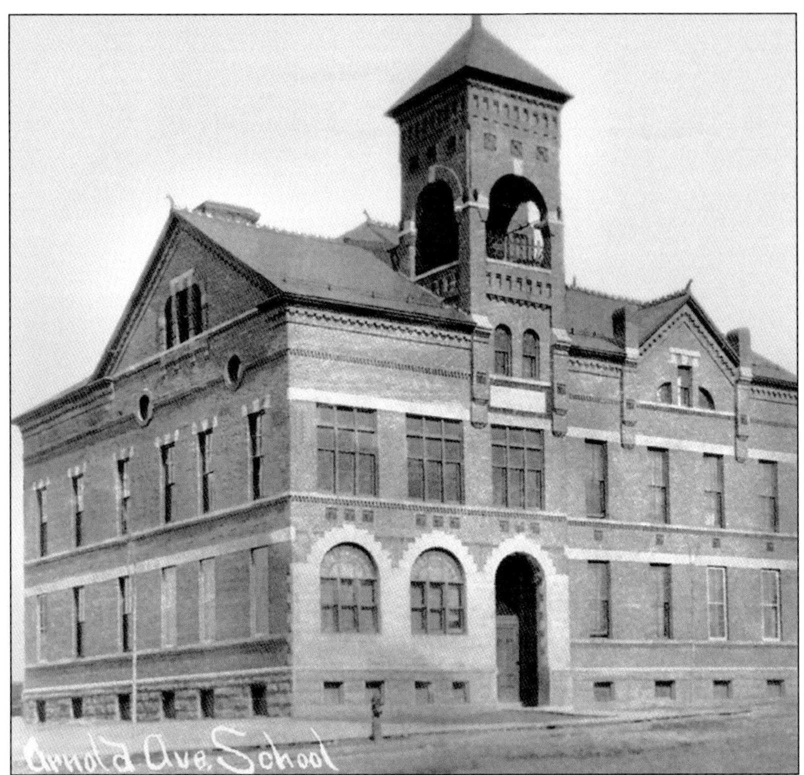


The Arnold Avenue School was built in 1891. The school and the avenue were not both named for Benedict Arnold—only the avenue was. Prior to 1930, schools were not named for individuals but rather numbered, named after location, or described. The Arnold named here was not the infamous traitor but a local congressman, town supervisor, and village president of the early 19th century.

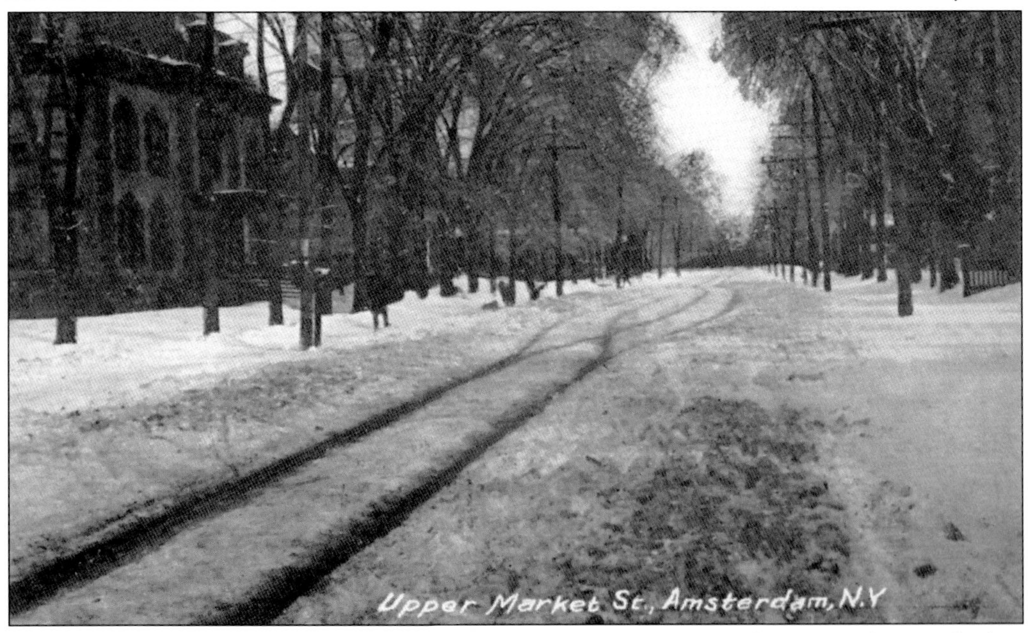


After it crests Market Hill, Market Street rises more gently towards the next ridge. In the late 19th and early 20th century, it became a popular location for professionals' homes, which were stately but smaller than the estates elsewhere. They were near enough to everything but far enough away to be peaceful and not on a heavily traveled road. This changed as the commercial focus moved from downtown to malls built outside the city.

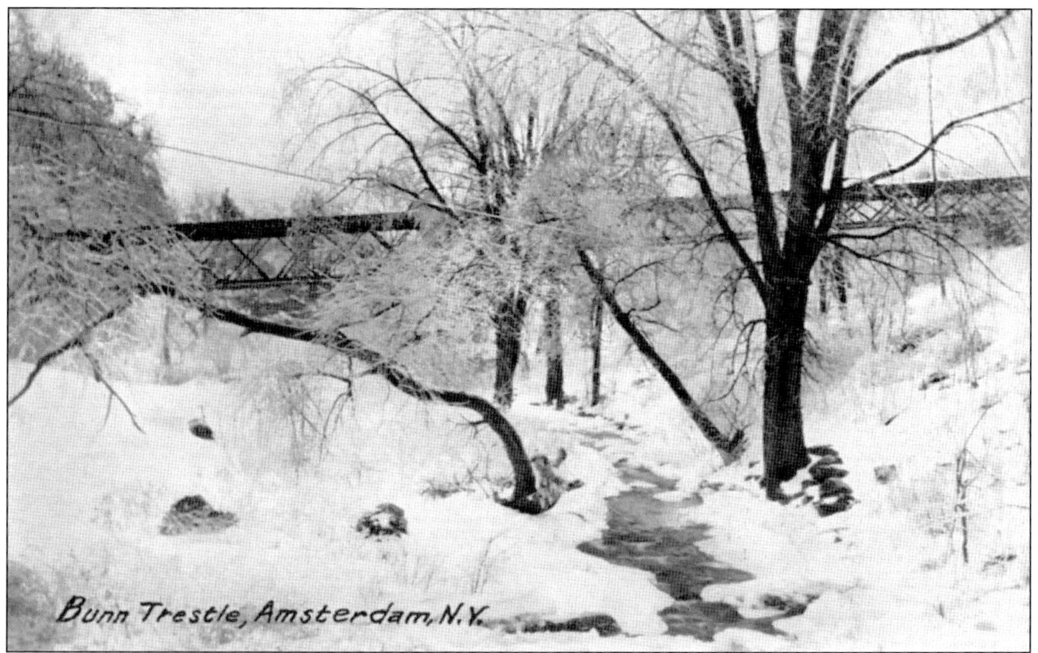


Looking out toward Brookside Avenue, the Bunn Trestle can be seen carrying the trolley line from the intersection of Market and Meadow Streets across Harmon Field and the Bunn Creek to a point about half way up Brookside Avenue hill. Erected in the spring of 1902, the abutments that supported the ends of the trestle remain in place today.

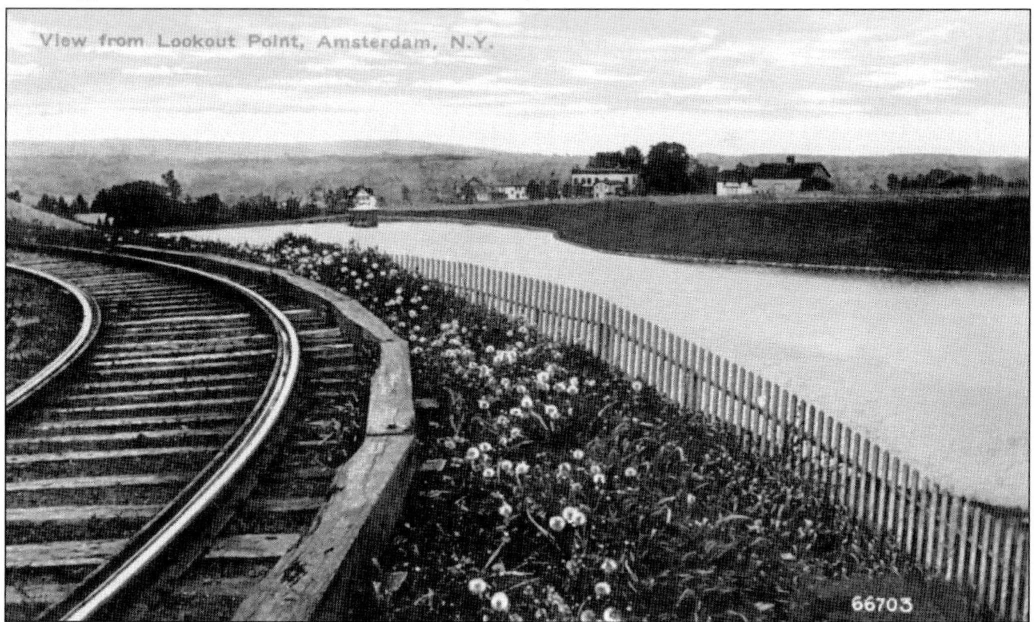


Wells and springs provided the first drinking water for Amsterdam. As early as 1820, an Amsterdam Aqueduct Association ran wooden pipes for water from Bunn Creek. This would not be sufficient for city needs, and a board of water commissioners was empowered to find solutions in 1880. Two years later, the city acquired 18 acres near Brookside Avenue to construct its first reservoir. It is pictured here alongside the tracks of the Fonda, Johnstown and Gloversville trolley line.

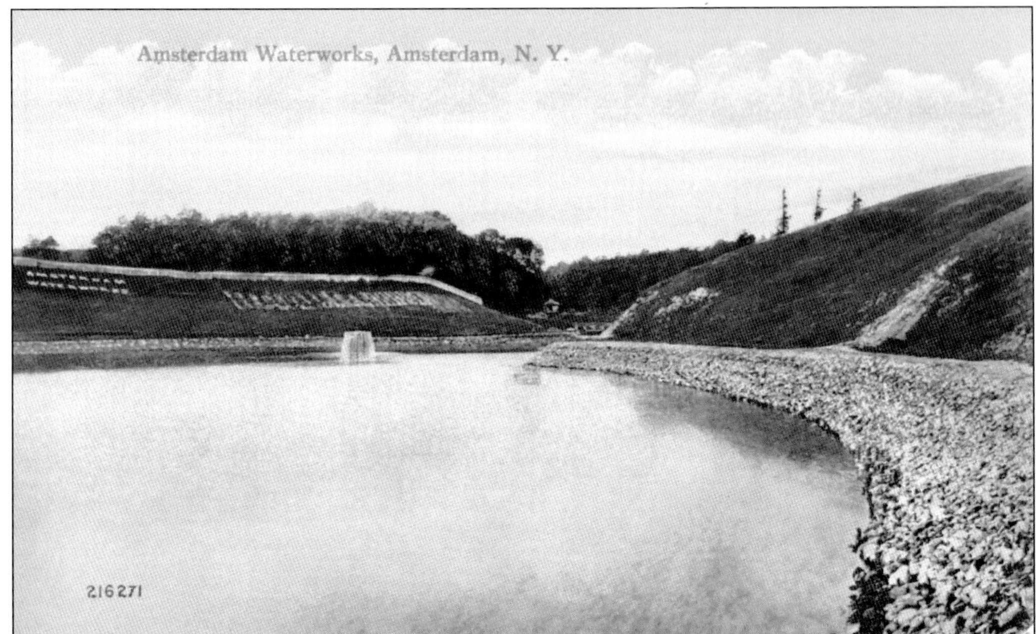


Amsterdam quickly outgrew its first reservoir and had to look elsewhere for water. Neither the Mohawk River nor the Chuctanunda Creek were acceptable sources due to pollution and flow considerations. In 1889, watershed in the Glen Wild area of Saratoga County was purchased and 12 miles of pipe were laid to the city.

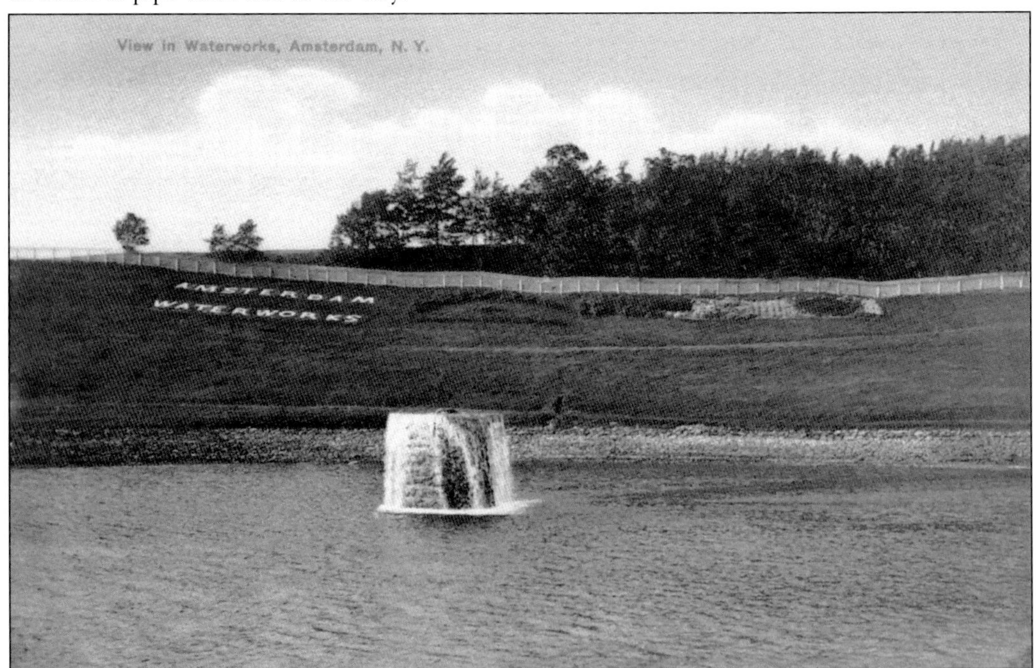


The city reservoir, originally known as the distributing reservoir, was designed to provide a storage capacity of 81 million gallons. The "fountain" structure in the view above provided mixing and aeration of the water to prevent stagnation. White painted rocks on the hill in the background for many years identified this as the "Amsterdam Waterworks."

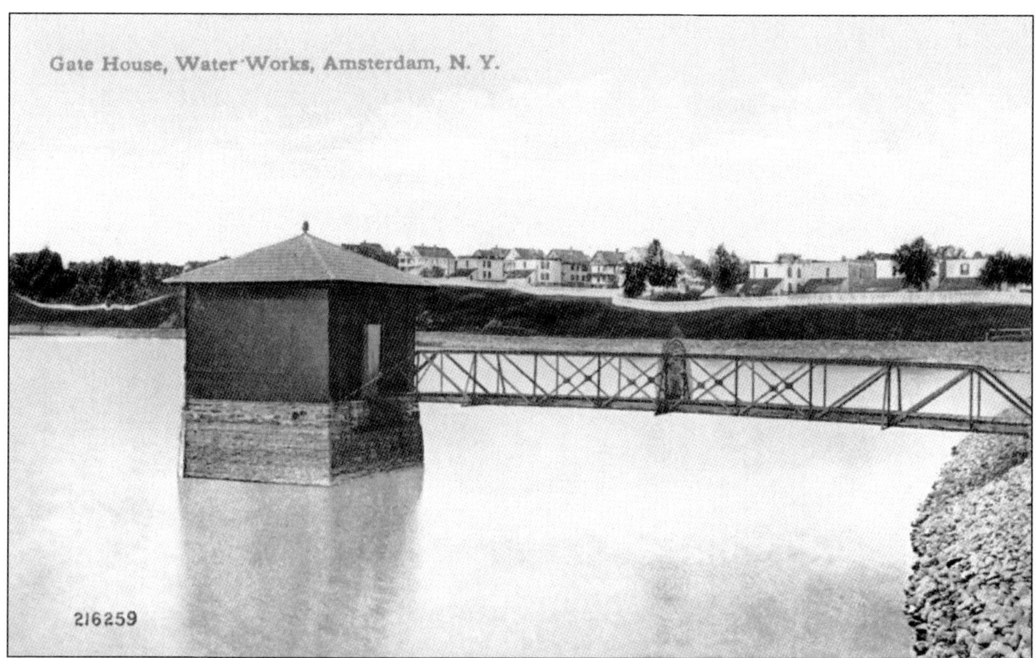


In 1899, Kellogg's Reservoir was created north of the city to improve supply and pressure, particularly for the fire hydrant system and elevations higher than the city reservoir. This was not entirely satisfactory, and in 1909, a second pipeline was run to Glen Wild. Kellogg's was abandoned three years later.

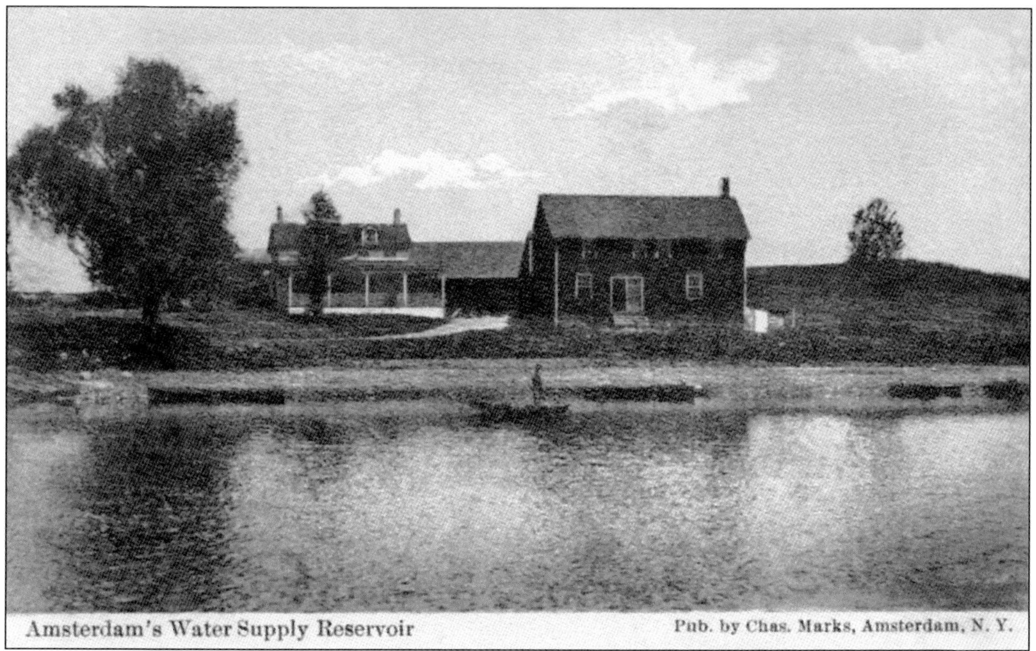


An additional expansion of the Glen Wild area into the Ireland Vlae left Amsterdamians with a bad taste in their mouths. Inadequate clearance of the land being flooded caused discolored and odorous water. Combined with chlorine and later fluorine, the result was called the "Amsterdam Cocktail." Filtration of the water supply was made possible by a federal grant in 1972.

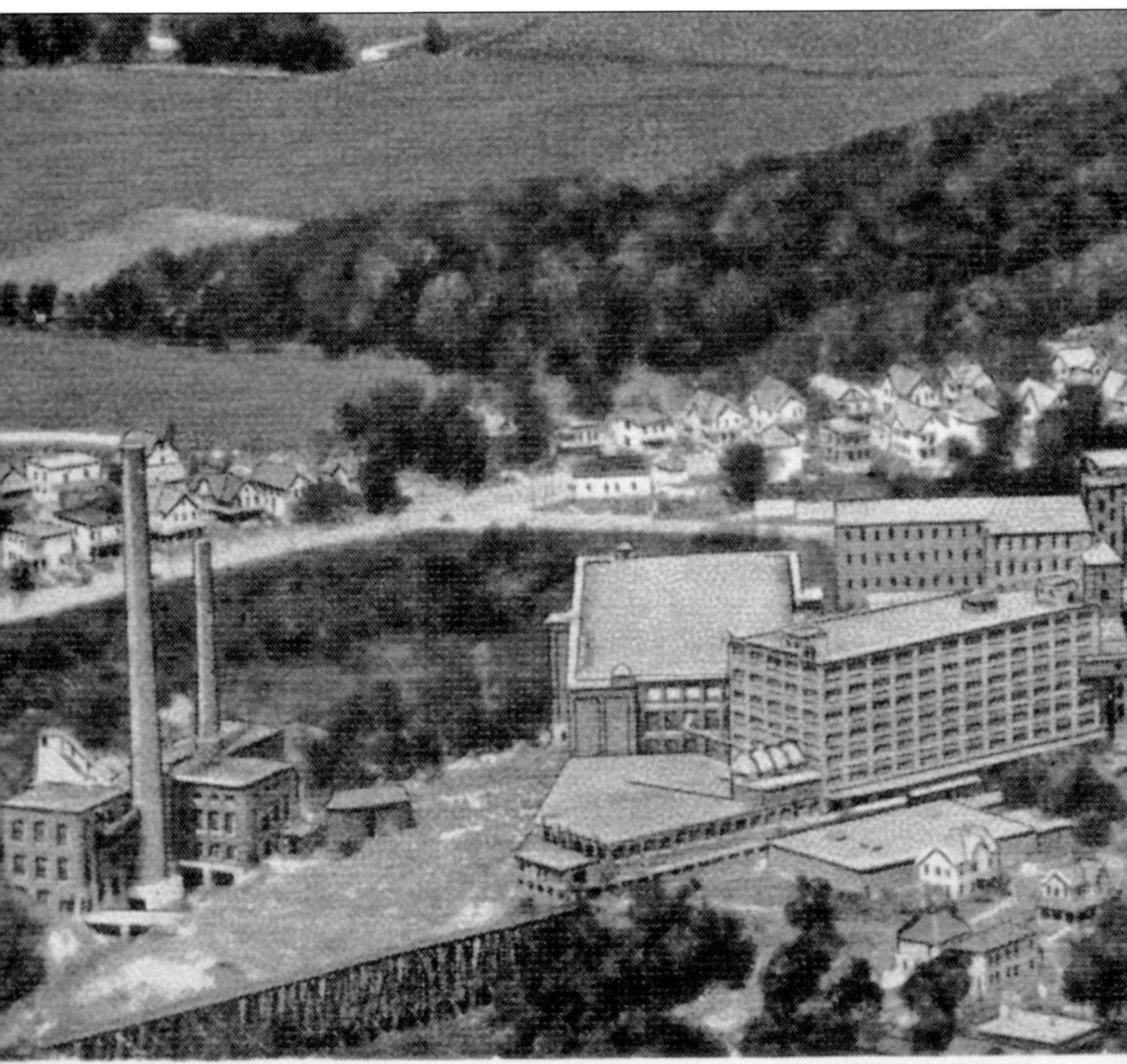


While mills and factories of all types were spread throughout the city, the carpet mills that were Amsterdam's foremost industries clustered into three locations: by the river, around the original Sanford Mills, and (above) higher on the Chuctanunda Creek. In 1886, four former employees of Sanford established their own mill in Port Jackson; it burned, and they immediately attempted again on the north side of the river. Reorganized in 1903 as McCleary, Wallin, and Crouse

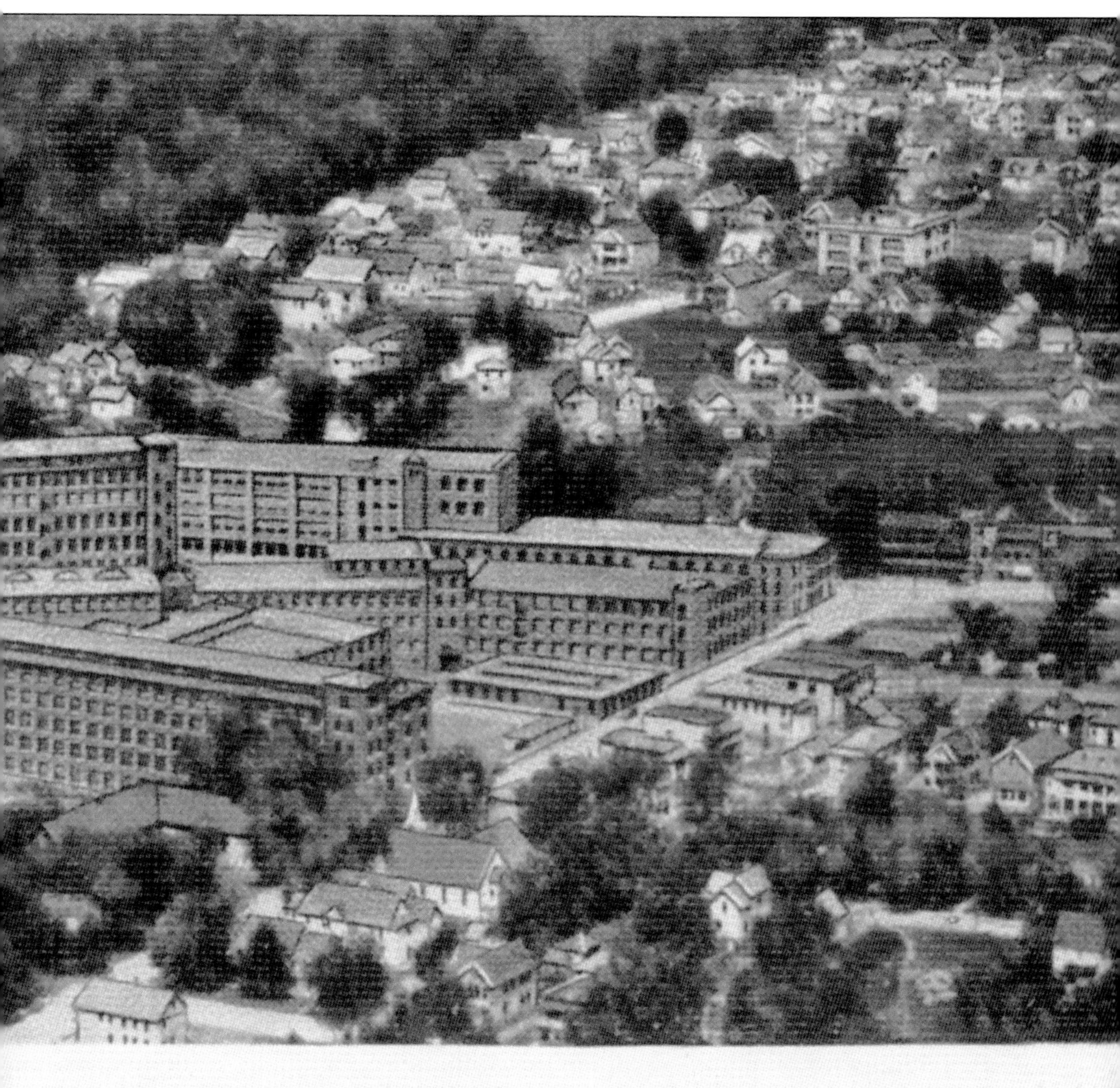

Mills (partner John Howgate died after falling in a millpond while attempting to clear ice from a mill water intake), in 1920, the firm merged with Shuttleworth to become the upper mills of Mohawk Mills. Most of the mill buildings across the top of the photograph were destroyed by fire or demolished. The power plant at the bottom right still stands, as do several of the central buildings, for which new purposes are sought.

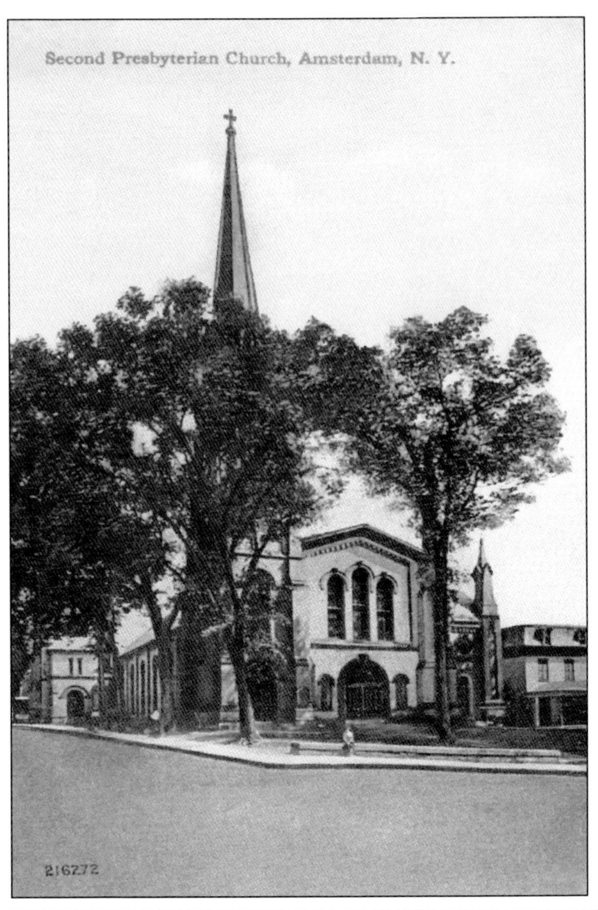


At left, the Second Presbyterian Church (see also page 28) became the United Presbyterian Church when the congregation of Emmanuel Presbyterian Church elected to close it and return to this location at the heart of the city. Truly the church that both mill owners and mill workers attended, its spire was an Amsterdam landmark for decades. When mill pioneer and philanthropist Stephen Sanford died in 1913, thousands attended the memorial services here. Below is Church Street near Livingstone (Grove) Street as seen before the construction of the library. At left are the Sanford Houses apartments, some of which survive above the library on the opposite side of the street.

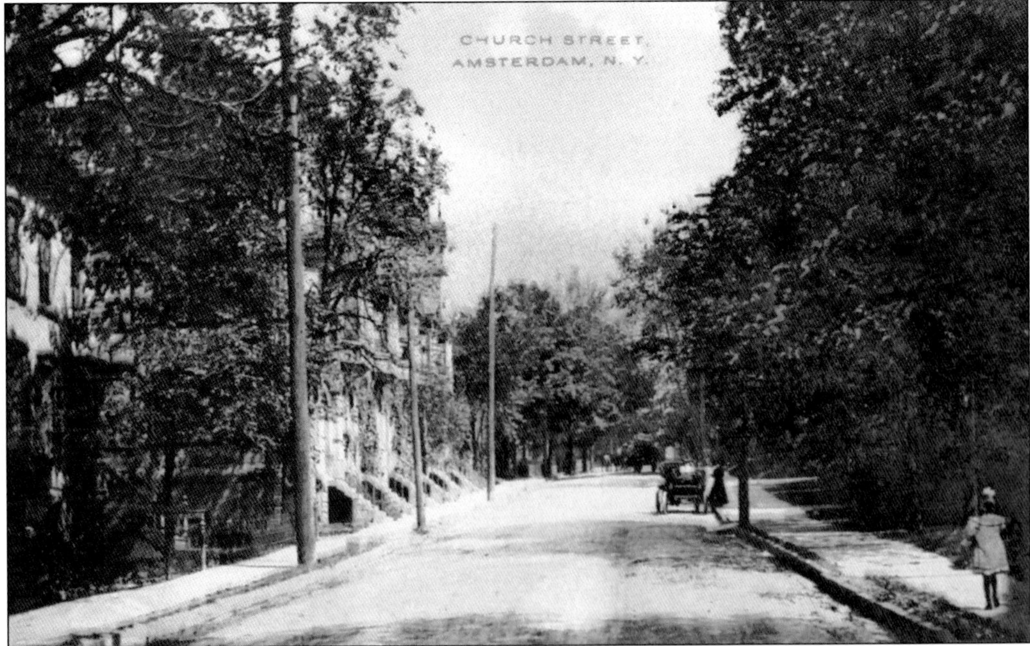

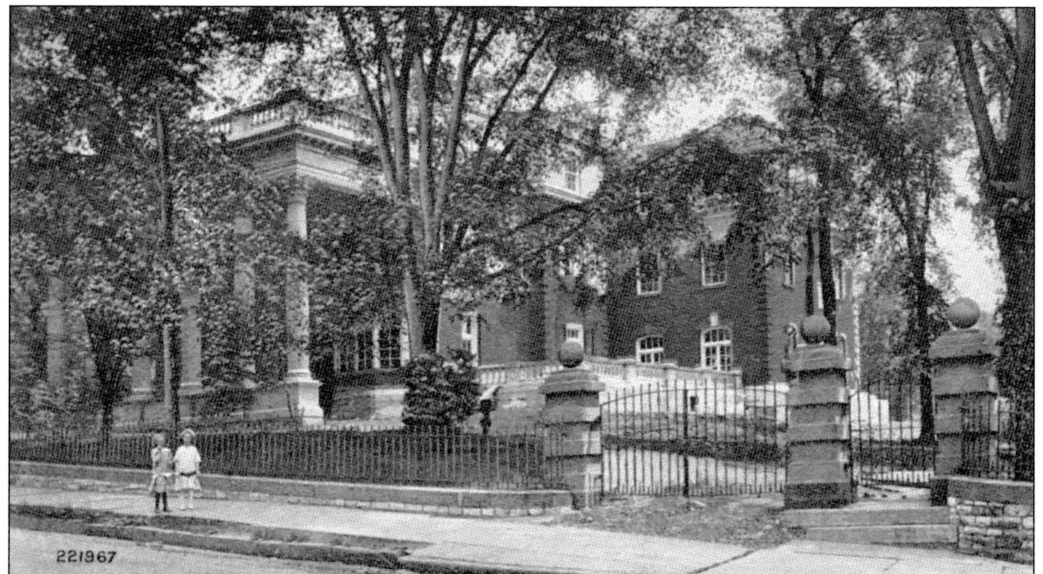


Originally constructed in the early 1850s, the Sanford mansion was radically altered in appearance in a four-year, $1 million rebuild starting in 1913. In 1932, it was donated to Amsterdam for use as city hall. Its front appearance remains much the same today except for the wrought-iron picket fence, which originally surrounded the entire 6.1-acre estate. It fell victim to an overzealous scrap drive in World War II.

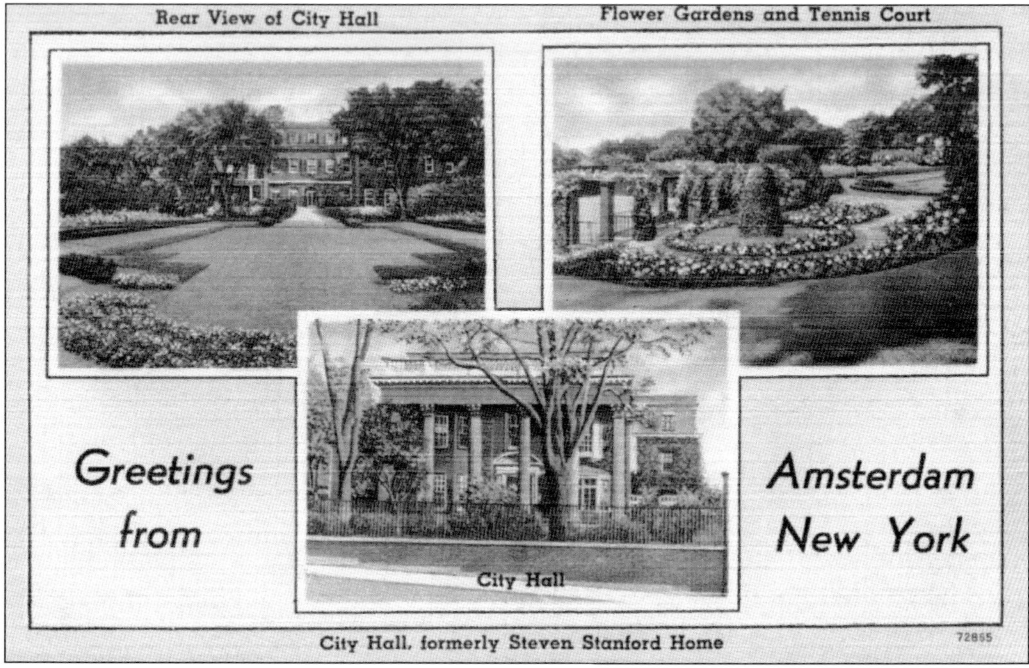


The Sanfords established formal gardens on their estate. City hall workers maintain the lawns and shrubs, but the floral plantings and elaborate ground covers have lapsed. The gardens were a longtime favorite location for prom dates and wedding parties to have their pictures taken; today they still come to have their pictures taken on the formal stairway in the building's main lobby.

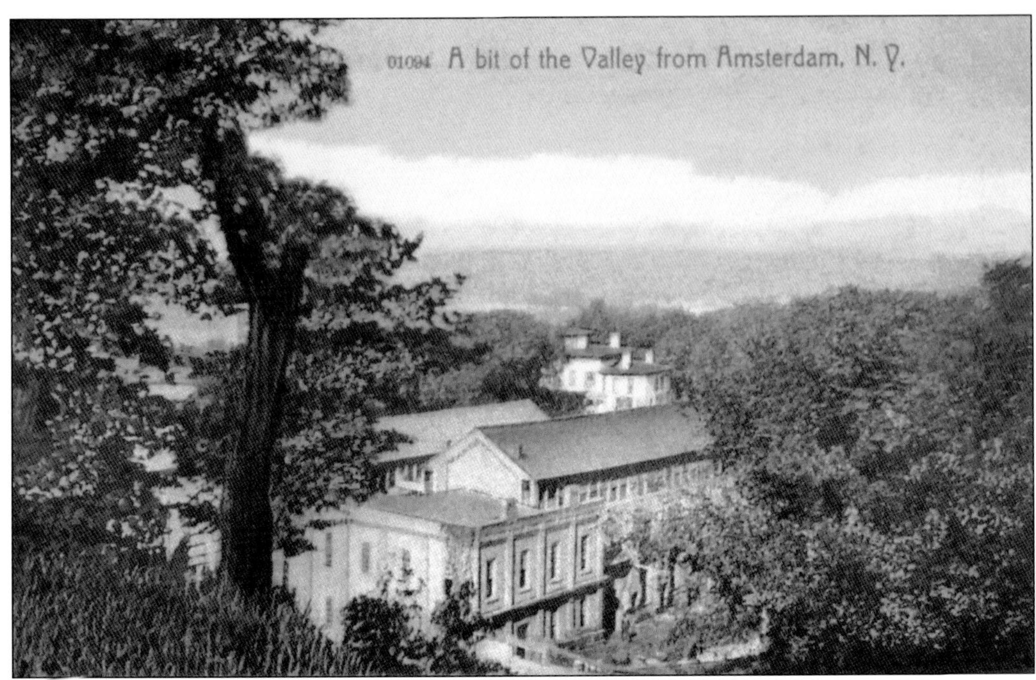


The original location of what was commonly called the Shuler Spring factory was approximately across from where city hall is today. Established in 1857, its first building was the one running across the front of the complex. It was reported that at one time, Shuler manufactured over 75 percent of the world requirement for elliptical springs. After the founder died, the complex was sold to the Sanford Mills in 1909, and the business relocated closer to the river at the foot of Eagle Street (see page 51).

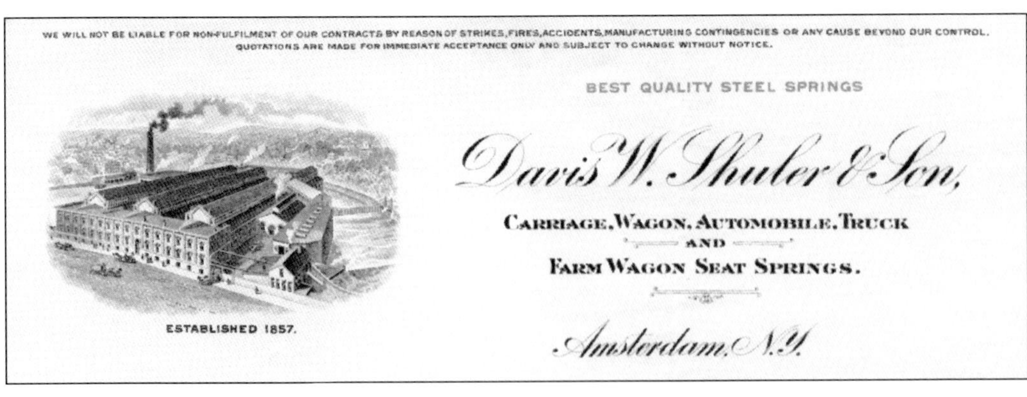

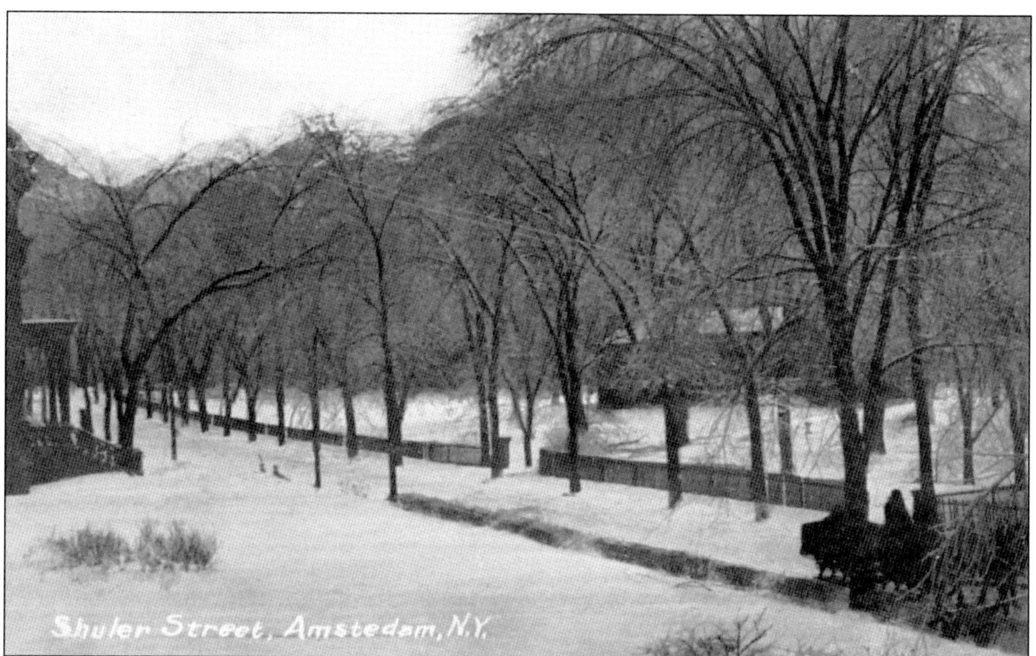


The Shuler homestead was located across the Chuctanunda Creek and was connected to the factory by a bridge over the water (shown at right). Other Shuler family members were engaged in coffin and furniture making, general commerce, and civic and other activities. As a family, they were typical of their time, believing that what was good for business was good for the city and vice versa.

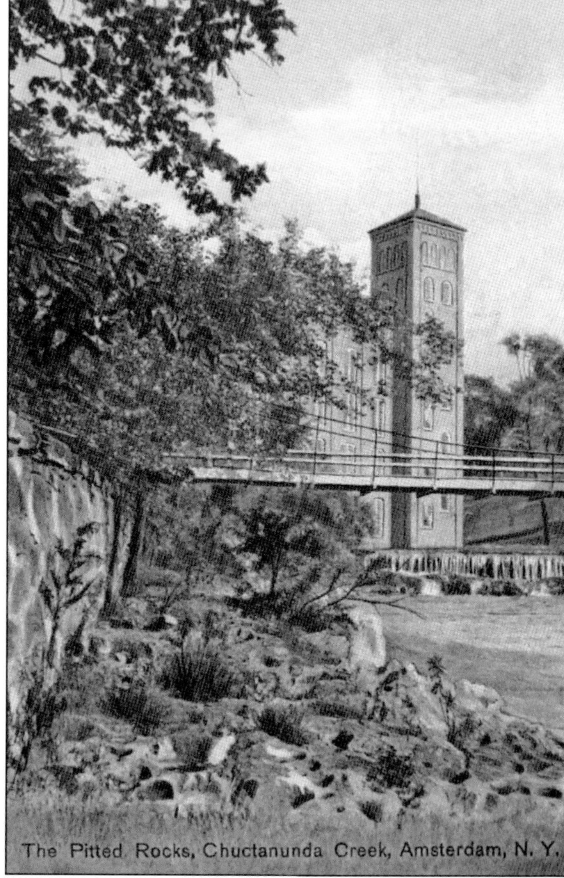


The Pitted Rocks are spherical scorings of the creek bed, resulting from the same geologic forces that caused the creek to take the path it did. A region of softer rock had been forced up between layers of harder rock, and as the force of runoff eroded the softer rock to form the channel, pieces of surrounding harder rock broke off and local currents turned them into swirling abrasives.

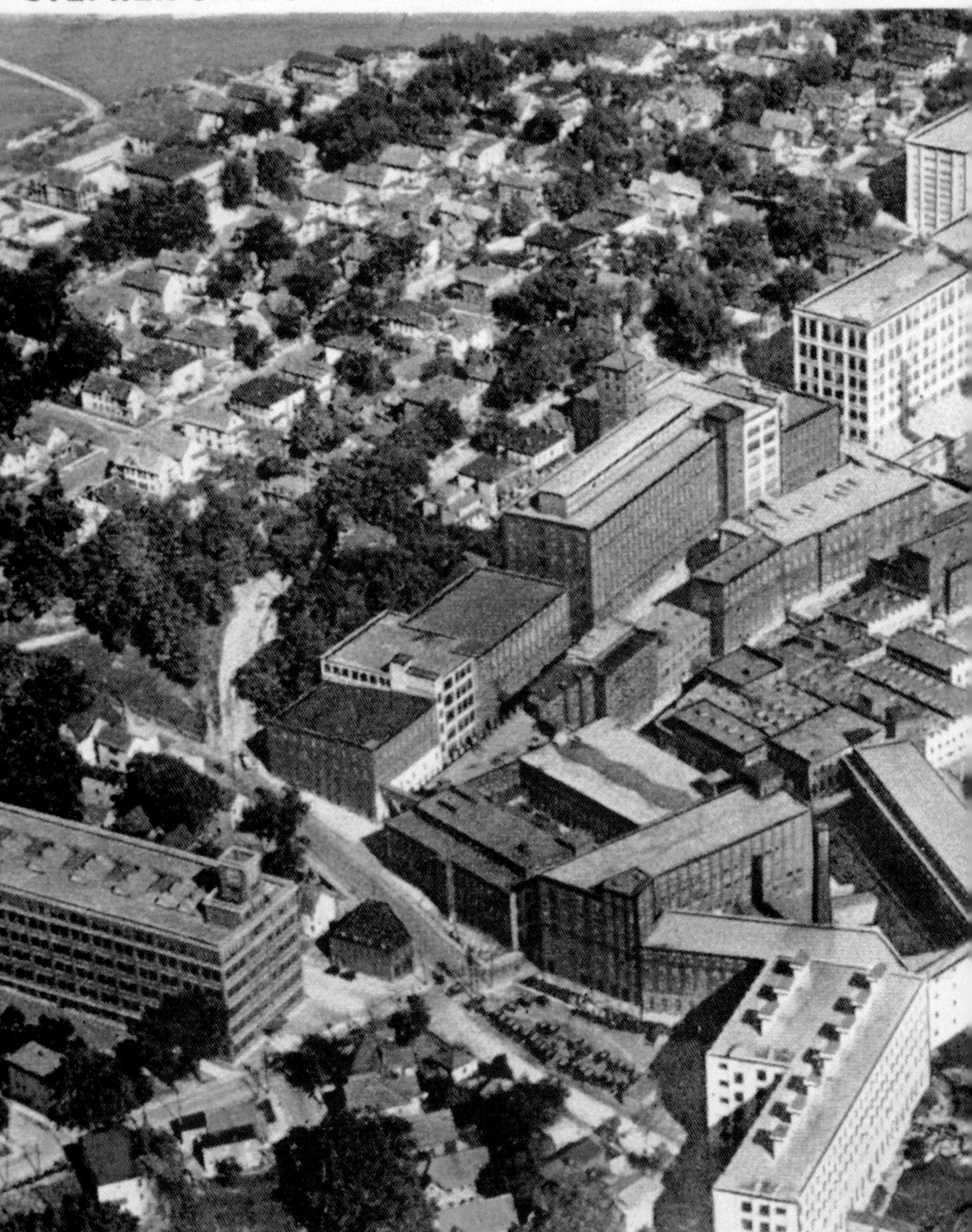
STEPHEN SANFORD & SONS, INC., RUG AND CARPET MA

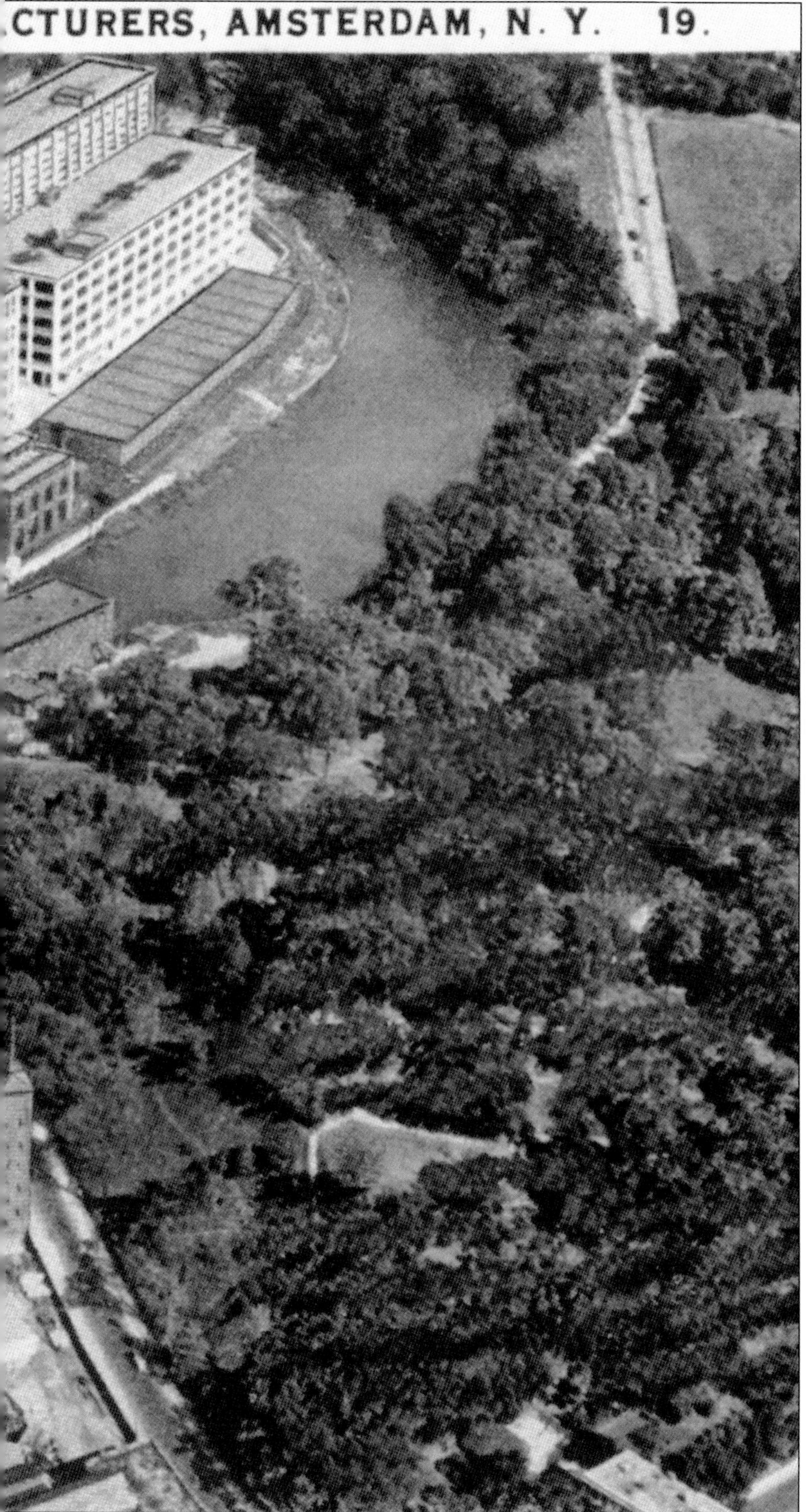


The Sanford Mills were the pioneering carpet mills of Amsterdam. Near the center of the picture were the original mills of the 1840s; much of the rest of the expanse, including the holding pond in the upper right (now a parking lot), was the result of the efforts of Stephen Sanford and his son John. Stephen's mansion and gardens are at lower right. Between the mansion and the pond is Green Hill Cemetery, an early rural cemetery that sought to create green spaces useful to the living as well as the dead. Stephen's mausoleum sits on a rise there in sight of his interests. At lower left is the local landmark Clock Tower building; generations set their watches by it and viewed its face as a welcoming sign when returning from travels.

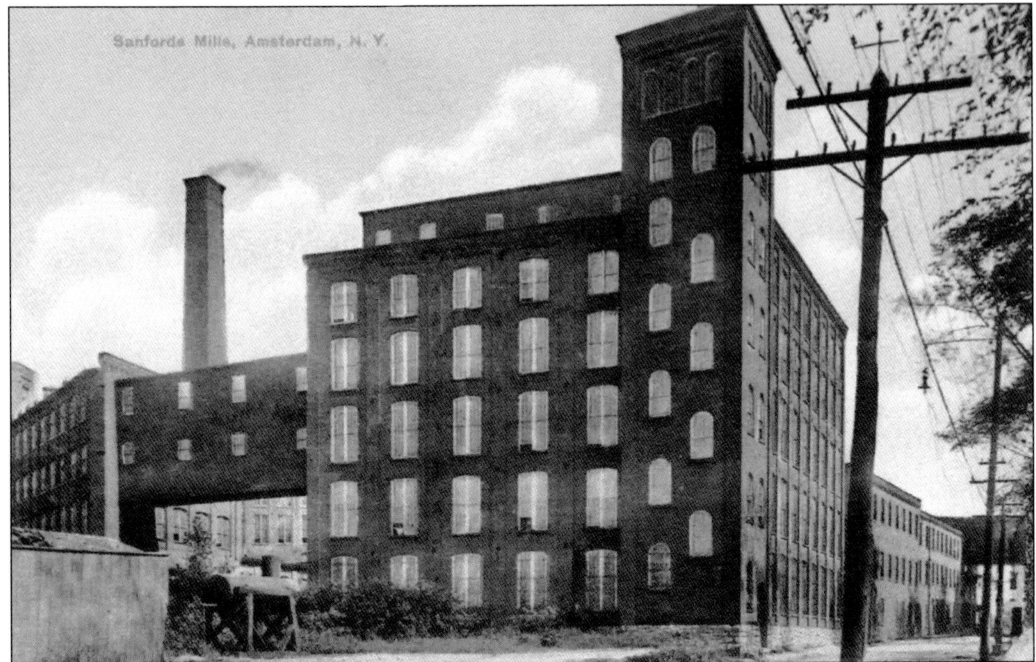


In 1840, William Greene and partner established a carpet mill north of Amsterdam. After two years, this partnership dissolved and Greene relocated to Amsterdam, where John Sanford soon joined him in business. Greene left the firm to start a knitting mill in the city, while Sanford brought his son Stephen home from the U.S. Military Academy to help run the business. Stephen assumed control of the firm when his father retired in 1855.

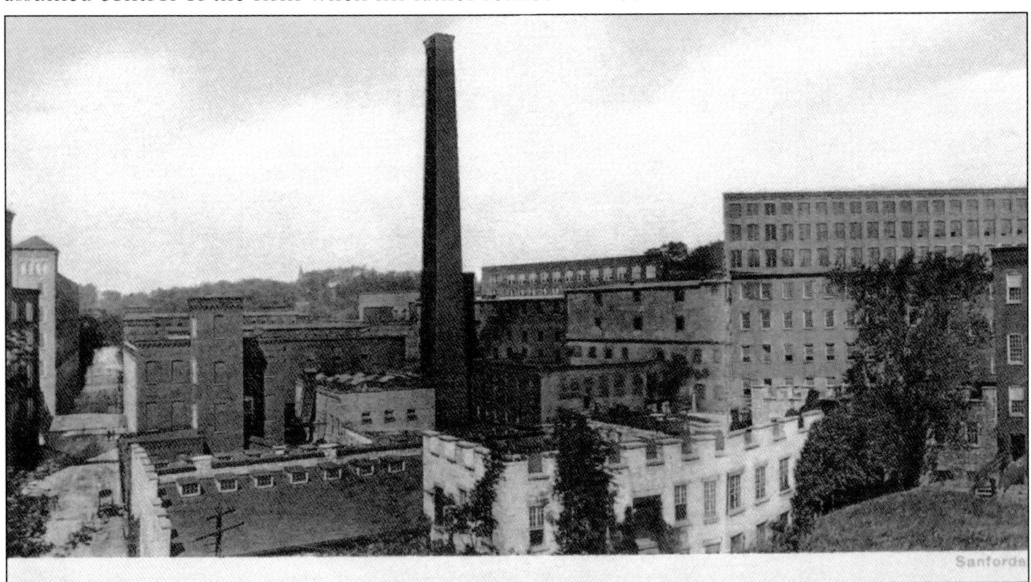


At left are some of the original Sanford mill buildings, dating to 1842. Many of these buildings are now home to the Noteworthy Corporation, inventors and manufacturers of the litter bag and other promotional items. Other firms have moved into former mill buildings with mixed success. Coleco (Connecticut Leather Company) manufactured its famous Cabbage Patch Kids dolls here before ceasing operations in the late 1980s.

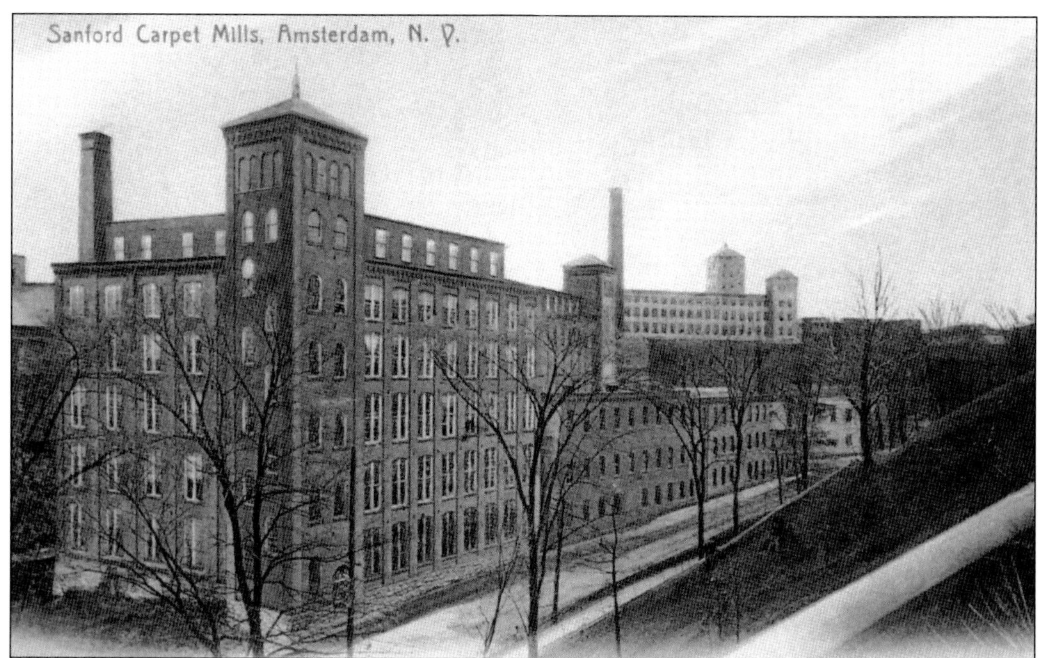


After running the firm by himself for a number of years, Stephen brought in his sons, and the name of it became S. Sanford and Sons. Son John brought the company to even greater heights before Stephen's death in 1913. The Amsterdam, Chuctanunda, and Northern Railroad (incorporated in 1899), extended its tracks to the Sanford complex by 1905. A new coal-fired power plant generated the steam and electric power that replaced waterpower in the mills.

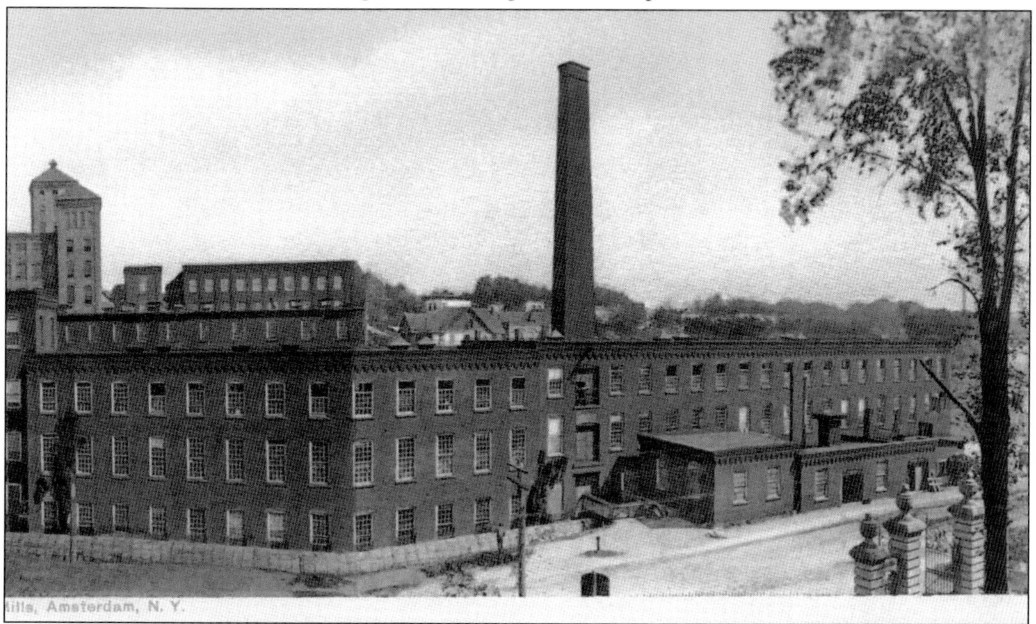


In 1929, Sanford's company merged with Bigelow to become Bigelow-Sanford, and corporate control migrated to Connecticut. Sanford involvement in Amsterdam came to an end as the family spent less time in the city they had made their fortune in. As one last gesture, John donated the family home to the city for use as its first permanent city hall.

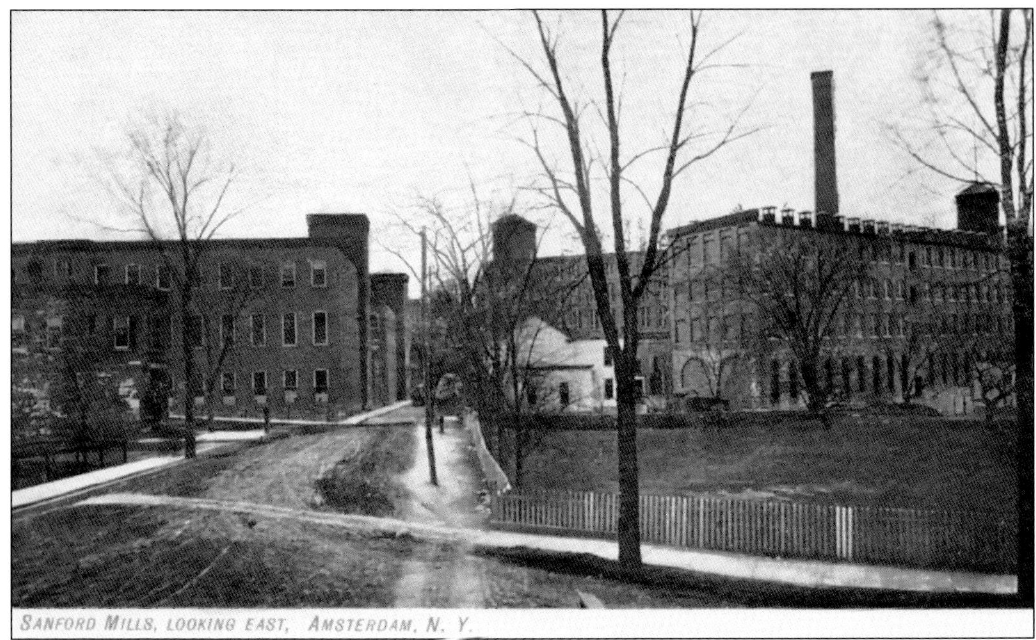


The Great Depression slowed but did not halt production at Sanford and Mohawk Mills. With the coming of World War II, the shifts that had been curtailed were put back and expanded to produce tarps, tents, and small parts for a myriad of wartime requirements. Women greatly increased their representation in the mill workforce.

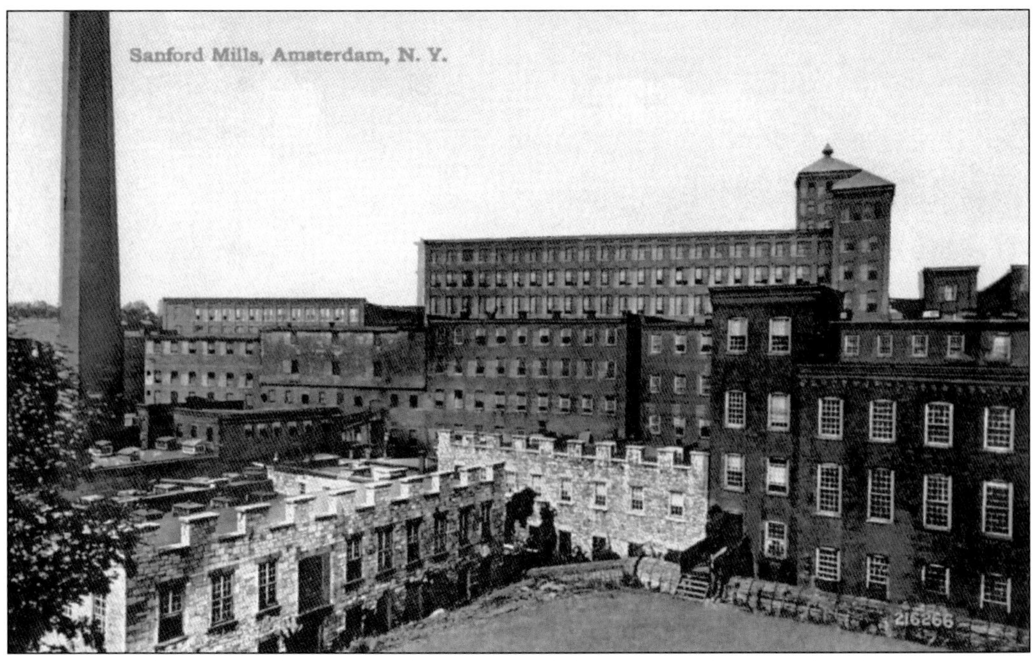


In 1955, Bigelow-Sanford announced it was consolidating manufacturing into its Connecticut facilities. Work at the Amsterdam mills diminished rapidly, as its equipment and functions were transferred to New England and then ultimately to the South and overseas, locations where production and especially labor costs were cheaper.

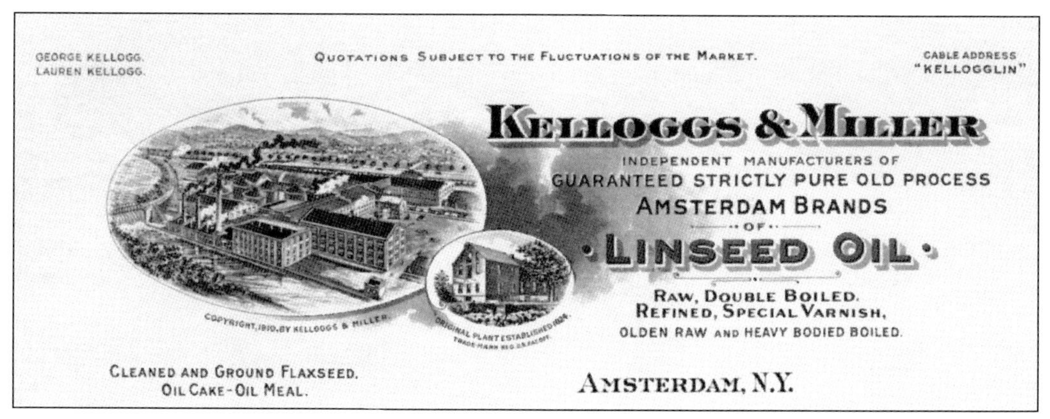


In 1824, Supplina Kellogg established a linseed oil mill in West Galway. The operation relocated to Amsterdam in 1850 to a former distillery on the Chuctanunda Creek just upstream of the Sanford carpet mills. The firm name was changed in 1871 to Kelloggs and Miller to reflect the involvement of other family members and James Miller. The mill pressed linseed oil, a drying agent for paint, varnish, linoleum, and other industrial products from flaxseed. Its by-product was a cake residue sold for animal feed. At its height, the plant employed 500 workers and produced 6,000 barrels of oil a week. The firm acquired additional factories in Chicago and Philadelphia before it was sold to the Bisbee Company in the 1930s. The Amsterdam plant closed in 1948.

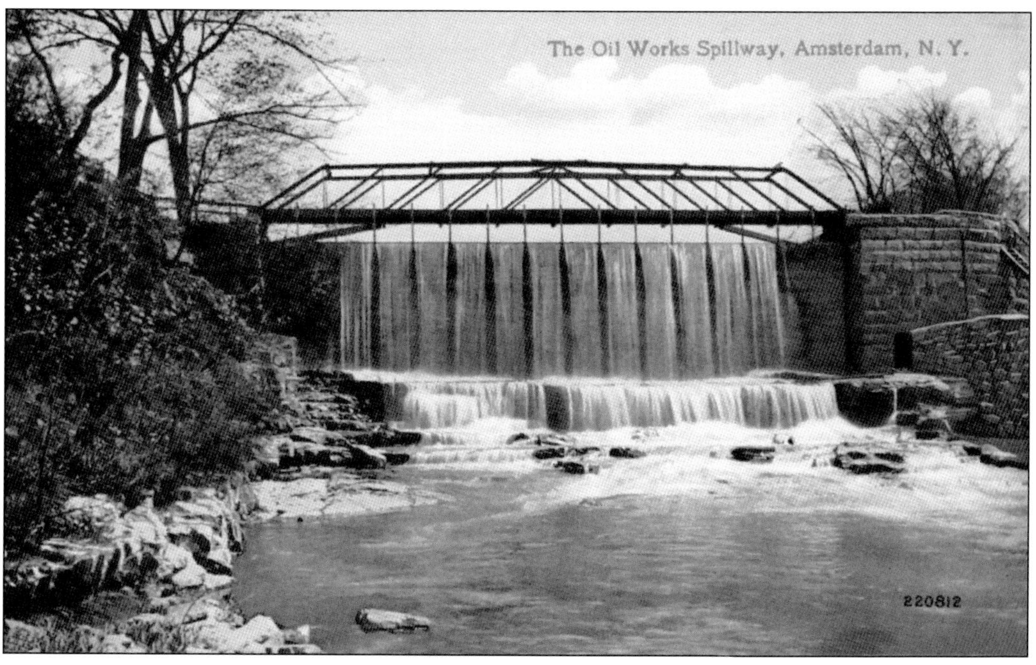

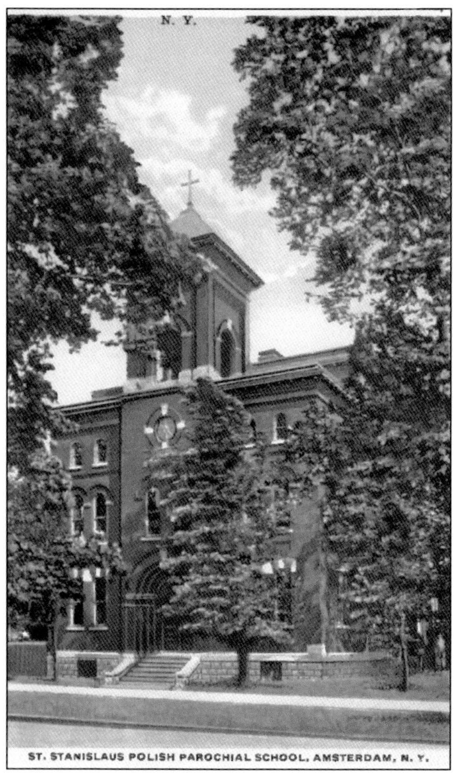


St. Stanislaus Roman Catholic Church was established in 1888 in response to the desire of the first wave of Polish immigrants to Amsterdam to have a church in which sermons and confessions could be heard in a language they understood (at the time St. Mary's Roman Catholic Church was English speaking and St. Joseph's was German speaking). The church, as shown below, was erected in 1897 on Cornell Street and added to in 1912. The school, shown at left, dates to 1906, with an additional third floor added in 1915. The convent and rectory were finished in 1934 and 1940, respectively. One outstanding feature of the church is a series of stained-glass windows created by internationally recognized ecclesiastical artist Guido Nicheri. The entire complex is listed on the National Register of Historic Places.

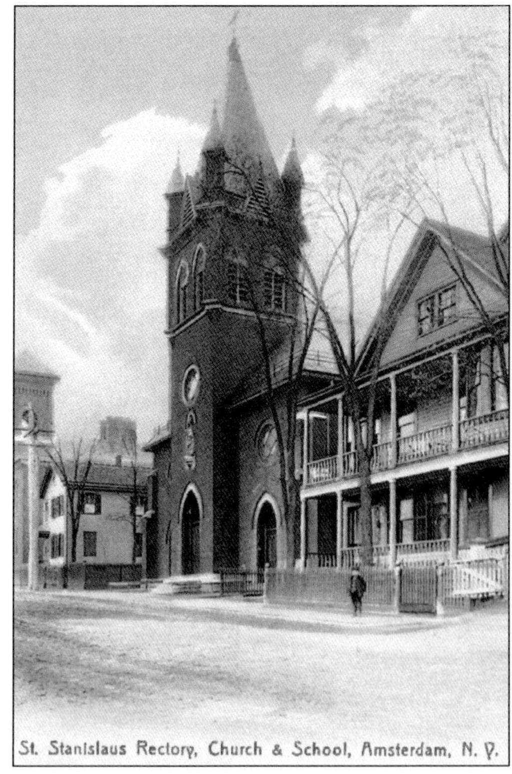

# *Seven*

# Special Places, Special Times

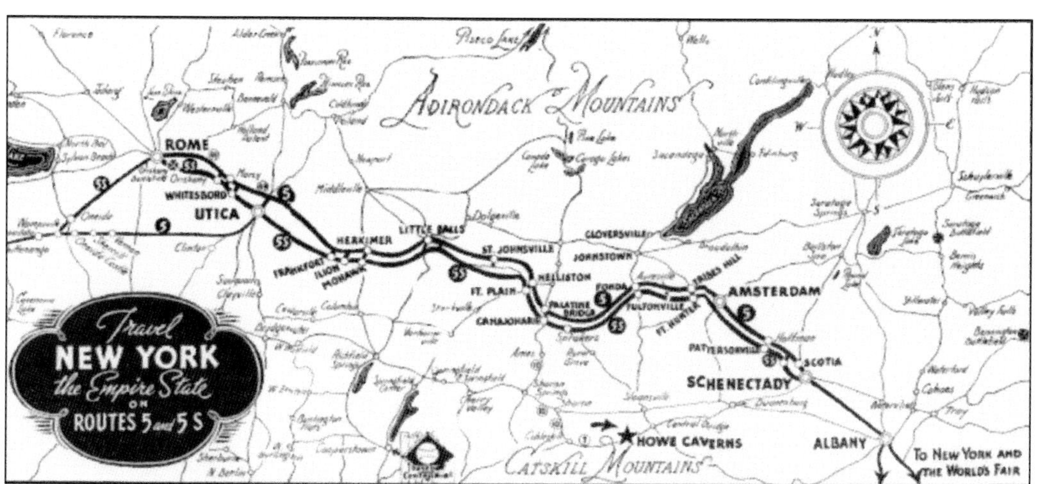


This 1939–1940 New York State tourism map shows Amsterdam in its relative position as the "gateway to the Mohawk Valley." Routes 5 and 5S mainly follow the paths of the Mohawk and Great Western Turnpikes, respectively, which were key to the opening of both the valley and the Western frontier. (Courtesy of Montgomery County Department of History and Archives.)

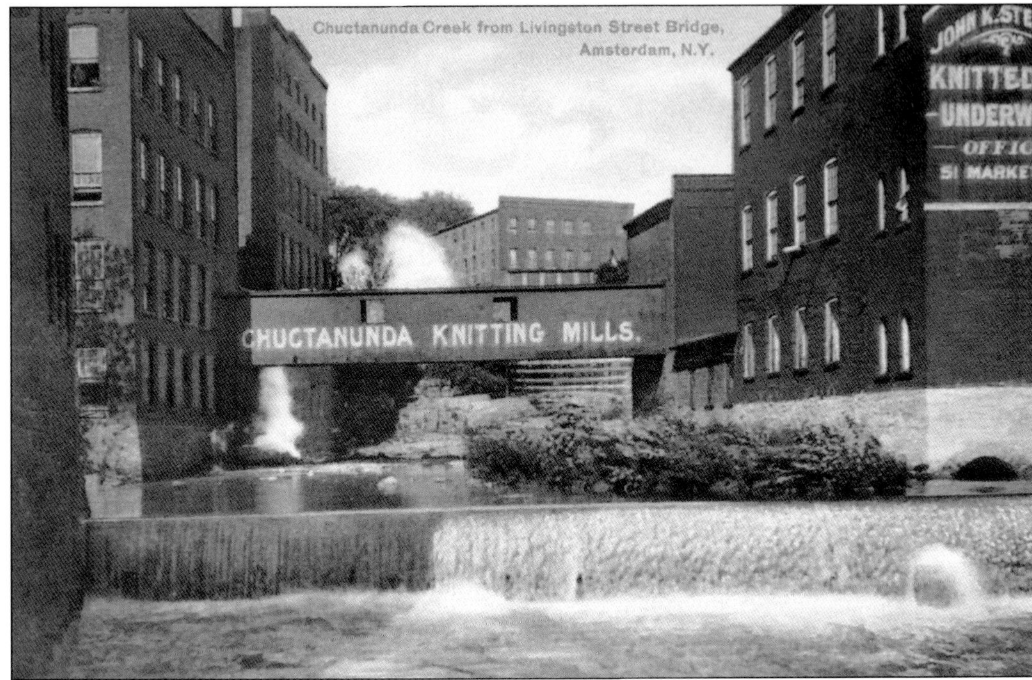


These two postcards, photographed northward from nearly the same position, demonstrate that the very thing that makes the Chuctanunda Creek beautiful and useful also makes it dangerous. Regarding the storm that created the rushing waters of the image below, one Amsterdamian wrote on her postcard, "Fear and excitement. Schools, Mills, stores dismiss in fear of the reservoirs. Wed night residents in the path notified to leave homes. Fire hydrants opened relieved pressure [*sic*]."

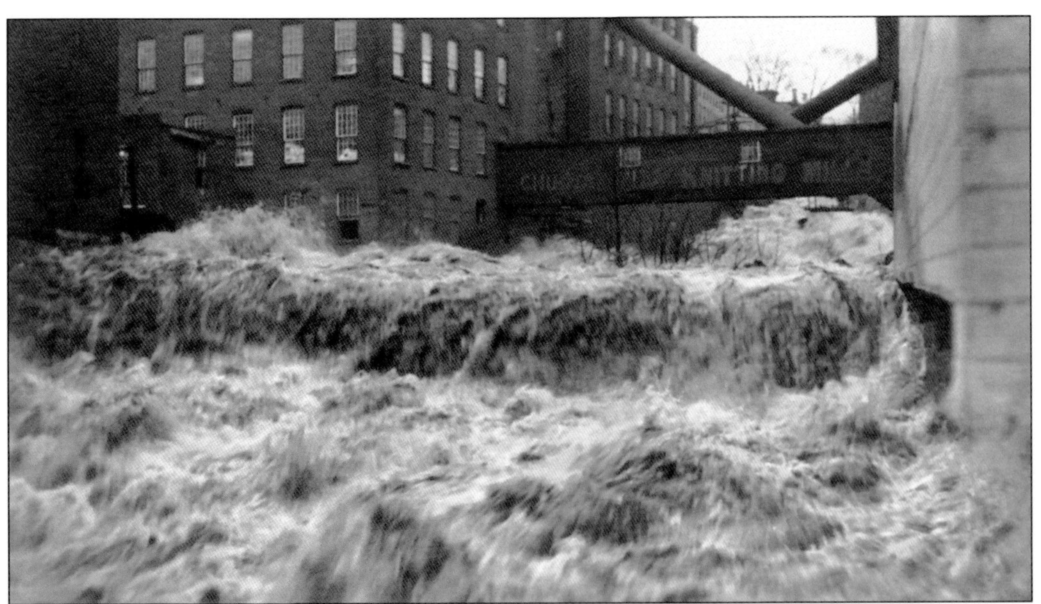

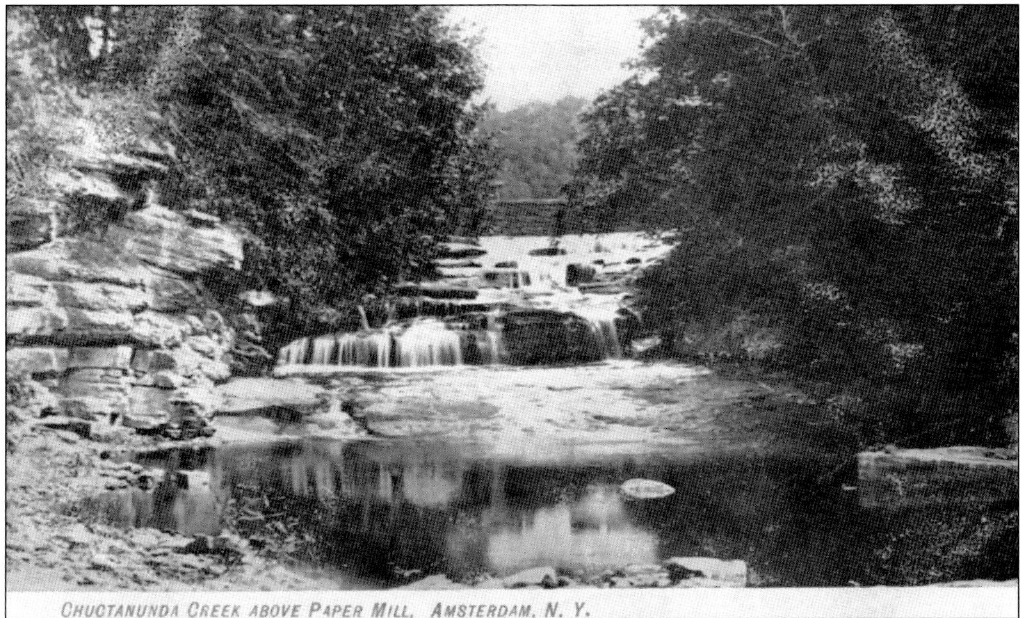


The Chuctanunda Creek is a source of both beauty and power along its 17-mile course from Galway Lake to the Mohawk River. Its power arises mainly from the 300-foot drop within its final 3 miles. The dam and falls shown above are just off Forest Avenue and originally provided power for the Stewart and Carmichael and later the Smeallie and Voorhees paper mills.

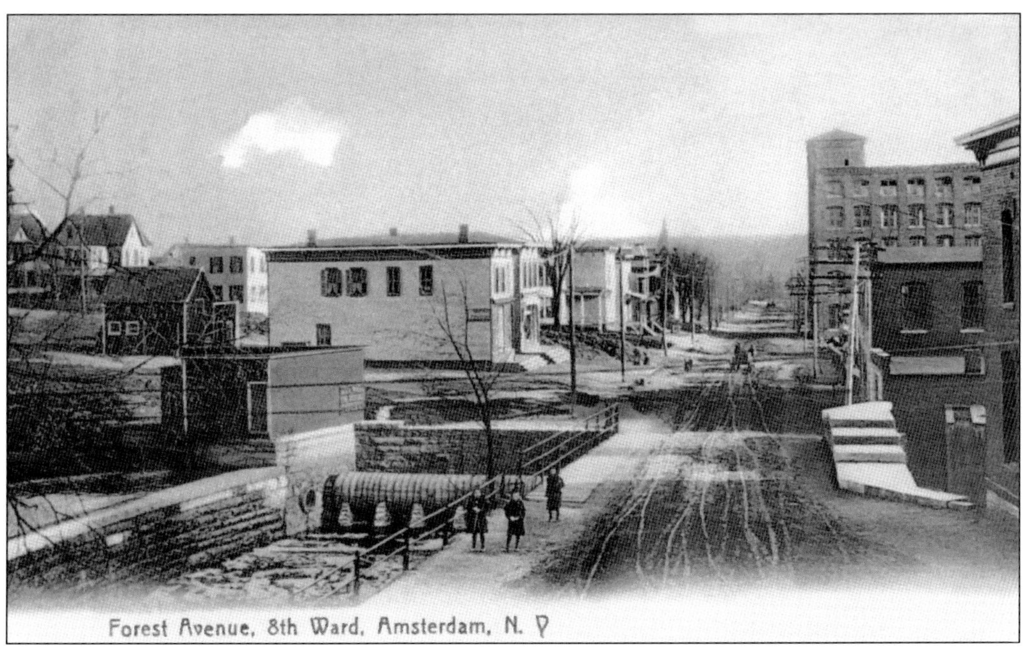


Rockton (originally Rock City) was a hamlet north of the city line when Amsterdam was chartered as a city in 1885. Rockton became the eighth ward of the city with two aldermen joining the common council in the spring of 1901. The dam at the right, remnants of which are still visible, supplied water to the McCleary, Wallin, and Crouse carpet mills.

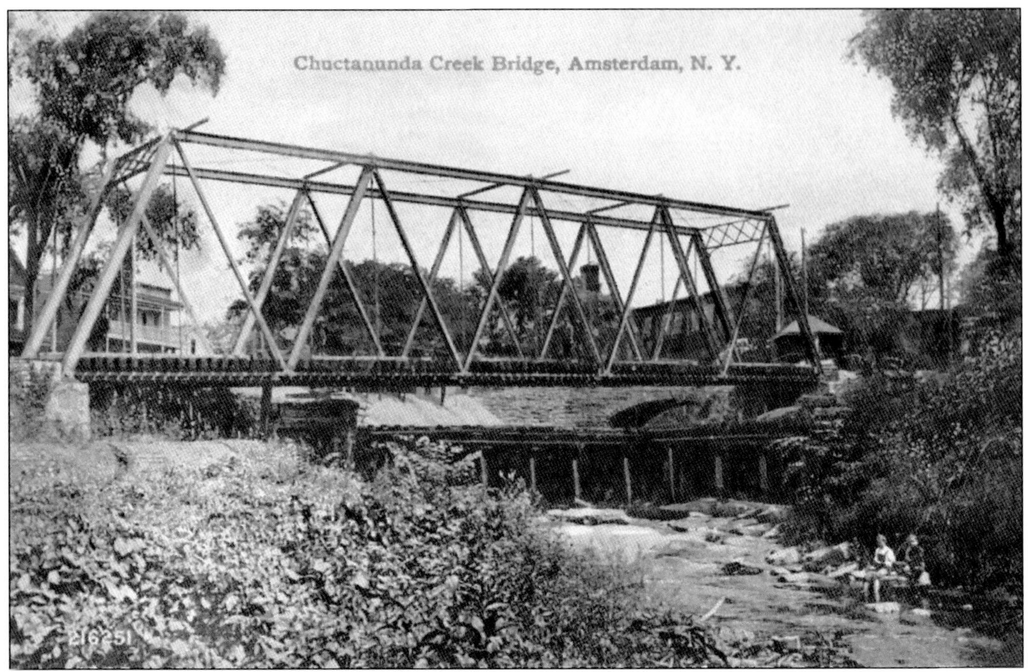


This is the trolley bridge crossing the Chuctanunda Creek from Lyon Street to the Rockton trolley wye. The milldam and penstock visible at left center are taking water to the L. L. Dean Park Spinning Mills.

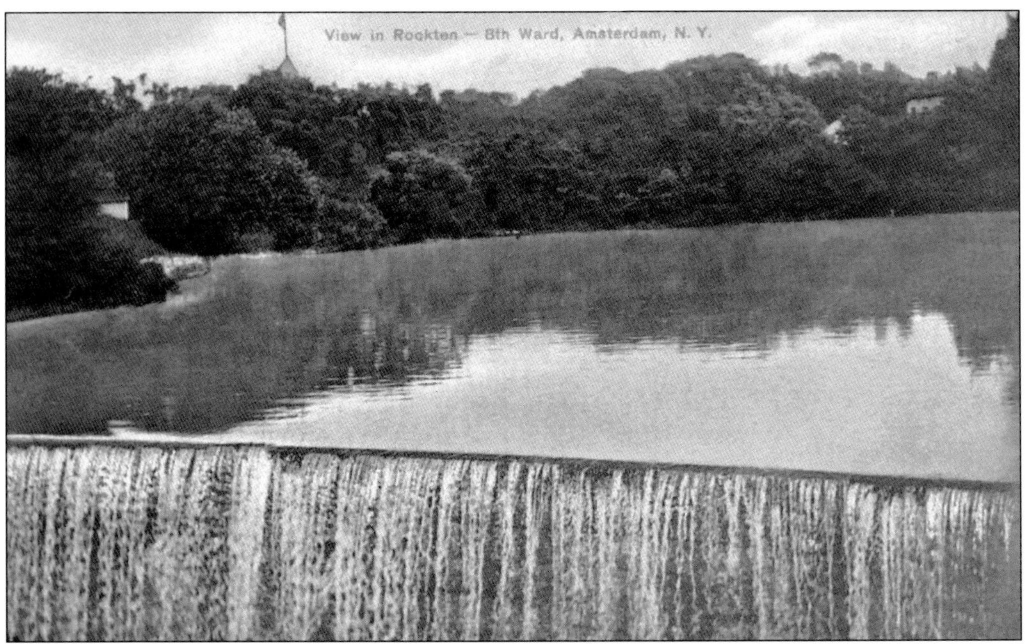


The power of the Chuctanunda Creek was harnessed by a series of dams along its course through the city. This dam, just north of the Rockton wye bridge, provided power for the textile and box mills along the east side of the creek and Hewitt Street.

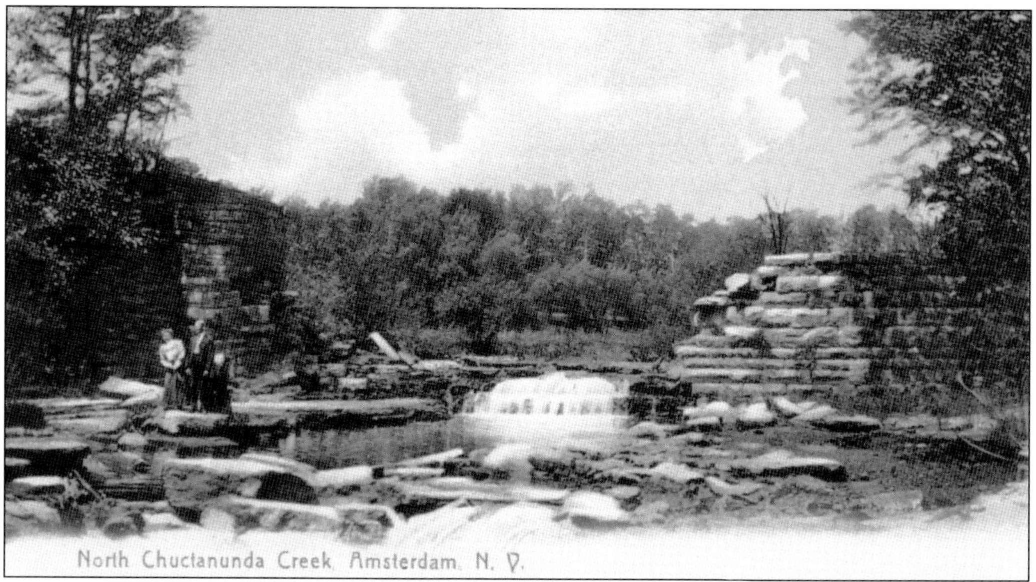
North Chuctanunda Creek, Amsterdam, N. Y.

Many residents of Amsterdam are unaware of the creek's beauty and that it winds continuously through the heart of the city and beyond. Periodic tours and lectures about its history, geology, and wildlife have rekindled awareness, and many hope someday that a nature and recreation trail can be established along its length.

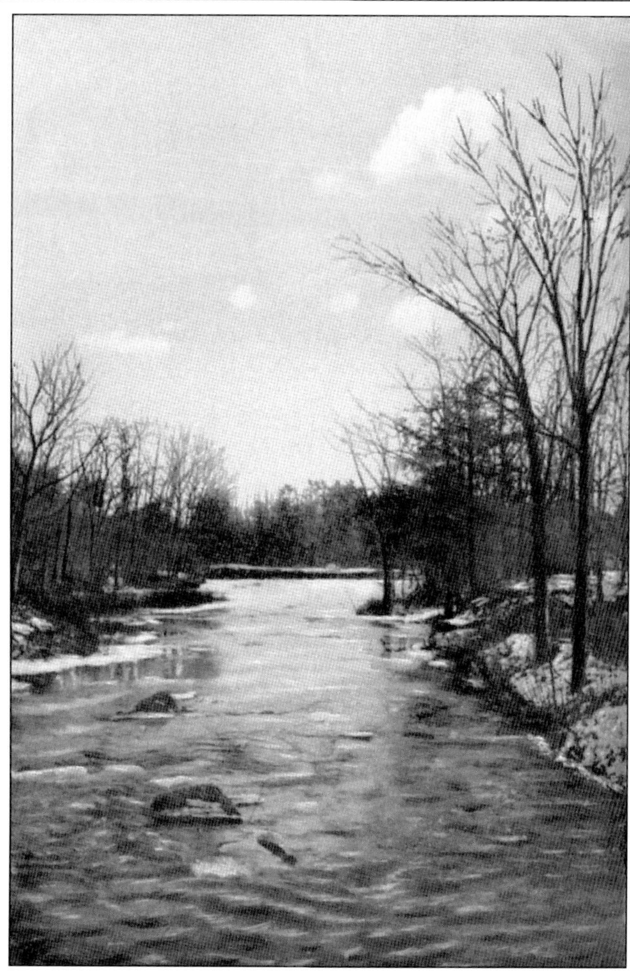

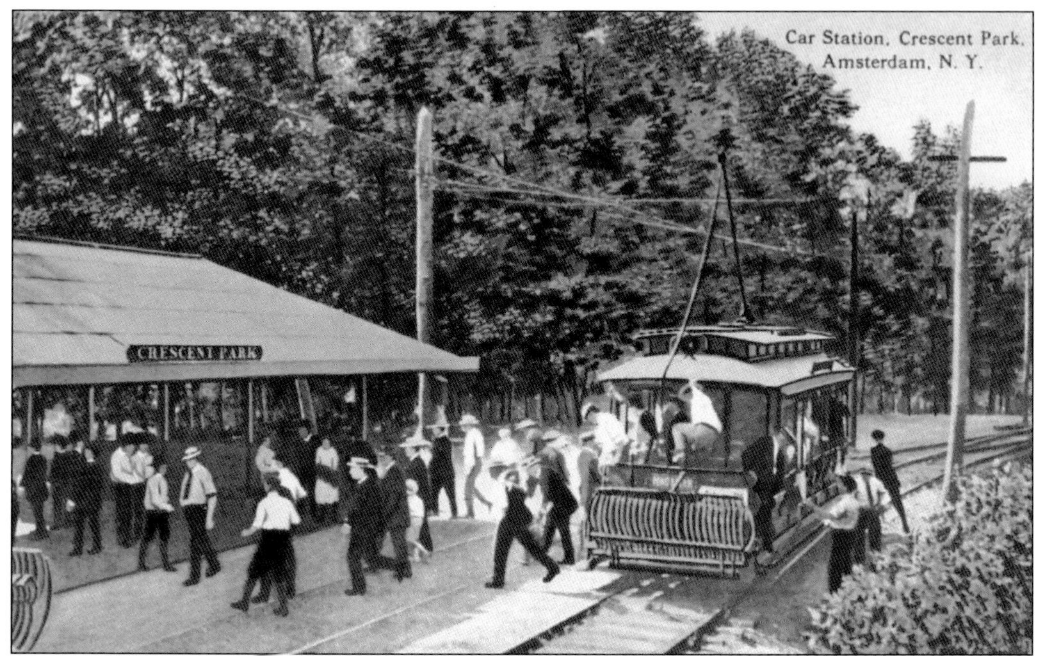


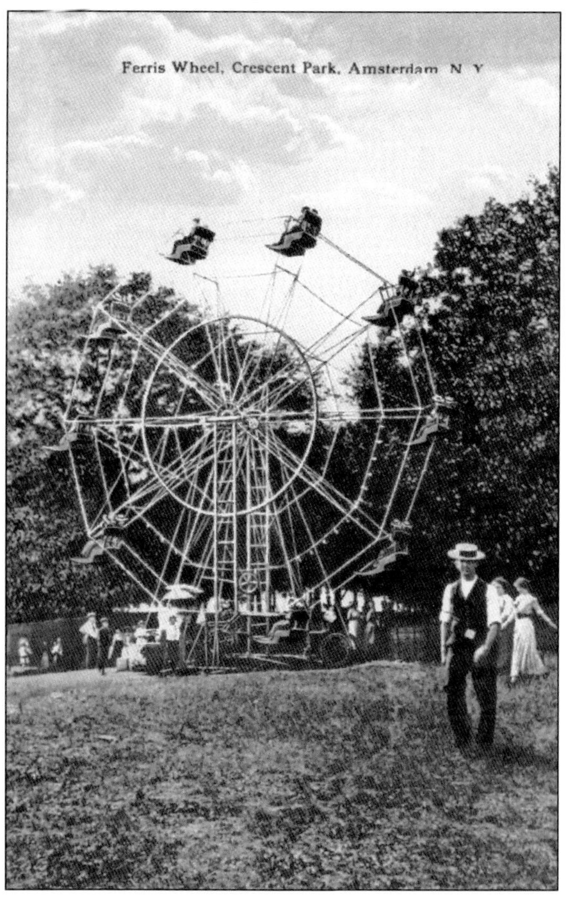


In 1914, a private realty company involving the McCaffrey brothers (see page 26) developed an area east of Locust Avenue as Crescent Park, an amusement park. Bordering the Chuctanunda Creek and served by the Hagaman line of the Fonda, Johnstown, and Gloversville Trolley, the park was a popular destination for those seeking escape from the noise of the looms and weariness of a six-day workweek.

In 1923, management of Crescent Park fell to Fred J. Collins, who purchased the property and renamed it Jollyland. He also added more rides and games, including a miniature railroad.

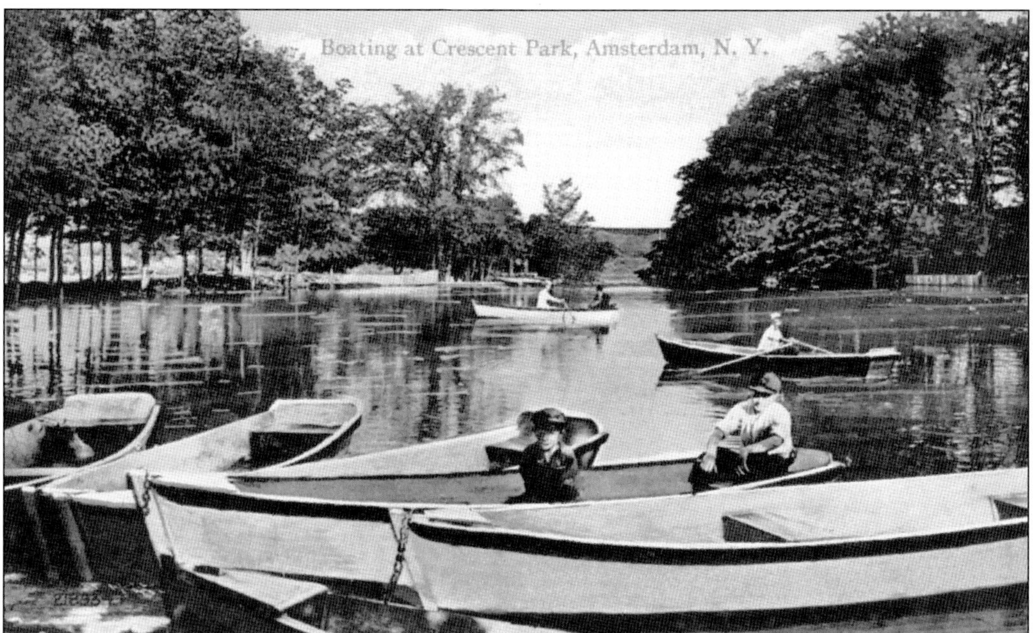


Subsequently purchased by a leading manufacturer and renamed Mohawk Mills Park, the park was donated to the city and renamed Shuttleworth Park in 1977. Long gone are the lake and dam, replaced by more modern recreational facilities, including a minor league baseball stadium.

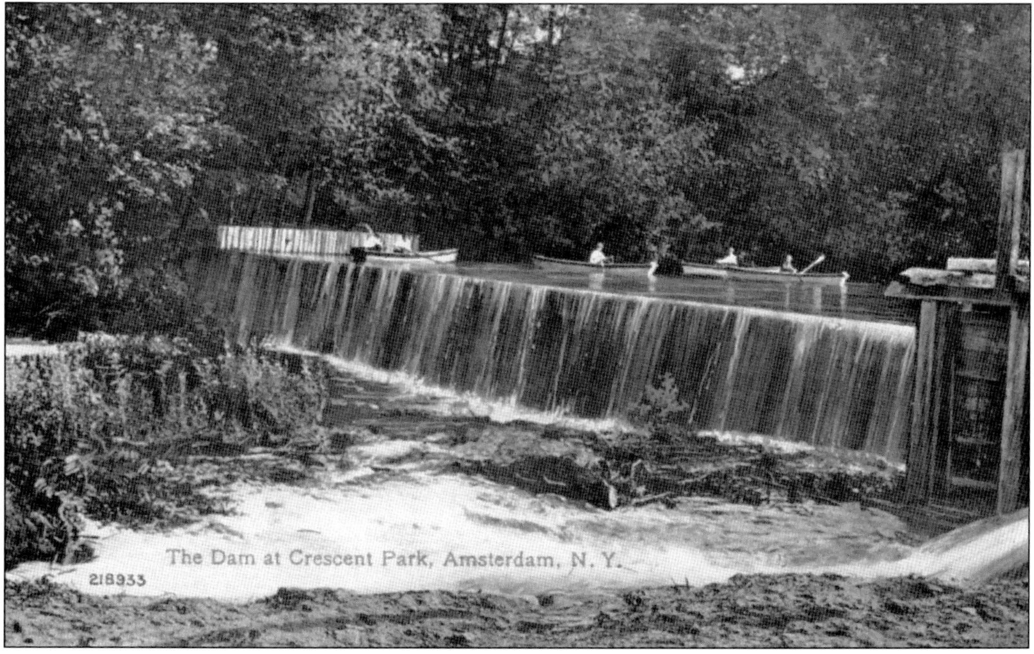


Other than a few large stone blocks behind the baseball field's center field, little remains today of the Crescent Park Dam, one of the few dams on the Chuctanunda erected for recreation rather than industry. Some of the former boating area became a winter ice skating rink.

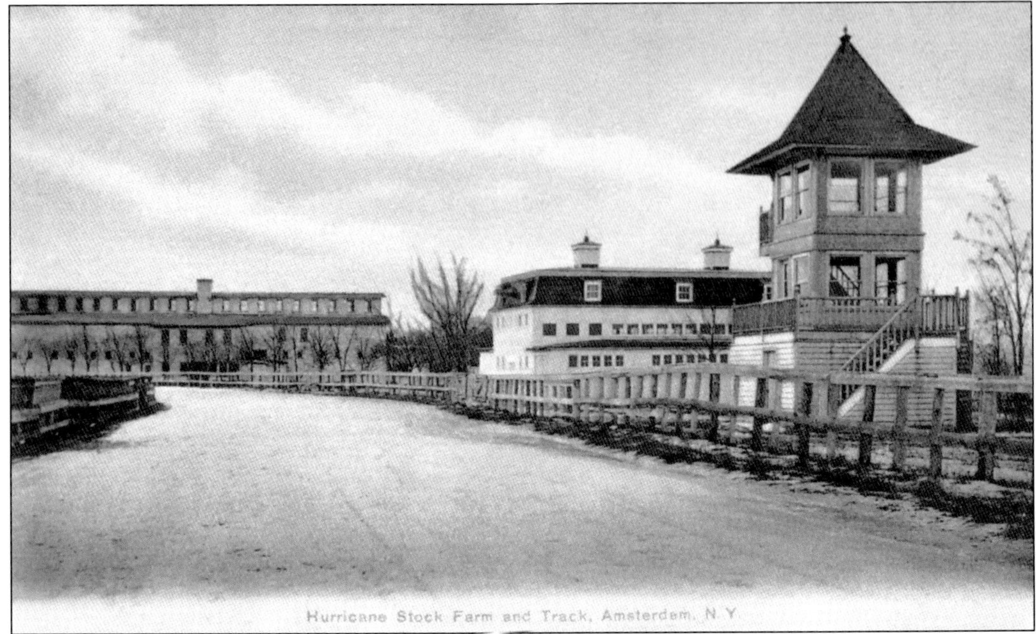


In the 1870s, mill owner Stephen Sanford took his doctor's advice to get a hobby and began buying up land along a windy ridge north of the city to create a farm to breed horses. He called it Hurricana Farm. In this view, the outdoor exercise track is seen in the foreground, and from left to right are the broodmare barn, the stallion barn, and the judges' stand. For several years in the early 20th century, Sanford invited employees to a yearly picnic at the farm, complete with exhibition races.

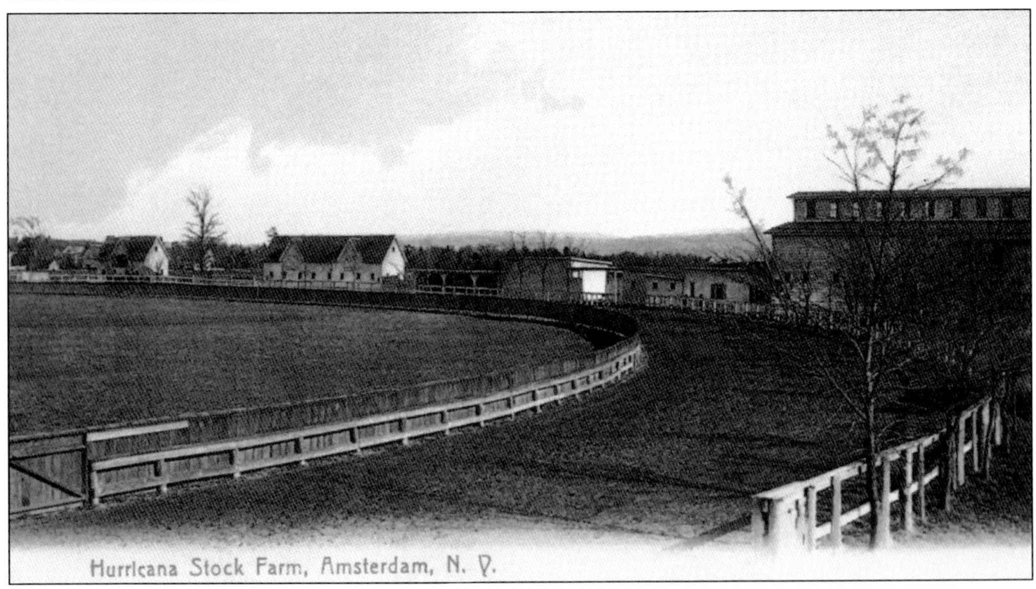


The farm not only supported the breeding of Sanford's own horses for racing at Saratoga and elsewhere (including the 1916 Kentucky Derby winner), but it also contracted out its services to other breeders. Thus in the 1930s, the name was changed to Sanford Stud Farms. One expert estimates that the majority of modern Kentucky Derby winners can trace their lineage through this farm.

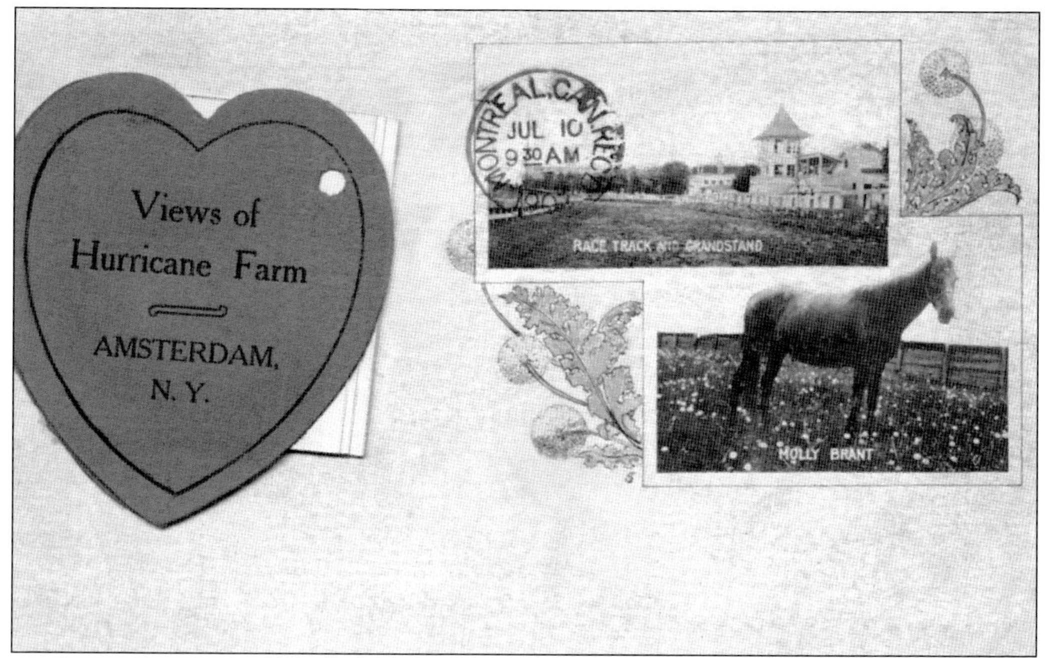


Sanford made a practice of naming his most beloved or promising horses after local features or persons. This rare Valentine's Day card shows one such, Molly Brant, who was named after the Native American wife of Sir William Johnson (see page 124). Other favorites who appear in a foldout strip behind the heart included Chuctanunda, Rockton, and Caughnawaga (the original name for the township including Amsterdam).

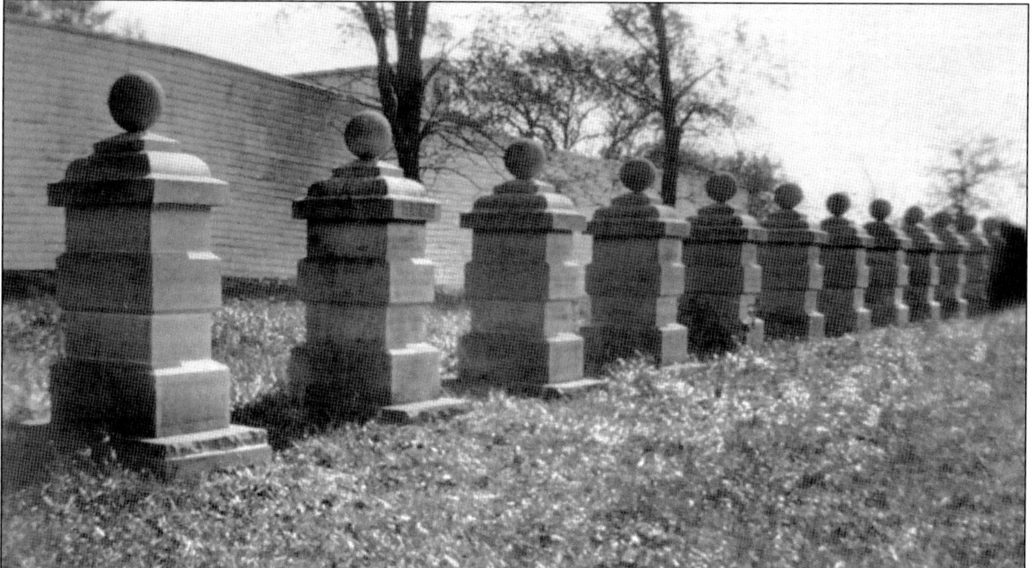

The farm closed in 1977, and portions were sold to make shopping centers along Route 30. The broodmare barn and several structures were ceded to the Town of Amsterdam, and a friends group is preserving them. These monuments to Sanford's favorite horses once adorned the farm. Contrary to local legend, these are not grave markers of horses, including the 25 horses killed in a barn fire in 1939. Only one horse, Monarchist, is known to be buried here.

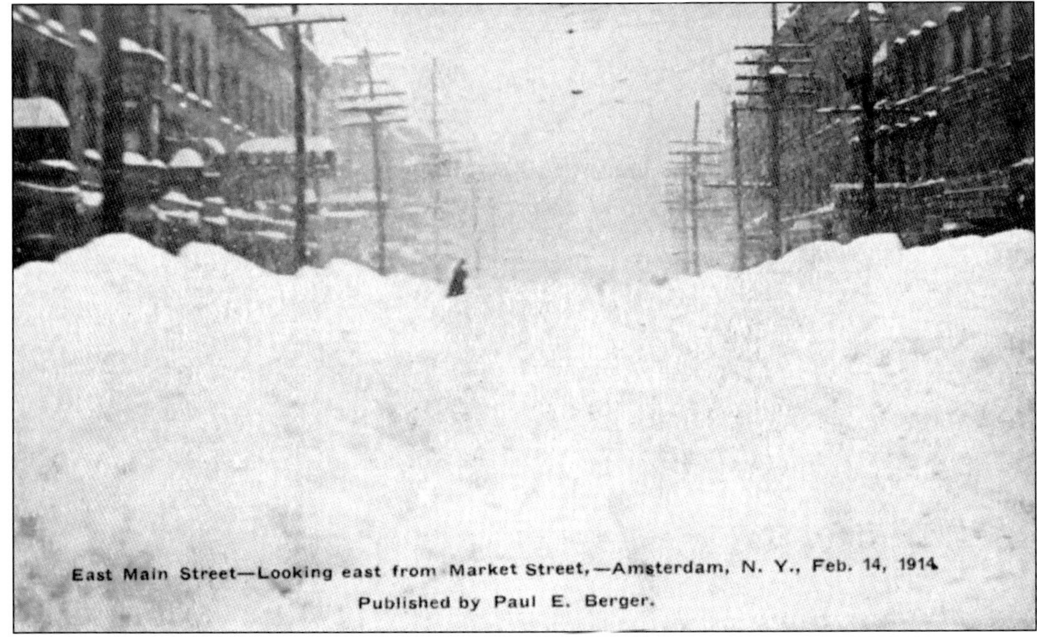


People attempt to cross downtown streets in the aftermath of the Valentine's Day blizzard of 1914. Winters may be harsh or moderate, but throughout its recorded history, Amsterdam has never been more than 10 to 20 years away from a crippling snowstorm. Snow removal remains a make-it-or-break-it issue for each mayor of Amsterdam.

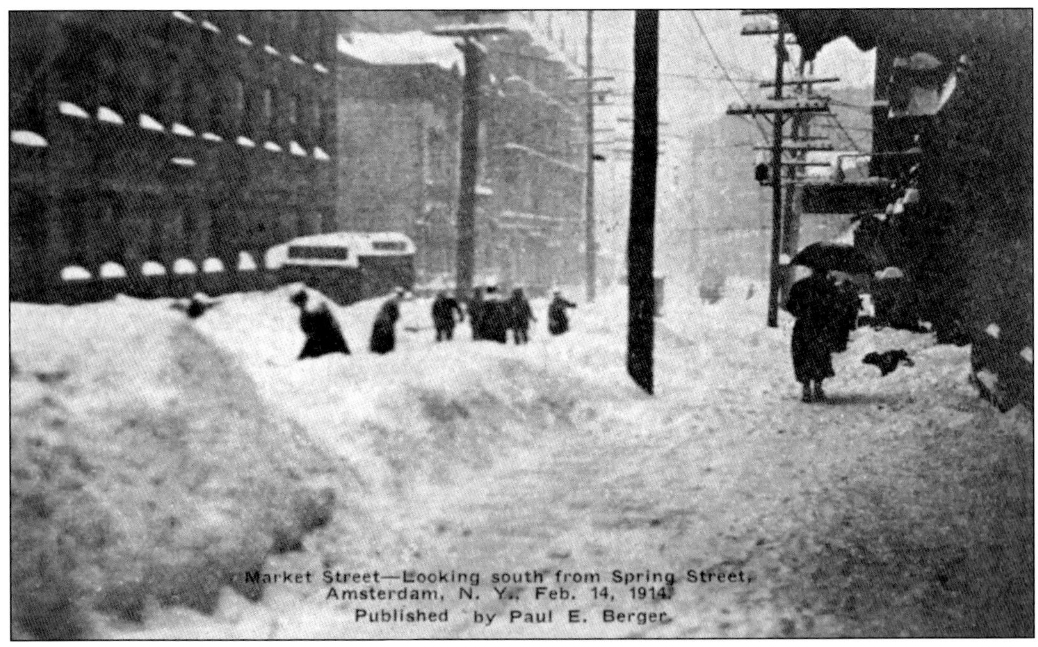

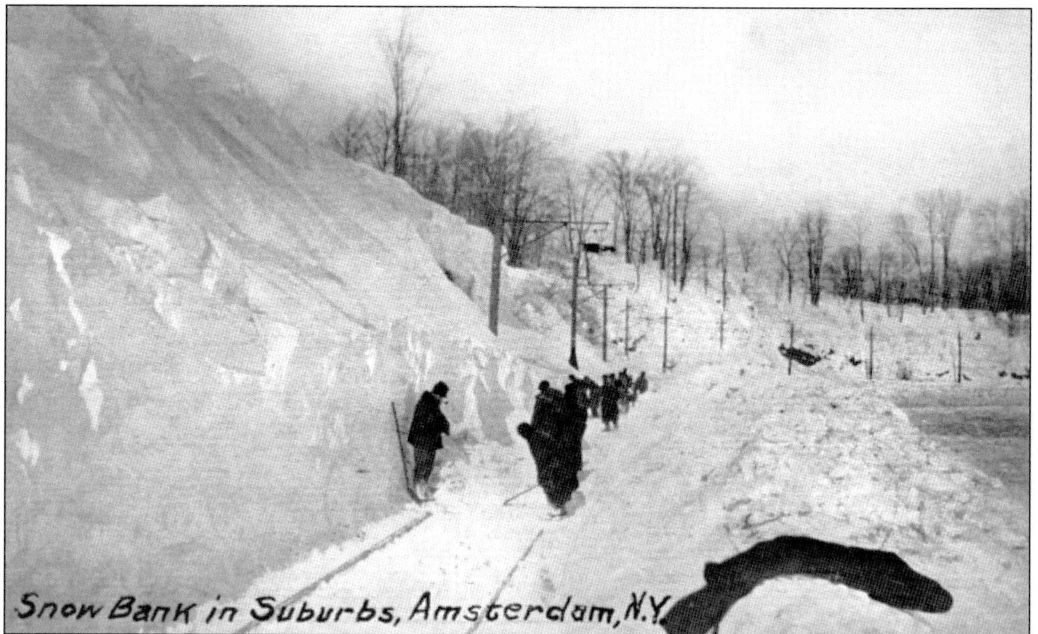


Work crews from the Fonda, Johnstown and Gloversville Rail Road dig out trolley lines on the outskirts of the city in 1914. This railroad was equipped with snowplow machinery, but even after they had passed through, individual shoveling crews were required to complete the clearing of the tracks.

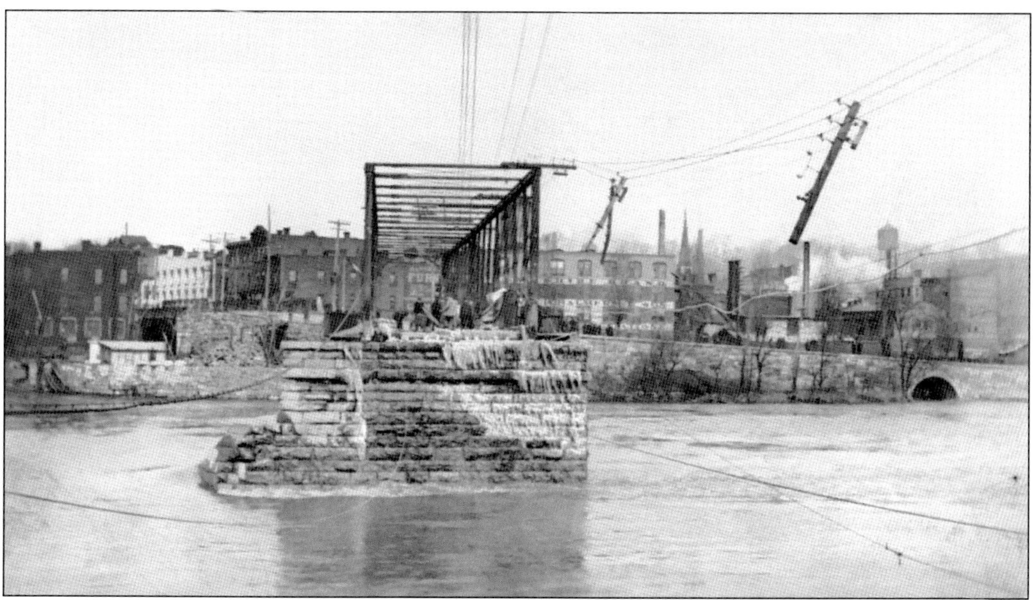

For many years, March 27 was "bridge day" in Amsterdam. On March 27, 1913, floodwaters tore the southernmost span of the bridge over the Mohawk River from its footings. Exactly one year to the day later, the trestle erected as a repair was demolished in another flood. Here workmen inspect the damage after the first flood.

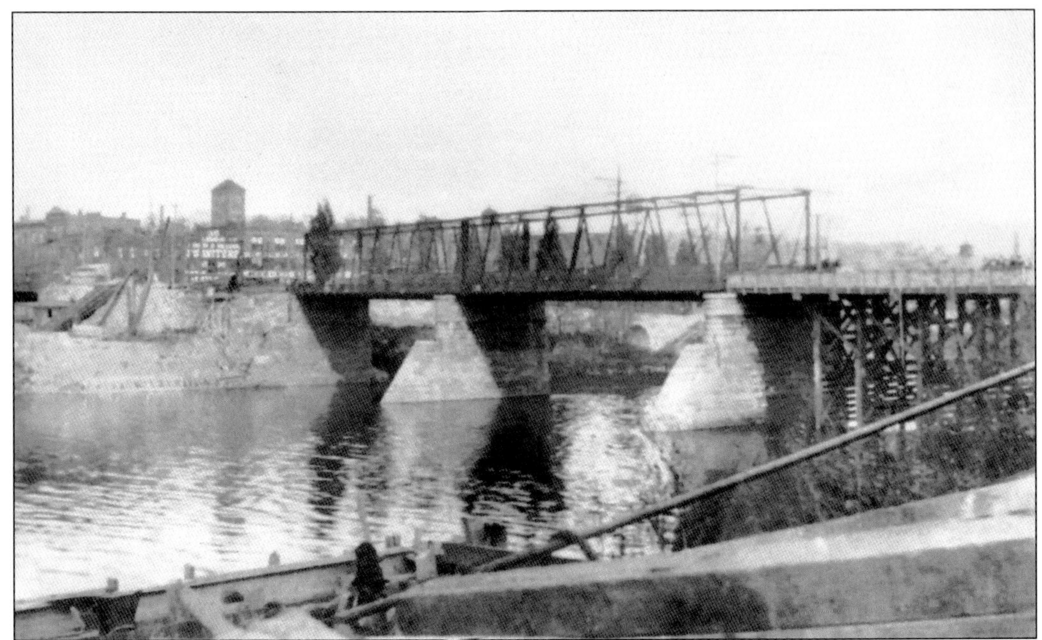

In this image, the 1914 repair trestle is emplaced. This was destroyed on March 27, 1914. After each time a span went down, individuals and businesses were left to find their own ways across the river either by going to another crossing up- or downstream or by using the temporary ferry services that sprang up. At least two deaths were caused by small boats being used as ferries in bad weather.

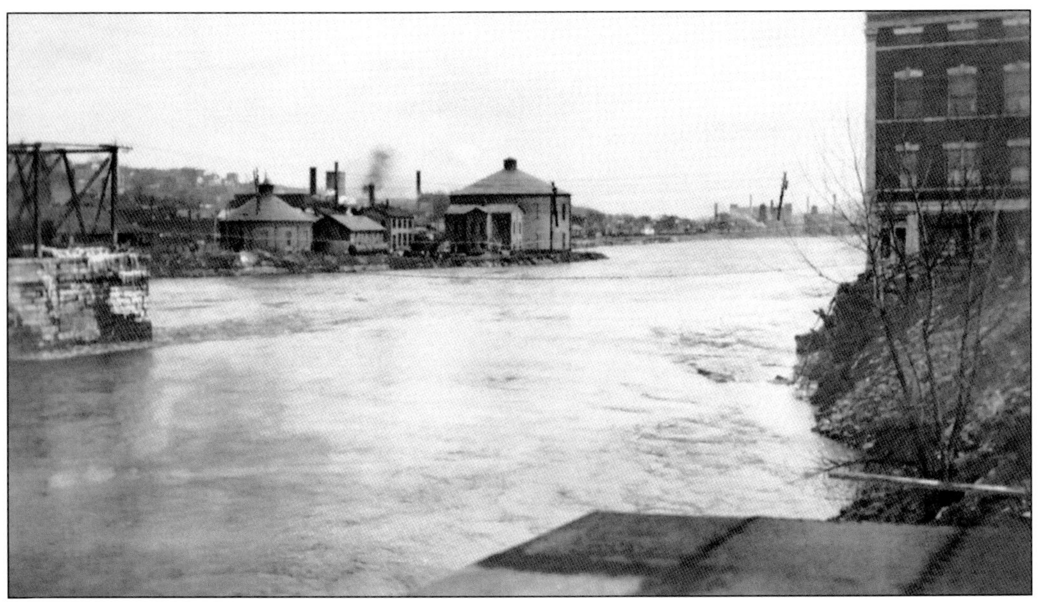

Here is the bridge as it was further damaged in 1914. In the foreground is a popular hotel and restaurant operated in the south side by an Italian immigrant family. On the north bank, the Chuctanunda Gas Light Works are visible. After the 1914 destruction, no more attempts were made to effect repairs to the 1876 bridge; a new and stronger one was built in 1916.

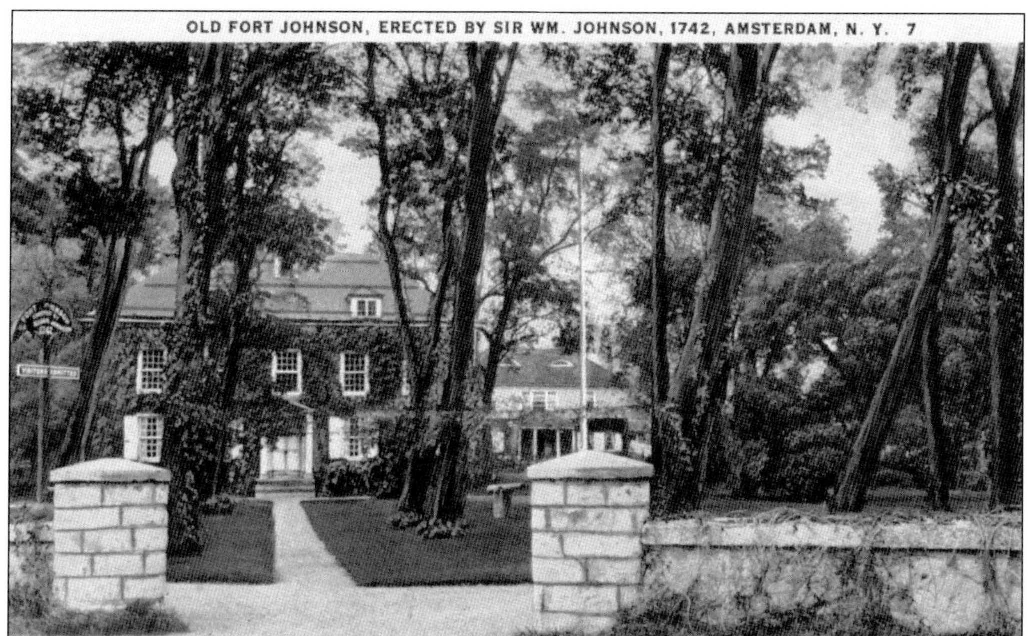


After immigrating to the colony of New York in 1739 to attend to his uncle's land holdings across the Mohawk River from what became Amsterdam, William Johnson sought to obtain his own land and business opportunities on the north bank. Using his knowledge of and good relations with Native Americans, Johnson embarked on a career that brought him land, wealth, military honor, nobility, and the especial trust of many Native American nations and the king of England. This was his second home on the north bank, built in 1749. An earlier home was built in 1743 a mile closer to present-day Amsterdam. Today the house is extensively restored and open as a museum. Old Fort Johnson is a national landmark.

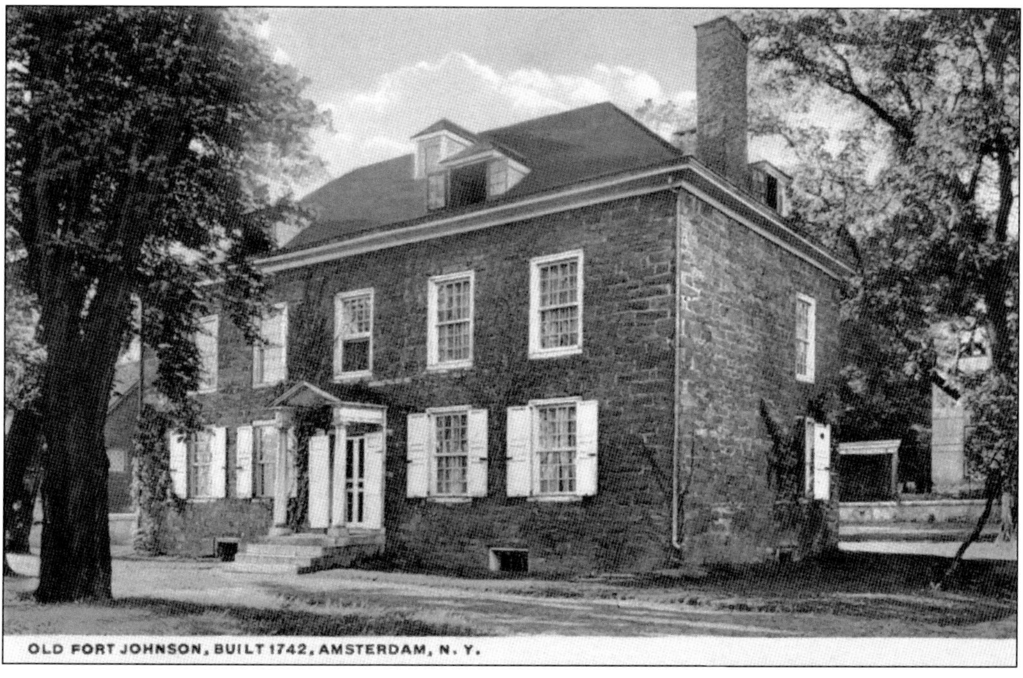

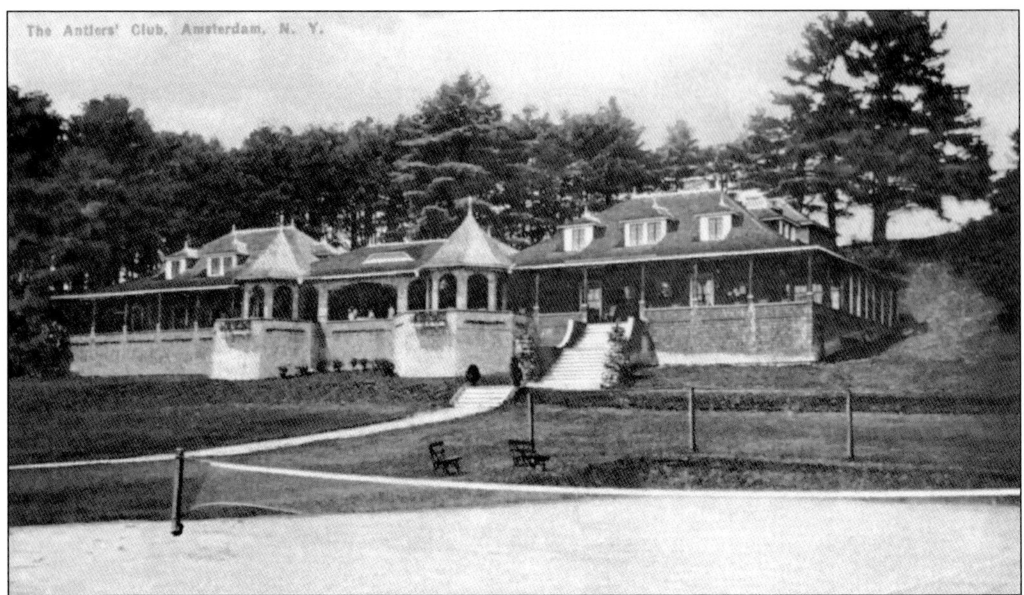


The Antlers was founded in 1900 as a private club for Amsterdam's well-to-do. Membership was by invitation only and restricted to "eligible males of the county over 21 and of approved character." With a professionally designed golf course and tennis courts overlooking the scenic Mohawk, it was the popularity of the clubhouse for social functions that lead to its expansion within four years of opening. The expansive clubhouse was destroyed by fire in 1965 and replaced with a smaller version.

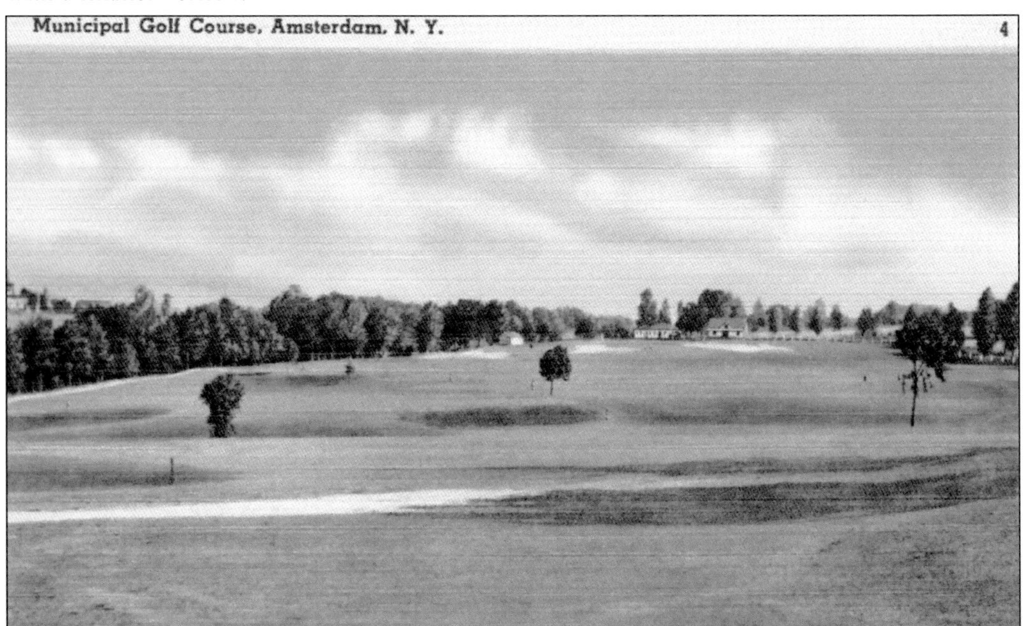


A golf course for Amsterdam had long been considered, and efforts commenced in 1929. Approximately 200 acres of farmland was purchased for $16,000. Federal Works Progress Administration funding paid for four-fifths of the construction costs ($123,000), and the Muni opened on July 19, 1938, with national titlists Gene Sarazen and Tom Creavy teeing off. Debate continues today as to the degree which the course should be supported by public funds.

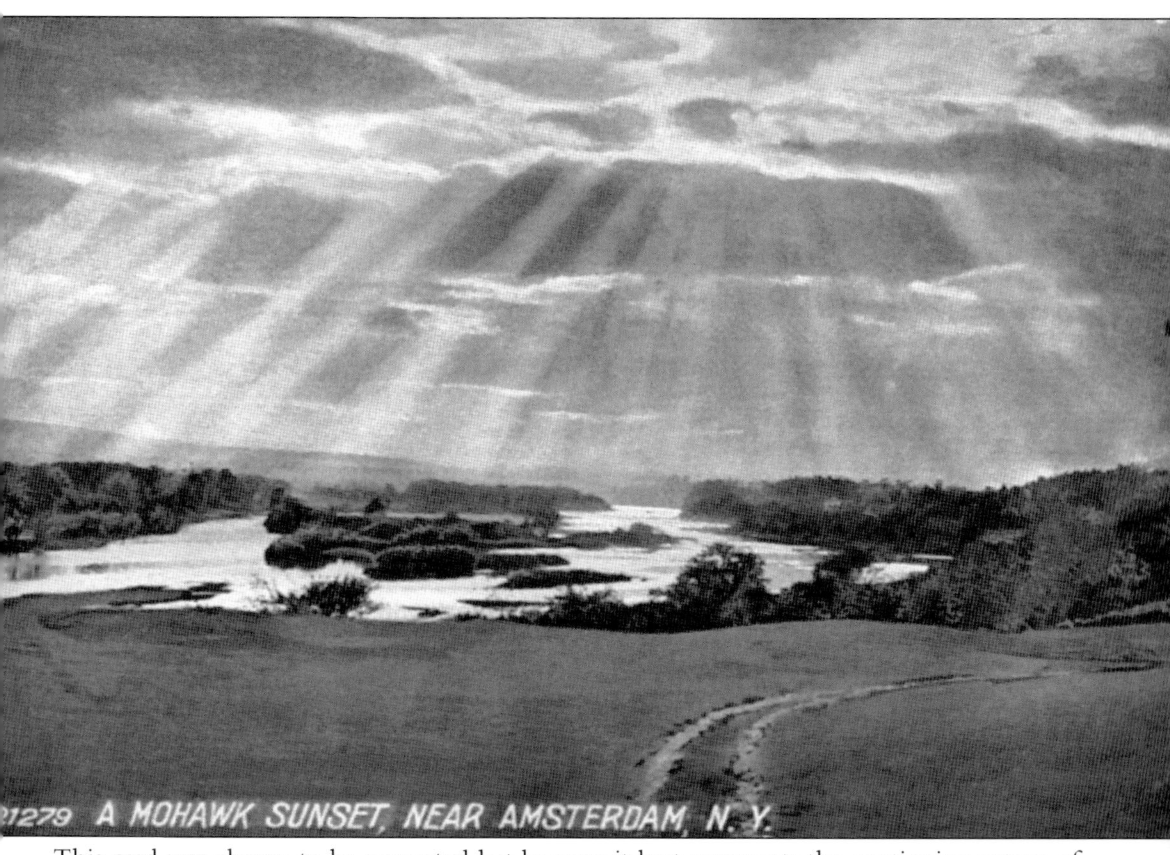


This card was chosen to be presented last because it best represents the continuing nature of Amsterdam history. As the postcard fad passed so eventually did the industrial heyday of the city. Now a new day awaits its dawning, and its outcome will depend on how Amsterdam capitalizes on the same forces—the land, the water, and the people—that made it great once before. (Courtesy of Rob von Hasseln.)

# Discover Thousands of Local History Books Featuring Millions of Vintage Images

Arcadia Publishing, the leading local history publisher in the United States, is committed to making history accessible and meaningful through publishing books that celebrate and preserve the heritage of America's people and places.

Find more books like this at
**www.arcadiapublishing.com**

Search for your hometown history, your old stomping grounds, and even your favorite sports team.


Consistent with our mission to preserve history on a local level, this book was printed in South Carolina on American-made paper and manufactured entirely in the United States. Products carrying the accredited Forest Stewardship Council (FSC) label are printed on 100 percent FSC-certified paper.

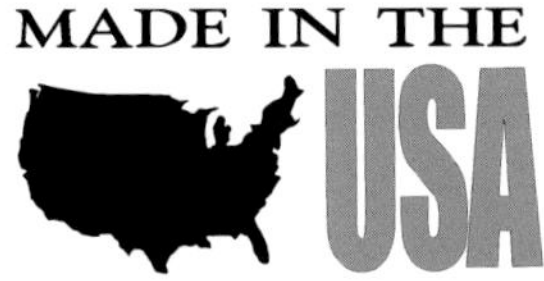